Learning by Choice in Secondary Physical Education

Creating a Goal-Directed Program

Kevin Kaardal, MEd
Vice Principal
Reynolds Secondary School
British Columbia, Canada

Human Kinetics

Library of Congress Cataloging-in-Publication Data

Kaardal, Kevin, 1962-
    Learning by choice in secondary physical education: creating a goal-directed program /
Kevin Kaardal.
        p. cm.
    Includes bibliographical references (p. 253) and index.
    ISBN 0-88011-688-9
    1. Physical education and training--Study and teaching (Secondary) 2. Physical
education and training--Curricula. I. Title.

GV363 .K32 2001
613.7'071'273--dc21   00-059681

ISBN: 0-88011-688-9

Acquisitions Editor: Scott Wikgren; **Developmental Editor:** Elaine Mustain; **Writer:** Elaine Mustain; **Assistant Editors:** Maggie Schwarzentraub, Melissa Feld, and Sandra Merz Bott; **Copyeditor:** Bonnie Pettifor; **Proofreader:** Erin T. Cler; **Indexer:** Craig Brown; **Permission Manager:** Courtney Astle; **Graphic Designer:** Nancy Rasmus; **Graphic Artist:** Yvonne Griffith; **Photo Manager:** Clark Brooks; **Cover Designer:** Jack Davis; **Photographer (cover):** Tom Roberts; **Photographer (interior):** Kevin Kaardal, pages 1 and 7, Tom Roberts for all other photos; **Art Manager:** Craig Newsom; **Illustrators:** Tim Offenstein and Sharon Smith; **Printer:** United Graphics

Printed in the United States of America   10 9 8 7 6 5 4 3 2 1

Human Kinetics
Web site: www.humankinetics.com

United States: Human Kinetics
P.O. Box 5076
Champaign, IL 61825-5076
800-747-4457
e-mail: humank@hkusa.com

Canada: Human Kinetics
475 Devonshire Road Unit 100
Windsor, ON N8Y 2L5
800-465-7301 (in Canada only)
e-mail: hkcan@mnsi.net

Europe: Human Kinetics, P.O. Box IW14
Leeds LS16 6TR, United Kingdom
+44 (0) 113 278 1708
e-mail: humank@hkeurope.com

Australia: Human Kinetics
57A Price Avenue
Lower Mitcham, South Australia 5062
08 8277 1555
e-mail: liahka@senet.com.au

New Zealand: Human Kinetics
P.O. Box 105-231, Auckland Central
09-523-3462
e-mail: hkp@ihug.co.nz

This book is an act of love. Love for a subject that is one of the most important things we do in schools–teach students how to be fit, enjoy leisure, play games, cooperate, compete with fairness and good sportsmanship, and experience the joy of choosing to live full lives. Love and sincere gratitude for being blessed enough to be a member of a profession that impacts so many lives in such significant ways. This book is also an act of love for the students I hope it affects. I hope it helps students love to participate in physical education, set goals, and make positive and healthy choices toward living active lives.

I dedicate this book to my daughters, Danielle and Maria, and my maternal grandmother, Rita Rogerson. To my daughters in the hope that they participate in physical education programs that help them learn to love being physically active for a lifetime. To my Nana, a master teacher, writer, and grandmother who showed me there is an adventure waiting for you every day.

Contents

Part II Reproducibles to Help Build Your Program

Acknowledgments

I would like to acknowledge six very special people who helped make this book a reality:

First, my wife, **Cynthia**, whose encouragement, patience, and support are boundless. Without Cynthia this book never would have been written and many of the approaches to teaching never would have been attempted.

My parents, **Stanley** and **Anita**, who always made me believe I could make a difference and accomplish what I wanted.

Theresa Maxwell, my friend, mentor, graduate advisor, and teacher educator at the University of Calgary. Her contributions to this book are paramount. She was the original editor, curriculum expert, and resource responsible for the final basketball unit and the original manuscript of this book.

Scott Wikgren, Human Kinetics acquisitions editor, who always believed in this project and had the patience to help me see it through.

Elaine Mustain, an incredible, creative, and patient Human Kinetics developmental editor, who energized both me and the manuscript when discouragement reigned and creative vision was blurred.

I would also like to acknowledge **Leroy Pelletier**, **Marg Schwartz**, **Daniel Cooney**, **Colin Lumby**, **Tony Makowski**, and **Larry Beauchamp**, who are professors, teachers, and national leaders in physical education. Their ideas and support formed the approach to teaching and assessment reflected in this book. Finally I would like to acknowledge the professionals I have worked with whose ideas and professionalism are reflected in every page of this book:

Larry Auger—A friend and educator who has shared and developed ideas with me. He gave me the treasure trove of files that became Success-Based Physical Education, and he helped me develop leveled track and field as well as approaches to golf and archery.

Avery Harrison—A master coach, educator, and friend who has been a sounding board and insightful contributor to the ideas presented in this book.

Michelle Holzner—A master teacher at Bishop Kidd Junior High School, who helped me develop and use dance, volleyball, stuntnastics, and cross-country units.

Raissa Adolphe—A master teacher at Bishop McNally where she co-developed our program that included the self-evaluation template, team teaching, peer teaching, heart rate days, tennis units, stuntnastics, group peer evaluation of performance routines, and volleyball units.

Leanne Timko—A terrific teacher and original member of the physical education team that developed Success-Based Physical Education. She co-authored the soccer unit, along with many other contributions.

Carl Gratton—Another terrific teacher and an original member of the team that developed Success-Based Physical Education. Among Carl's many contributions were the 30-minute walk-run, a modular approach to delivering physical education in a traditional timetable, and the dance unit.

Colette Pereschitz—A team member at Bishop McNally and a great teacher. She helped keep an active-living focus in the program and a comprehensive approach to health in the school. Colette developed walking units.

Ed Marchand—The principal responsible for developing the success-based approach to instruction at Bishop McNally.

Craig Foley—A vice principal of Bishop McNally. He supported the development of the success-based program, and as physical education supervisor, he helped promote its principles.

Maureen Hall—A vice principal of Bishop McNally. She facilitated the development of the unit template in the book.

Neil O'Flaherty—Head of the physical education department at Bishop Grandin School. His contributions included developing a leveled soccer unit and flag football task cards as well as the approach to modularizing physical education in a traditional school timetable.

Wally Kozak—A master teacher and co-author of the Student Self-Evaluation template.

Elio Gerimia—A wonderful teacher at Bishop Kidd Junior High School. Elio helped develop cross-country units.

Frank Durante—A terrific teacher who is now department head at Bishop McNally. He developed another way of giving students choice in their own summative evaluations.

And *Tom Urbanik*—He taught me the teacher-directed approach to leveled teaching. I based part of the volleyball unit on his work.

PART I
How to Create Student Excitement and Achievement

Part I describes a program that has worked for thousands of people, instilling in them a love for and an ability to pursue active living in the long run. It also summarizes the principles that will enable you to create your own physical education curriculum that will likewise inspire and enable your students to become active for life, and thus be happier and healthier than they would be had they not been in your classes. It provides many examples of the principles in action, clarifying the ideas that are discussed. It will equip you to use the handouts presented in part II, and to be able to create additional materials of your own.

One note that may help head off confusion: A crucial feature of the goal-directed program is that it allows students to choose the level of difficulty at which they will participate in many units. The levels are designated by the letters A, B, and C. I have chosen to make A the easiest (lowest) level, and C the most difficult (highest) level in a deliberate attempt to disassociate the level designations from grading systems that regard "A" or "1" as the best, and succeeding letters or numbers as progressively worse. I do not want students or teachers to have the idea that working at the most difficult level is more valuable than working at the easiest level. If this statement suggests to you that the program described in the following pages lowers standards of excellence, please read on. You'll discover that rather than lowering achievement for all, goal-directed education consistently raises the level of accomplishment for all students, from the most gifted to those who are physically challenged.

I am excited to share these ideas and experiences with you, and I hope that you will be similarly excited as you put them into practice in your own programs.

CHAPTER 1

Physical Education Can Be Exciting

Imagine . . .

- 100 percent participation in every physical education class;
- students asking to run for a half hour instead of the standard 12 minutes;
- a previously silent, shy student sharing with the teacher that she has set a personal performance record;
- students rushing to set up and put away equipment; and
- students eagerly volunteering to lead the class warm-up and stretching.

Think of working with students who . . .

- are cooperative and responsible;
- have ownership of their own physical education program;
- select their activities, organize themselves, plan personal objectives, follow through, and stay on task throughout the class period; and
- can accurately assess their performance, identify their strengths, and set goals for their improvement.

Dream of physical education classes in which you and your students consistently experience

- excitement,
- fun, and
- celebration!

Sounds like a fantasy—but it isn't. I have seen all these things and more at Bishop McNally High School and Bishop Kidd Junior High School in Canada, where the staffs involved themselves and their students in an effectively communicated approach to physical education instruction and assessment.

How Did It Happen?

Creating these successes didn't happen overnight, and it didn't happen as a result of one person's genius. It happened because many people helped me along the way, not the least of whom were my students, who showed me the way through their reactions to what I tried over the years.

The long process of learning to build successful physical education programs started in my student days at the university. It began when I was assigned to design an individualized unit that could be completed independently by students with the teacher acting only as a *facilitator*. I designed such a unit for basketball, and I was pleased when my professor gave it high marks.

Fast forward a bit. . . .

The next fall I began my first teaching job. I taught 7th to 12th grade physical education in a rural school and decided to try the individualized unit, which I'd written at the university, in a setting outside my practice teaching. When the students, the principal, and provincial evaluators all liked the results, I decided to develop more individualized units. Over the next three years, I designed and refined units for artistic gymnastics, cross-country running, racquetball, volleyball, outdoor education, badminton, soccer, slow-pitch softball, and track and field.

Then I moved to the city (Calgary, Alberta) to work for the Catholic school board, which hired me to teach at Bishop Kidd, an inner-city junior high school. "Oh, a Catholic school!" you may say. "They don't have to take just anybody, and they can kick kids out if they make trouble. No wonder his units worked." Not so. In Alberta, Catholic schools are publicly funded institutions and are open to all students. Thus, the children at this school had the same demographic diversity as the students at inner-city schools; they came to school with the same joys, gifts, and problems that inner-city students face everywhere. It was in that school that I learned to teach.

On arriving at Bishop Kidd, I was fortunate to be partnered with a terrific teacher, Michelle Holzner. Willing to experiment, Michelle helped me immensely in the refinement and development of the individualized gymnastics unit.

Michelle developed an individualized dance unit, including a remarkable dance production that 80 percent of the school's students enthusiastically participated in. The Provincial Department of Education evaluated our physical education program and was impressed with the individualized units and our student-centered and leveled approach to teaching basketball, gymnastics, cross-country running, racquetball, volleyball, outdoor education, badminton, soccer, slow-pitch softball, and track and field. They were especially enthusiastic about the school's dance production. All this led to national recognition from the Canadian Association for Health, Physical Education, Recreation and Dance, as our program was the first junior high school in the Calgary Catholic School District to receive a Quality Daily Physical Education Award.

Because our students loved the individualized units, Michelle and I began to look for other ways to individualize our instruction. To help us, Physical Education Supervisor Leroy Pelletier sent me to the American Alliance for Health, Physical Education, Recreation and Dance (AAHPERD). There I was introduced to Tom Urbanik, a teacher from Pennsylvania. Tom's work was a revelation to me, because through him I learned that my ideas about individualizing weren't the only game in town. His approach was more teacher-centered than mine, but it worked just as well. From Tom I learned you don't have to replicate "my" program to have successful individualized PE instruction. You can use your own teaching style as long as you include

- "preassessment" of the students' skills;
- students in appropriate levels (having three levels for each skill seems to work well);
- multiple instructional and practice stations for each unit, including peer instruction;
- the teacher as facilitator; and
- assessment keyed to whatever level a student is currently in.

Then at last the opportunity came to set up a program from scratch: I was hired as one of the lead teachers to plan a program at Bishop McNally High School in Calgary. As coordinating teacher for physical education, I was able to hire some excellent physical educators. Together we set up a goal-directed program we called

"Success-Based Physical Education." How successful were we? The fact that more than 80 percent of our students registered for the physical education classes that were *optional* for grades 11 and 12 confirmed we were on the right track. Another strong indication of success was the student response we received to a questionnaire given out at the end of the year. Students were requested not to sign their surveys so their answers would be anonymous and therefore (we hoped) honest. Over 500 questionnaires were returned, and here are some of the results:

- 97.8 percent of the respondents agreed or strongly agreed with the statement: I really enjoyed taking physical education this year.
- 92.7 percent of the students agreed or strongly agreed with the statement: I enjoyed the active-living focus of this program because it adds meaning to the units we are learning by showing how they improve my fitness level and quality of life.
- 93.8 percent of the students agreed or strongly agreed with the statement: I enjoyed the leveled approach to skill development and evaluation because it allowed me to work at a pace and rate I could be successful at.
- 93.2 percent of the students agreed or strongly agreed with the statement: I found using the student self-evaluation process helpful in allowing me to identify my strengths and maximize my mark to its highest potential.
- 75.2 percent of the students agreed or strongly agreed with the statement: I believe the expanded opportunity that allows students to receive marks for mastery in a game or unit outside of class is a valuable part of the physical education program.

And the rest, as they say, is history. Maybe not the kind that makes headlines in the national news or that's featured in the next generation's textbooks. But the kind that makes a difference in students' lives. What I've learned through experience and been taught by scores of colleagues and students is how to create and manage PE programs that have kids coming back for more; that result in students becoming active for lifelong fitness—and that are just plain fun to teach.

Can It Happen to You?

When I have given presentations or in-services, these are the most frequently asked questions I hear:

- Many of my students couldn't possibly work independently, so how can this system of instruction work?
- How do you get students to accept the responsibility of working independently?
- How does the teacher who adopts the role of "facilitator" ensure that learning is occurring?
- If you're not watching all the students all the time, how do you keep them on task?
- When you have so many students, how can you possibly give them the kind of individual attention required to establish individual goals, help them meet their goals, and monitor their progress toward those goals?

In short, with one physical educator and a couple hundred kids, the whole thing looks impossible.

But really, it isn't. In this book I'll share with you the strategies that have worked for me and for the teachers I've worked with. In part I, we'll cover four major areas:

• We'll examine the idea of goal-directed physical education, discussing how to establish goals, then how to write a curriculum based on them. You'll see how you can start with those units you have expertise in; develop the units by first identifying the core skill progressions you believe are required to participate in the activity you are teaching; then break them down into progressions. You will learn how to analyze these progressions and divide them into levels, then how to add other choices and modified games.

• We'll look at a variety of teaching techniques you can use to implement the units you've written, depending on your students and what works best for you.

• We'll answer those frequently asked questions about what seem to be barriers at first glance.

• Finally, we'll spend a lot of time talking about fair, effective, and appropriate assessment, because I've found that that's key to running programs in which students feel they can achieve fitness, enjoy physical activity, and learn the skills that will enable them to enjoy a wide variety of activities that will keep them physically active throughout their lives.

In part II, I'll share material that you can reproduce and use as much as you like. There you'll find

• the cores of units for basketball and soccer that you can use almost as they are, once you've absorbed the material in part I. You may want to make your own modifications and add a few things, but the essential programs are there; and

• bits and pieces of other units that will help solidify your understanding of the "how-to" material in part I and that you can use in developing your own complete units.

By using the materials in part II and modifying them to suit your unique outlook and style, you'll learn by doing and will be well on your way to implementing your own version of success-based, goal-directed PE.

I'm not saying that what I'm proposing in *Learning by Choice in Secondary Physical Education* is easy: it takes a lot of work to develop the kind of PE program that excites kids *and* that you're excited about, too. But it's certainly not impossible. With some careful planning, common sense, educated risk-taking, and clear program goals in mind, you, too, can develop and teach PE programs that involve and excite young people—and that turn many of them into exercisers for life. Learning a few key concepts from some really great physical educators, working hard to put those concepts to work in teaching situations, observing the effects of what I tried, learning from outstanding peers, and changing strategies as I went along resulted in some pretty great physical education experiences for me. In this book, I've shared the materials and ideas I believe will help you, the students you teach, and the communities you live in to have those same great experiences and reap the health benefits (both physical and mental) I've seen along the way.

Hope you enjoy the journey!

CHAPTER 2
Goal-Directed Physical Education

If you want your students to be more excited about physical education, it may be time to revamp your program. But you can't start on unit and lesson plans until you have thought about your overall curriculum. The clearest way I know to think about structuring your curriculum is to take a *goal-directed* approach. Before we explore how you go about structuring a goal-directed curriculum, let's explore some basic assumptions that must underlie your curriculum planning if you're to have an effective and exciting program.

Three Basic Assumptions

Goal-directed physical education is quite similar to outcomes-based education in several of its basic assumptions: that the vast majority of students can learn and succeed, that schools can create conditions that will promote success, and that success breeds more success.

1. **Most students can learn and succeed.** The vast majority of students can learn and progress, given enough time, a teaching strategy that meets their learning style, and an appropriate definition of success for each individual. For example, although a person with a moderate mental disability may not be able to master complex logic problems, that person can succeed at acquiring skills for living independently, happily, and healthily. Some kids have the drive and the physical and mental potential to be great athletes. Others just want to be healthy, and as long as they're doing enough exercise to stay that way, they'll be perfectly content. Assuming that your goal as a physical educator is to get kids started on the road to lifelong fitness through exercise, it's legitimate to define success for each of these groups according to their goals and abilities. Of course, you've also got students who couldn't care less about athletics, health, or exercise. Your job is harder with these kids, because you've got to give them the motivation that will move them into a group with legitimate movement-for-life goals.

2. **Schools can control the conditions to create success.** If administrators and faculty implement the changes necessary to accommodate emotional, social, physical, and cognitive differences among students, schools can offer physical education programs that foster success for the vast majority of students. What are some of these changes?

- We should structure our programs so students are given choices about how to fulfill the mandated curriculum. For example, during a racket sport or activity unit, one teacher might teach squash racquetball, another badminton, another tennis, and the last paddle ball. Each teacher would teach the unit they are strongest in, and students could sign up for the activity that interests them most. This process would be repeated for each general unit in the curriculum, giving students choices about the overall design of their own programs.

- Our curricula must provide units that match the primary motivators of physical activity for different students: some youngsters enjoy the social nature of games; others enjoy the competition inherent in traditional sports; still others derive a sense of personal satisfaction from physical activity and becoming more fit. Thus, your program will have to include activities such as walking, gardening, or fishing, as well as more traditional activities. You must encourage all students to participate meaningfully in sports or other active pastimes that will help keep them moving and healthy for as long as they live.

- Our programs should empower students through giving them choice among the levels at which they'll participate in those units (beginning, intermediate, advanced, or elite). The staff must work hard to see that students select tasks at levels in which they can, with honest effort and skilled instruction, be successful.

- All students, from those with physical and mental challenges to the elite athlete, should be provided with opportunities to be challenged and to develop their skills. The Canadian Association for Health, Physical Education and Recreation (CAHPER, 1993) notes that "Physical Education is not athletics, school teams, or elite sports for a few gifted students. . . . [It] is for all students . . . females and males, able-bodied and persons with disabilities alike." For each of these groups, instructors, administrators, and families need to maintain high expectations of learning and performance within each individual's ability.

- Students who are genuinely unable to meet the requirements of the unit in the normal time allotted should be given further opportunities to complete the work—within reason. Also, students who have already mastered the material in the unit should be given opportunities to go beyond what is offered in the customary curriculum.

- Teaching techniques should be varied to meet the different needs of students. These techniques may include intratask, task station, peer teaching, and the use of contracts.

- Our instructional programs should include skill progressions and drills that are diverse and appropriate to the readiness of each student to learn, incorporating opportunities for students to work at different levels. Teachers need to act as facilitators, to celebrate their students' successes and promote their strengths.

- We must take the mystery out of marking by using criterion-referenced assessment tools. All assessment should be based on observable criteria and be repeatable if necessary. The curriculum must include clear, written objectives and outstanding examples of performances that can be reviewed to see what a good product is.

- Multiple assessment strategies should be used to give an accurate picture of students' progress and to accommodate most students' learning styles and intellectual strengths.

The remainder of part I will discuss how to make these changes to create the conditions for student success, and part II will give you reproducible tools to help you implement them.

3. **Success breeds success.** As you work on changing your approach to teaching and your students experience greater levels of success, you will find that your desire to modify your program is reinforced. You will be encouraged to try more changes, and your students and administration will be more eager to buy into those changes than they were to try the first ones you proposed. Every success you experience will make even greater success more likely,

and your students will discover the same thing as they participate in your program. It's a good sort of roll to be on!

Factors That Foster Success

Clearly, goal-directed PE requires significant differences from the traditional way of looking at the educational process. Before we can talk about how to structure a curriculum based on goals, we will consider in this chapter some of the factors already listed that will affect that curriculum, namely

- student choice,
- inclusion, and
- extended and expanded opportunities.

Teaching technique factors will be covered in chapter 3, and assessment issue factors will be discussed at length in chapters 4 to 6.

Student Choice

If a goal-directed curriculum is to foster lifelong participation in physical movement for health, students need to practice making wise personal decisions about physical activity. Thus, students must be exposed to many types of physical skills and offered choices for which they must consider their personal inclinations, their physical abilities, and what motivates them. The physical education program must help them find activities and acquire attitudes through positive physical experiences that will encourage them to continue to be physically active after they leave school. You can create meaningful choices for students concerning what they will learn, how they will learn, and how they will be assessed.

What Students Will Learn

Often, you can allow kids to select which activities they will do to meet each dimension of the curriculum. Here are some ideas:

- If your school is large enough, instead of organizing your program by class year (7th grade, 10th grade, and so on) and semester, you could define classes by content (soccer, in-line skating, swimming, hiking, softball, basketball, bicycling, and so on) and unit length (two weeks, three weeks, whatever works for your school). This system is called the "modular approach." At registration, students could fill out a chart similar to the one presented in form 2.1 to ensure that their class choices fulfill the overall PE requirements. This chart is based on the assumption that 10 units would be completed

The Logistics of Giving Students Curriculum Choices

With students potentially registering for activities with different teachers every few weeks, monitoring attendance can be a concern. To keep your administration happy, have students simply sign up for "physical education" at the main school registration, then have them choose units later, during each student's first PE class of the term. Once each student's choice chart is filled out, you can use a spreadsheet to track which activities students enroll in. Organize the spreadsheet alphabetically by last name, and include three other categories: student identification numbers, class section, and enough blank spaces where you will type the units the students have signed up for. You can sort your database by activity and quickly get the attendance lists you need. This assists in planning and assures that students are accountable to attend the activities they have signed up for. (A quick way to get your database started is to copy or export the school administration PE class lists to a notepad or folder on a local network drive. Save it as a text file. Then import it to the database or spreadsheet program you are using.)

At the end of each day, the teachers from all the activities meet and exchange attendance data and record it on the attendance lists generated by administration, which are based on the official school attendance lists. With this extra step of internal registration and attendance occurring only within the physical education department, the process is invisible to the rest of the legal operation of the school.

Student name: **Class:**   **Teacher:**

Curriculum Dimension	Minimum Number of Units Per Dimension	Activities Selected
Games	1	
Fitness	1	
Dance	1	
Gymnastics	1	
Individual activities	1	
Outdoor pursuits	1	
Aquatics	1	
Your choice	3	

during a 22-week semester, and the "Minimum number of units per dimension" column defines the overall curriculum requirements. You, of course, would modify the chart to fit your school's requirements. Such a system requires leveled instruction, which I will discuss later in this chapter.

• A "Physical Education Course Selection Chart" can be used within a conventional semester-long PE class defined by year. This is particularly appropriate at schools that are not large enough to handle the modular approach. At the beginning of the semester, the students could be given the charts and fill them in based on a list of available units. These would serve as ballots that would be tallied and used to determine the units for that semester. The advantage of running a program this way is that students work harder at tasks they enjoy. The disadvantage of this approach is that students are less likely to be introduced to new activities than they are in a totally teacher-mandated course.

• Another option for increasing student choice is to offer a "Heart Rate Day" periodically during which students have a choice of whatever heart rate–increasing activity they wish to do. The students are able to plan their own activities as long as those activities have potential aerobic benefits. The only additional requirement is that they track their heart rate for the period.

• Plan all-school days during which students are provided a variety of physical activities to choose from. When I was at Bishop Kidd Junior High School we had five such days: a fall outdoor education day, two winter outdoor education days, a spring outdoor education field trip, and a track and field day. The program involved every student in the school, and teachers from academic subject areas planned cross-curricular goals that could be met on our outings.

The possibilities for increasing student choice of curriculum are endless. I have discussed only a few, but if you brainstorm with others who are interested in this area and are alert to new possibilities as you gain experience, you will come up with many others.

How Students Will Learn

Because students bring both different levels of skill and different effective methods of learning, you can also offer them choices about how they will learn.

Fitting in Off-Campus Activities

If an off-campus activity will take more than one class period, this extended time can be accommodated in a number of ways that minimize disruption to other subjects' classes:

• Schedule the activity back to back with the period before or after the lunch hour.

• Schedule the activity to begin before the first period or to end after the last period so that only one class period is affected.

• If the activity requires students to miss any classes other than physical education, require that they be up-to-date on their work in order to be included in the trip.

• If parent volunteers are not easily available, limit the number of available slots to the number the supervisors and teachers available for a unit can easily handle.

• You can let them select the level at which they will participate in a given activity. Thus, the same student may choose the elite level for football but the beginning level for in-line skating or gymnastics.

• By using learning stations (usually presented as task card teaching, which will be discussed in depth in chapter 3), you can offer students choices about the order in which they learn skills and the activities they use to learn or practice those skills.

• You can often organize your program so students can decide for themselves whether they will learn a particular skill through self- or peer instruction, teacher-led instruction, or independent study. These options will be discussed at length in chapter 3.

How Students Will Be Assessed

Here again, the possibilities for offering students legitimate choices are limited only by your (and their) creativity. Options might include class demonstrations, student-created performances, conventional tests, journals, portfolios, class-organized tournaments, self- or peer evaluation, instructor observation, or oral interviews. These options are fully discussed in chapters 4 through 6, but there are other ideas out there just waiting to be discovered. If you listen to your colleagues, students, and own creative thoughts, you'll add to this list every year.

Inclusion

Many excellent resources are available on inclusion, but because it's so basic to an effective program, I'd like to at least mention it. In an inclusive program the lessons and evaluation are designed to ensure all students can participate. The following are examples:

• Basketball can be modified by putting everyone in wheelchairs. This challenges the able-bodied and teaches them about the gifts of students who use wheelchairs.

• In track and field high jump, the bar is replaced by an elastic band or string placed between the high jump bars at an angle. Beginners jump over the low end, and experts, the high end. The teacher assesses the students' performances based on how well they execute the technique of jumping, whether it's the flop or the western roll.

• Inclusion means students of various skill levels playing in a game together but getting to modify the rules in regard to their participation according to their abilities. For example, in a volleyball game, the beginning performer may serve from the middle of the court, while the expert must serve from the back, using a specified technique and aiming for a specified target on the opposing court.

Inclusion is such an extensive subject I cannot cover it within the restrictions of this text. There are many excellent resources available, some of which are listed in the box entitled "Resources on Inclusion in Physical Education."

Extended and Expanded Opportunities

In most schools today, credit is given for time spent in a subject, as long as a minimum 50 percent is achieved on course work and tests. But in goals-driven physical education, students get credit when they demonstrate they have achieved the specified goal. Having students achieve mastery or exit goals at levels that reflect each student's unique abilities will sometimes require that students have extra time available to work at improving and mastering a given set of skills:

• Extended opportunities must be planned for students who need more time to set up and engage in remedial activities necessary to meet the desired outcome. Extended opportunities prevent students from being pushed ahead be-

Resources on Inclusion in Physical Education

Active Living Alliance for Canadians With Disabilities. 1993. *Moving to Inclusion,* Ottawa, Ontario: Fitness Canada.

Burton, A.W., and D.E. Miller. 1998. *Movement Skill Assessment.* Champaign, IL: Human Kinetics.

CAHPERD (www.cahperd.ca)

CAHPERD. 1994. *The Canadian Active Living Challenge Resource Book and Tool Kit.* Ottawa, Ontario: CAHPERD.

CAHPERD. 1992. *Gender Equity Through Physical Education.* Ottawa, Ontario: CAHPERD.

CIRA (www.intramurals.ca)

Eichstaedt, C.B., and B.W. Lavay. 1992. *Physical Activity for Individuals With Mental Retardation.* Champaign, IL: Human Kinetics.

Lieberman, L.J., and J.F. Cowart. 1996. *Games for People With Sensory Impairments.* Champaign, IL: Human Kinetics.

Morris, D., and J. Stiehl. 1999. "How to Change Any Game." Pages 15-38 in *Changing Kids' Games,* 2nd ed. Champaign, IL: Human Kinetics.

Morris, D., and J. Stiehl. 1999. "Helping Others Change Games." Pages 39-52 in *Changing Kids' Games,* 2nd ed. Champaign, IL: Human Kinetics.

National Consortium for Physical Education and Recreation for Individuals With Disabilities. 1995. *Adapted Physical Education National Standards.* Champaign, IL: Human Kinetics.

Winnick, J.P. 2000. *Adapted Physical Education and Sport,* 3rd ed. Champaign, IL: Human Kinetics.

fore they understand prerequisite concepts, as sometimes happens in traditional methods because of time constraints.

• Expanded opportunities must be offered to gifted and highly trained students to encourage and enable them to pursue skills on an elite level.

Such opportunities can sometimes take place at off-campus locations, giving the additional advantage of connecting the students' learning to their lives outside of school.

Extended Opportunity

Giving students enough time to meet their goals or the goals set out in the program is key to goal-directed physical education. For example, if a student is unable to master a given badminton stroke or a headstand in the time allotted for the units associated with these skills, that student can be given extra time to practice these skills and improve his mark. Students can practice under supervision at lunch, before school, or after school. Practice can take place at local community centers or at home if the skill can be safely performed there. After the agreed-upon extra time, the student is reassessed. In this way, not only do we give students an opportunity to master skills they have not yet succeeded at, we also reinforce the idea that physical activity and skill development are important lifelong processes that take place over extended periods of time.

A false start

When I was first involved in offering extended opportunity, our department embraced the ideas involved in "mastery learning" in their entirety. This meant we required students to earn 65 percent or better on one unit before they could move on to the next one. We also allowed students unlimited opportunities to improve their marks. But soon we discovered that this approach was not practical. Allowing students to continue to work on unit one while the rest of the class was working on unit three was more difficult than we had anticipated, despite the development of individualized packages for instruction. Also, many students—knowing that they would get unlimited opportunities later to get it right—did not bother to do a good job when assignments were first made if the work did not fit conveniently into their schedules.

This resulted in enormous amounts of work being turned in at the end of the term and had three negative effects:

1. It became very demanding for teachers to complete marking their assignments and prepare report cards.
2. Because they had delayed doing their best work until later in the term, students were not getting feedback on work they completed until it was too late to make changes.
3. Many students procrastinated until they were unable to complete the courses.

A plan that worked

Under the leadership of our principal, Mr. Ed Marchand, our staff reviewed our approach and made a number of practical adjustments that resulted in a new expanded opportunity policy that proved to be quite successful. We posted our new policy and frequently referred students to it so they would be quite clear on what was expected of them. We began by establishing that reassessment opportunities were not to be had for the asking:

"Re-assessment is a privilege, not a right, and will be considered only when students have demonstrated a reasonable effort to complete the task on time and to the best of their abilities."

We also established six guidelines for extended opportunity:

1. Late assignments without prior arrangement may not be accepted. The opportunity for deadline extensions for outcome completion and reassessment is much more likely to be provided if the student discusses the need for it with the teacher in advance of the deadline. If accepted, the initial deadline and "incomplete" mark will be considered the initial assessment.
2. Work that is incomplete or is assessed at less than 65 percent will not be accepted. This rejection will constitute the initial assessment.
3. Students may be reassessed on skill performance tests and written tests at any time within the unit. After the unit is

completed, students have two weeks to reassess their skill performance and two weeks to reassess their written tests, assignments, and quizzes.

4. Reassessment opportunities are not always possible due to the inavailability of facilities or inclement weather. Extensions beyond the two-week post-unit deadline will occur only if the student has completed the appropriate remediation or skill practice by that original deadline and are at the discretion of your teacher.

5. For reassessed work students will receive the full mark they achieve on the skill performance test and a maximum of 80 percent on their written assignments.

6. Work will be accepted only after these dates at the teacher's discretion. All unfinished work will be given an "incomplete."

After the new policy was instituted, we found that most of those students who were prone to procrastination got the message and worked very hard the first time through. The number of reassessments decreased, and on-task time increased even for that small percentage of students who continued to procrastinate. We also began to get requests for reassessment from students who had worked hard to improve or master a skill instead of from those who were off task and required discipline during the unit. It was a lot more rewarding to spend time reassessing the work of students who were genuinely interested in a unit but needed more time or individual attention than marking the same work twice from someone who had put in minimal effort! What a great feeling it was when students asked for extra help! It meant they were interested in physical education and wanted to improve. This is, after all, what education is about—getting students excited about learning and improving their performances.

Expanded Opportunity

Expanded opportunities can be offered to students who are already proficient in the current PE unit. Why bore these athletes by forcing them to practice skills they've already mastered? Instead, let them use the class time to work on an area of the program where they are weaker, or to play a leadership role by acting as a teacher assistant or peer tutor, or even for doing their homework for other courses.

Expanded Opportunity Criteria

Any student taking part in Physical Education 9, 10, 11, or 12 may challenge the outcomes of any unit or curricular dimension offered if the student meets the following criteria:

1. Can demonstrate mastery of level C or D performance outcomes.

2. Is actively involved in an alternative program offering the unit being challenged.

3. Demonstrates that a minimum of 25 hours of combined practice and competition for the activity have been completed during the challenged unit for each credit earned.

4. Completes a research report that demonstrates understanding of the basic skills and how they are applied within offensive or defensive strategies (where needed) for the sport involved.

5. For physical fitness units, completes the Individualized Fitness Unit in six weeks and earns at least 210 points.

Students successfully challenging unit outcomes may either use the time to gain leadership hours by acting as a teaching assistant or to work on other subjects in a study center. If they choose to participate, they will receive a mark and be offered the opportunity to opt out of a unit that meets the same curricular requirement.

This idea worked very well for us at the high school level. A student participating on Provincial Elite teams or varsity teams at school could "challenge" activities by turning in a portfolio (usually involving video), supporting the claim that she had already mastered the material in the unit. She was required to provide the portfolio at least a week before the beginning of the unit. If the portfolio evaluation determined that the student's claim was legitimate, she was offered an expanded opportunity. For example, a varsity football player might choose to complete a weight program during the flag football unit or an elite volleyball player might serve as a teacher assistant during the volleyball unit. Students struggling in math but excelling in basketball have done extra math assignments in class to ensure they maintained their varsity eligibility. We found that very few students opted to use their extended opportunity for studying for other subject areas. Those who did were already getting plenty of physical activity during their varsity practices.

We had clearly outlined procedures for evaluating the challenge portfolios and for ensuring the student would continue his elite activity throughout the unit he was challenging. The student would have one or a number of the games he played with his elite team videotaped. The student athlete and coach would then review the tape and assess the student's play against the team's goals. After the coach and athlete decided a percentage-based grade using criteria they agreed on, the student athlete would give the teacher the tape, grade, and rationale for the grade arrived at by the student and his coach. Next, the teacher would evaluate the athlete's performance based on how well it met the goals of the unit being challenged and would combine this mark with the student and coach's grade. To help nonteaching coaches assess their athletes against the goals of the school program, the teacher would send the goals for that dimension of the curriculum to the evaluating coaches, along with evaluation sheets like forms 2.2 and 2.3 on which they could record students' work.

Cross-sport challenging

A student can use participation in almost any sport to challenge a unit, even if that sport is not offered at your school. For example, be-cause ice hockey is a goal-oriented game, and the strategies and skills used in ice hockey would meet the curriculum goals outlined for all goal-oriented games such as soccer or basketball, a student could use his ice hockey experience to challenge either of these goal-oriented sport units. In the same fashion, ice hockey could be used to challenge handball, ultimate Frisbee, field hockey, or any other goal-oriented game.

An advantage of allowing cross-sport challenging is that by doing so we level the playing field for all our gifted students. If, for example, a physical education program consists of basketball, volleyball, baseball, soccer, football, wrestling, badminton, tennis, track and field, and cross-country running, athletes who excel in one or many of these activities are rewarded with high marks. However, many students may meet the exit outcomes for many of these sports by achieving excellence in sports not offered in school, yet their achievements are not recognized. If our programs are designed to encourage students to be active for a lifetime, we need to expand what we will assess and recognize that learning happens outside the classroom.

Physical activity leadership challenging

Expanded opportunities need not always be sport participation. Leadership in physical activity may also be explored. "Requirements for Leadership Unit" on page 18 outlines the expectations for such a program. Form 2.4 may be used to evaluate such leadership projects. A calendar for planning the activities for the challenge unit may be drawn up, using the planning calendar from the sample fitness unit as a model (see page 213).

Writing a Goal-Directed Curriculum

Now that we've established the principles you should keep in mind as you implement your goal-directed curriculum, let's talk about writing that curriculum. A goal-directed curriculum simply means that

- the school system's ultimate goals for physical education (generally government-mandated at some level) will be met if the course objectives for each year are met;

Dear Coach,

Your athlete, _____ , has challenged the _____ dimension of our physical education program and wishes to receive credit for athletic endeavors outside of the classroom. In order to receive credit the athlete must demonstrate that he or she has competed at a high level for 25 hours within the dimension he or she is challenging. Please verify the athlete's participation in practice or competition by completing and signing this attendance schedule as well as the Athlete Evaluation (form 2.3).

Thank you for your assistance.

Sincerely,

_____

Attendance Schedule

Date: _____	Date: _____	Date: _____	Date: _____	Date: _____
Time in hours and minutes:	Time in hours and minutes:	Time in hours and minutes:	Time in hours and minutes:	Time in hours and minutes:
Date: _____	Date: _____	Date: _____	Date: _____	Date: _____
Time in hours and minutes:	Time in hours and minutes:	Time in hours and minutes:	Time in hours and minutes:	Time in hours and minutes:
Date: _____	Date: _____	Date: _____	Date: _____	Date: _____
Time in hours and minutes:	Time in hours and minutes:	Time in hours and minutes:	Time in hours and minutes:	Time in hours and minutes:
Date: _____	Date: _____	Date: _____	Date: _____	Date: _____
Time in hours and minutes:	Time in hours and minutes:	Time in hours and minutes:	Time in hours and minutes:	Time in hours and minutes:
Date: _____	Date: _____	Date: _____	Date: _____	Date: _____
Time in hours and minutes:	Time in hours and minutes:	Time in hours and minutes:	Time in hours and minutes:	Time in hours and minutes:

Coach's signature:_____

From *Learning by Choice in Secondary Physical Education: Creating a Goal-Directed Program* by Kevin Kaardal, 2001, Champaign, IL: Human Kinetics.

Form 2.3 Athlete Evaluation

Athlete's name:_____

Sport: _____

Please describe the unit goals the student has met by comparing his or her play with our physical education program document:

_____

_____

_____

_____

_____

Strengths:

_____

_____

_____

_____

_____

In which percentile, compared to other athletes you have coached at this age level, does this athlete rank?

Top 5%   **Top 10%**   **Top 15%**   **Top 20%**   **Top 25%**   **Top 30%**   **I rank this athlete in the top _____%**

Areas to improve in:

_____

_____

_____

_____

_____

General comments:

_____

_____

_____

_____

_____

Coach's signature _____ Coach's phone # _____ Date _____

From *Learning by Choice in Secondary Physical Education: Creating a Goal-Directed Program* by Kevin Kaardal, 2001, Champaign, IL: Human Kinetics.

Requirements for Leadership Unit

In addition to the other requirements listed below, at the end of the learning experience, the student will give a presentation clearly demonstrating his or her learning in the following three areas:

1. Knowledge—subject content
2. Competence—understanding of content
3. Affective orientation—desire to learn, motivation, willingness to change

Requirements and Exemplars for Levels

Level A

• The student will provide 5 hours of leadership in the physical education department as evidenced by the student's participation in assisting, organizing, or running intramural events; acting as a minor official at school athletic events such as league games or tournaments; or helping set up equipment for athletic events.

• Students will complete a student leadership report describing their leadership experience and recording their roles, responsibilities, and the time spent providing leadership. This must be signed by the physical education teacher who is accountable for the activity.

• Exemplars: Teacher examples, completed reports that received 80 percent or better, completed intramural leadership planning guides that receive an 80 percent or better.

Level B

Same as level A, except student will provide 7.5 hours of leadership.

Level C

Same as level B, except student will provide 10 hours of leadership and add serving on the active-living executive council or other additional leadership activity.

Level D

Same as level C, except student will add acting as a teaching assistant.

• course objectives will be met as a natural result of meeting unit goals; and

• unit goals will automatically be met if lesson goals are met.

You can see, then, that by beginning with your ultimate goals, you can design a program "backward" to build in the necessary components step by step. This concept is popularly called "designing down and delivering up" (Wiggins and McTighe 1998). The simplest way of explaining this process is to list the basic steps of designing down in order:

1. You determine what the appropriate goals are.

2. You decide how your students can demonstrate (and thus how you can assess) that they have met those goals by their exit grade (10th grade in some places, 12th grade in others).

3. You decide what units (including sports, activities, and concepts) can be taught that will give students the opportunity to meet these goals and demonstrate their competence.

Form 2.4 Physical Activity Leadership Report

Name: _____ **Class:** _____

Teacher: _____ **Level:** A   B   C   D

Total hours required: _____

Leadership activity	Hours completed	Teacher's signature

Total hours earned: _____

Briefly describe your leadership roles and responsibilities.

_____

_____

_____

_____

_____

_____

_____

_____

_____

Describe your experience. What would you keep the same? What would you change to improve the activity or your performance of your role?

_____

_____

_____

_____

_____

_____

_____

_____

_____

_____

From *Learning by Choice in Secondary Physical Education: Creating a Goal-Directed Program* by Kevin Kaardal, 2001, Champaign, IL: Human Kinetics.

4. You plan sport- or activity-specific content for each unit, including evaluation tools that will enable students to demonstrate, and you to assess, their mastery of material at the lesson and unit levels.

5. You plan lessons and learning activities.

6. You follow the same process for elective physical education courses, beginning with enriched versions of the exit goals for the required physical education curriculum.

"Delivering up" simply means that once you design your program, you begin with students at the step 5 level (lessons and learning activities) then work backward toward the goal with which you began the design process.

Grant Wiggins summarizes designing down by saying you must identify the desired results, determine what is acceptable evidence that those results (goals) have been met, and then plan learning experiences and instruction that will engage the students and enable them to reach those goals.

Establish Goals

The place you've got to begin for establishing goals is with yourself. Whatever goals you are pursuing have to be goals you believe in—or you cannot succeed as a teacher. So first you must answer two questions:

- Why should physical education be taught?
- Why do I want to teach PE and how does this relate to mandated goals?

Why Should Physical Education Be Taught?

Because you're a physical educator you've no doubt thought about this question a lot. But reviewing some of the excellent reasons why PE is important may help rekindle your own vision of what you want to accomplish as a teacher, enabling you to understand the overarching goal that you will want to direct your curriculum toward.

Physical education is essential to a complete education. No other school subject has the potential to so directly and positively affect a person's physical health. With sedentary lifestyles now the norm and obesity on the rise, physical education is more crucial than ever. The *Surgeon General's Report on Physical Activity and Health* (USDHHS, 1996) states that physical inactivity is the major cause of heart disease, adult-onset diabetes, and some cancers. Inactivity, it says, is as risky to your health as smoking is! Research has indicated that regular physical activity helps lessen symptoms of hypertension and depression, improves weight control, and enhances bone growth and muscle development. Thus, it is clear that promoting healthy living though physical education courses has the potential not only to improve quality of life for students but also to save society millions of dollars in healthcare costs as well.

People who are healthy perform better on *all* the tasks in their lives, including academics, because, compared with unhealthy people, they exhibit increased concentration, enhanced memory, greater alertness, and improved learning capabilities. Furthermore, physical activity greatly reduces stress. Because healthful habits and skills established in youth carry forward, physical education is an essential part of a person's lifelong learning and must begin at the very outset of our communities' public schooling efforts.

Disabling Conditions Prevented or Improved by Exercise

According to Dr. Carlos J. Crespo, public health adviser for the National Institutes of Health and a health statistician for the Centers for Disease Control and Prevention, research has shown that the following conditions can be prevented or improved by exercise:

- Heart disease (including hypertension and stroke)
- Diabetes mellitus
- Various types of cancer
- Osteoporosis
- Falls (especially for older persons)
- Musculoskeletal disabilities associated with aging
- Low back pain
- Obesity
- Poor mental health

Youngsters in good physical education programs are more confident and positive about school, physical activity, and themselves. They learn how to socialize and exhibit less aggressive and hyperactive behaviors. Through organized physical activity, children learn to establish and follow rules of conduct, work cooperatively, and compete with an appropriate focus on strategy and skill, with winning secondary to participation. Dance and gymnastics provide opportunities to express thought and emotion and respond to music physically. Learning new leisure activities teaches students how to enjoy their free time actively. These benefits help counter students' being sedentary, lonely, or overly dependent on videos or computer games for recreation. According to "CAHPERD QDPE Fast Facts," it's even been shown that attendance improves at schools with quality physical education.

Thus, when physical education is well-taught, with an emphasis on lifelong movement as a key to fitness, it benefits the whole student, the whole curriculum, and the whole society. What greater motivation could you find for putting together a dynamic PE program?

Your Personal Motivations and Physical Education Goals

Having explored why PE should be taught, you should next define your primary personal reasons for teaching. For example, I believe lifetime fitness should be the prime focus of a good physical education program. Thus, I understand my mission as a physical educator is to impart to students

1. a strong motivation to live fit, active lives, including the ability to enjoy and appreciate physical activity;

2. the skills necessary for participating in lifetime physical activities, including the basic motor skills required for a wide variety of physical activities and the ability to assess their own or a peer's strengths and weaknesses related to participating in, leading, or understanding physical activity;

3. the ability to plan and participate in a personal fitness program;

4. knowledge of safe practices, rules, strategies, basic principles of movement, and psychological concepts related to performance enhancement in individual and team activities; and

5. the ability to cooperate and compete, using codes of fair play.

Next, consider how your personal motivator fits in with government-mandated goals. In Alberta, for example, the Alberta Learning 2000

Students who exercise regularly are, on average, better adjusted and more socially adept than those who do not.

Physical Education Curriculum team has prescribed the following four desired outcomes:

- General Outcome A: Students will acquire skills through a variety of developmentally appropriate movement activities (e.g., dance, games, types of gymnastics, individual activities, and alternate-environment activities such as aquatics and outdoor pursuits).
- General Outcome B: Students will understand, experience, and appreciate the health benefits that result from physical activity.
- General Outcome C: Students will interact positively with others.
- General Outcome D: Students will assume responsibility for leading an active way of life.

(Note that to be consistent with the terminology in the rest of this text, and thus to avoid confusion, I will refer to these "general outcomes" as "exit goals," and the Alberta Learning 2000 "suboutcomes" as "secondary goals" from this point on. Although the Alberta Learning 2000 terminology is different from the terminology that I use, the function is the same.)

It's easy to see that my personal desires fit in well with the goals that were handed to me by the system:

- Exit Goal A matches my second and fourth goals: Teach students the skills necessary for participating in lifetime physical activities . . . and the ability to assess their own or a peer's strengths and weaknesses related to participating in, leading, or understanding physical activity; and impart to students knowledge . . . related to performance enhancement in individual and team activities.
- Exit Goal B matches my first goal: Motivate students to live fit, active lives, including the ability to enjoy and appreciate physical activity.
- Exit Goal C matches my fifth goal: Impart to students the ability to cooperate and compete using codes of fair play.
- Exit Goal D matches my first and third goals: Motivate students . . . and equip students to be able to plan and participate in a personal fitness program.

Thus, it's clear to me that if I "design down" based on the provincial goals, I will be achieving my personal goals while acting out of my own passion. Thus, I can wholly endorse and use the goals that have been mandated for me as I design my curriculum. Now there's motivation to plan with enthusiasm!

If you take the time to think about what you care deeply about—what motivates you to teach physical education—you will generally find that, as in my case, it will agree nicely with the stated goals of your school system for physical education. After all, the people who write those goals generally care about kids and understand the importance of physical activity as much as you do! But don't think you can skip this exercise: it is important to establish your personal motivator(s) first, because until you've done so, you will have no vision for your students. And without a vision to inspire you, no matter how "by the book" you are about establishing a goal-directed curriculum, the day-to-day challenges of teaching physical education will grind you down rather than push you and your students up to higher levels of achievement and satisfaction. Moreover, if you find there is some discrepancy between your personal goals and the goals of your system, now is the time to come to terms with that. Unless you've thought through this problem carefully and come to some solution, your inner conflict will keep you from being the best teacher you can be.

In the Absence of Mandated Goals

What if there are no mandated goals? In the United States, for example, there are no government-mandated standards on the national level, and local school systems vary tremendously in whether they provide goals for physical education. Some systems have detailed plans, while others have no stated goals at all, with the majority lying somewhere between these two extremes. But whatever you are given to work with, you must come up with clear, comprehensive goals if you are to accomplish anything. If nothing is provided, you must provide your own, and this is best done by working with interested people within your community: other teachers, parents, school administrators, and experts from academia and the sports and fitness community. Take advantage of state standards (most states have them), National Association for Sport and Physical Education (NASPE) standards, or standards from various other governments such as the Key Stages mandated by the British government or the *Physical Education Guide to Implementation* from Alberta Learning 2000.

Write Secondary Goals for Exit Goals

Before you can begin the process of making unit and lesson level curriculum choices, you must break the exit goals down one more level, into 4 to 10 secondary goals that can be directly addressed by unit choices. If you have a comprehensive guide such as the Alberta Learning 2000 materials, you will not need to do this, because there will already be secondary goals provided. If you do not have such a guide, you must do this task yourself. The object is to break down goals until you reach a level for which you can describe general tasks that can be met by unit curriculum choices. This can generally be done by establishing a primary goal, setting exit goals that will feed into the primary goal, and determining secondary goals that will feed into the exit goals. "Establishing Primary, Exit, and Secondary Goals" illustrates how I might do this for one goal if I did not have the Alberta Learning 2000 curriculum statements to guide me.

Decide on Appropriate Units

Now you can begin to think about what curriculum content must be mastered (and in what order) to achieve each of your secondary goals. In chapter 3, I'll discuss how you can "level," or individualize, the components for planning and participating in personal fitness activities to meet each student's unique fitness needs.

Some units are so standard as to be almost a given. You can begin by listing the obvious activities and then seeing what goals each will meet. For example, softball is a game that is an excellent lifelong activity, so you'll probably want to offer it. Using the Alberta Learning 2000 goals, I can see that a softball unit can be designed to meet the following secondary goals:

- Secondary Goal 10 (of Exit Goal A) for grade 10: Students will adapt and improve activity specific skills in a variety of games.
- Secondary Goal 8 (of Exit Goal B) for grade 10: Students will select and perform appro-

priate physical activities for personal stress management and relaxation.

- Secondary Goal 3 (of Exit Goal C) for grade 10: Students will demonstrate etiquette and fair play.
- Secondary Goal 5 (of Exit Goal C) for grade 10: Students will develop and apply practices that contribute to teamwork.
- Secondary Goal 6 (of Exit Goal C) for grade 10: Students will identify and demonstrate positive behaviors that show respect for self and others.
- Secondary Goal 8 (of Exit Goal D) for grade 10: Students will be prepared for participation in community activity programs for all ages and will understand the influences that affect participation.

It is clear that softball can be used to address all the secondary goals just listed. Softball or slow-pitch is a game people can play for a lifetime and that contributes to health by helping players socialize, reduce stress, and have fun. It requires the development and refinement of basic motor skills like throwing, catching, funneling, using lateral movement to close space, and intercepting and fielding a hit ball, batting (using an implement to strike a moving object), and sprinting around the bases. If designed properly, this unit can also help students practice etiquette and fair play and develop and apply practices that contribute to teamwork and behaviors that show respect for self and others. Because softball is such a common pastime of active adults, it would also lend itself easily to promoting students' participation in community activity programs for all ages. (Notice that this description clearly indicates the value of this particular unit as it relates to the students' life outside of school. Be sure to take every opportunity to make this connection in the students' minds so they can grasp the real value of mastering these softball skills.)

If you examine the goals for the slow-pitch softball unit on page 233 and the Affective Evaluation Chart on page 84, you will see that if students reach those goals, they will clearly be starting to fulfill the Alberta Learning 2000 secondary goals listed earlier. See "Soccer—Goals for each Level" (page 34) for a second example of what the completed goals for a leveled unit would look like.

Establishing Primary, Exit, and Secondary Goals

Step I: State my primary goal.

Enable as many students as possible to achieve lifetime fitness though active living.

Step II: State my exit goals.

By the time students exit my program, they will have gained the following:

1. A strong motivation to live fit, active lives, including the ability to enjoy and appreciate physical activity.
2. The skills necessary for participating in lifetime physical activities, including the basic motor skills required for a variety of physical activities and the ability to assess their own or a peer's strengths and weaknesses related to participating in, leading, or understanding physical activity.
3. The ability to plan and participate in a personal fitness program according to their unique abilities.
4. Knowledge of safe practices, rules, strategies, basic principles of movement, and psychological concepts related to performance enhancement in individual and team activities.
5. The ability to cooperate and compete using codes of fair play.

Step III: Select one of my exit goals and develop secondary goals for it.

Exit Goal 3: Students will have the ability to plan and participate in a personal fitness program according to their unique abilities.

Secondary goals:

1. Students will understand and design workouts based on energy systems—aerobic, muscular endurance, muscular strength, and flexibility.
2. Students will maintain a personal fitness program for a minimum of eight weeks.
3. Students will be able to demonstrate safe warm-up and cool-down practices.
4. Students will understand the health benefits of and energy systems used when participating in a variety of physical activities and will incorporate some of these activities into their eight-week workout plan.
5. Students will understand how to self-assess their current fitness level.
6. Students will be able to set reasonable, achievable fitness goals based on their unique abilities.
7. Students will be able to measure their own progress toward achieving their goals and make appropriate adjustments to their fitness plan.
8. Students will develop healthy, long-term, positive attitudes toward attaining and maintaining a fit body as part of total wellness.

Step IV: Repeat step III for my remaining exit goals.

Once you have listed the units that come immediately to mind as well as the goals that each addresses, you should look for balance among what you have offered. Does it include activities such as bicycling, gardening, and hiking not usually offered in physical education but that may pull in students who will otherwise think physical activity is not for them? Can you offer these activities easily in your community? Are there activities that will allow for successes for the nonathlete? Are there activities that will challenge the gifted athlete? Are there new and novel activities being offered, considering the demographics of the majority of your students and the opportunities they would have to participate in these new activities? What is your school board's policy on offering an activity? Is the activity considered too risky to offer? White-water canoeing, for example, would be very risky, placing the teachers, students, and school board at risk; therefore, you probably shouldn't offer it in a physical education program. Common sense, the teacher's expertise, and legal constraints will be determining factors in what activities and sports you offer. Brainstorm with others involved in curriculum planning and consult some of the many excellent materials available on curriculum planning. You will find some of these listed in the bibliography.

Plan Unit Contents and Lessons and Learning Activities

You should begin planning each unit's content by analyzing what skills and strategies must be taught for the students to master the activity. This is covered in chapter 3. As you establish the necessary skills and strategies for each unit, you must also decide how each can be assessed. This is discussed in detail in chapters 4 through 6.

The final step in curriculum design is planning individual lessons and the activities involved in each. Chapter 3 presents information on how to do this, taking different teaching techniques into account.

The design-down model of goal-directed physical education helps everyone involved—teacher and students—connect the skills learned in class to activities and tasks outside the gymnasium or athletic field and to life beyond high school. Physical education should give students repeated positive experiences in developing skills they will find useful in many settings. Learning to cooperate with peers in a team environment, for example, is useful at home, in other classes, and in the work world. Or consider practice in analyzing skilled performance: having the confidence to do this analysis can help students if they eventually have children of their own and want to participate with them in physical activity, help them be successful in sport, or get involved in community sports as volunteer coaches. Learning to be active for life will, of course, improve the quality of students' experiences in all areas of life for as long as they live. If you keep these ideas in mind as you fashion goals and design curricula, you are likely to develop programs that not only excite your students but also set them on the path to lifetime fitness.

CHAPTER 3

Individualized Teaching Techniques

Physical education at Hugh Sutherland School began with a cross-country running unit every year. It whipped kids into shape at the outset, and it also helped us select a cross-country team. During my first year at Sutherland, I upheld the tradition and ran a fairly conventional unit. But many students did not enjoy it. The kids who loved to run thought it was great. The majority, however, did not love to run, and it was a chore to get them to do it. They complained and felt like failures because they couldn't complete the distances I had set—5K for everyone in grade 10, 8K for everyone in grade 11, and so on. I knew my unit wasn't working very well when some of our school's top academic grade 11 students complained I was torturing them by making them run 8K in class as their final cross-country test. What was even worse, I found that a significant number of students resisted physical education for the rest of the year—something I wasn't used to happening in my classes. Here I was trying to turn kids on to being active for a lifetime, and the way I delivered my first unit had turned them off for months. The principal, who was a kind and wise man, suggested I develop an alternative delivery system that accommodated everybody's ability—much like the individualized units I was using elsewhere in the program. I knew the time had come for a change. By the time the second year rolled around, the other physical educator at Sutherland and I had come up with a different approach, and I was excited to see how our new plan would work.

This was how we changed the unit: Students were allowed to choose the distances they ran. They signed a contract such as the one shown in form 3.1 and were expected to run the distance they agreed to for each class. Students were allowed to choose when they ran or how many times they ran in a given class period, but all students had to meet the objectives they had written on their contracts. We also added aerobic games to the unit and played running and tag games to increase the level of fun. We had a 1K running track that surrounded a park with fields, tennis courts, and basketball hoops, so we could play soccer, basketball, or road hockey.

Organizing the unit to allow for instruction and practice geared to each individual turned out to be the key in transforming the cross-country experience at our school. Providing different levels of activity and allowing students to choose their own levels for

Name: _____

Class: _____

Level A

100% = 3.5 km per class

90% = 3.0 km per class

80% = 2.5 km per class

70% = 2.0 km per class

60% = 1.5 km per class

50% = 1.0 km per class

Less than 50% = Less than 1.0 km per class

Level B

100% = 4.0 km per class

90% = 3.5 km per class

80% = 3.0 km per class

70% = 2.5 km per class

60% = 2.0 km per class

50% = 1.5 km per class

Less than 50% = Less than 1.5 km per class

Level C

100% = 5.5 km per class

90% = 5.0 km per class

80% = 4.0 km per class

70% = 3.0 km per class

60% = 2.5 km per class

50% = 2.0 km per class

Less than 50% = Less than 2.0 km per class

I wish to be evaluated at level _____ . My goal is to run _____ km per class.

To keep a running total of the kilometers you have run, check off one number below per kilometer completed. This will help you gauge your progress toward your personal goal.

1	2	3	4	5	6	7	8	9	10	11	12	13	14	15	16	17	18	19	20	21	22	23	24	25	26
27	28	29	30	31	32	33	34	35	36	37	38	39	40	41	42	43	44	45	46	47	48	49	50	51	52
53	54	55	56	57	58	59	60	61	62	63	64	65	66	67	68	69	70								

From *Learning by Choice in Secondary Physical Education: Creating a Goal-Directed Program* by Kevin Kaardal, 2001, Champaign, IL: Human Kinetics.

instruction, participation, and assessment turned our program around completely. Kids no longer moaned about PE but ran with enthusiasm. Most of them actually had fun while they got into better aerobic shape. And we were still able to choose our cross-country team.

Once I moved to Bishop Kidd, where we were set up for team teaching, the cross-country unit became even better. Here are some of the improvements we instituted:

• One of our teachers set out a number of cross-country run routes of varying distances in our schoolyard. He drew these on a map, and we set cones with different colored pinnies on them to signify each course.

• One teacher would monitor and encourage the runners on the routes we'd set up while another directed running games the students could choose to participate in to fulfill their contracted running obligation. For example, in Fox and Hound the "hound" (either a student or the teacher) had to chase the "foxes" (the rest of the class) to try to tag them or pass them on the cross-country route. Foxes had to only run the distance they had contracted for on the route.

• The other two teachers would set up aerobic games, such as soccer, ultimate Frisbee, and flag and capture games, that the students could play before or after they ran.

I'll never forget the culminating day of the cross-country unit for my 8th grade classes during the fourth year that I ran it at Bishop Kidd. At the end of the day, the vice principal came up to me and teasingly said, "Kevin, I have a bone to pick with you. Not only were all your 8th grade students late to their next classes from PE today, they also couldn't count! They were all so excited that they told me that they'd run anywhere from 4- to 8Ks in PE today!"

I was delighted to tell him that the kids were late because they all were trying to set personal best distances for running or running and walking continuously for the entire 50 minute period, and no one wanted to stop in the middle of the 1K course. And in fact, they could count quite well: they had all completed those distances.

"4- to 8K!" he exclaimed. "How do you get kids to do that?"

I explained that, at the suggestion of a colleague, I had started out three years earlier by giving each kid one Popsicle stick for every lap they completed. I had my doubts it would make any difference in the students' performances. After all, they were only Popsicle sticks. No Popsicle, no prizes, just a concrete way to count how they were doing. But it seemed to work: every student in my class that first year achieved a personal best! Later another colleague suggested using playing cards instead of Popsicle sticks and giving the student with the best hand at the end of the class a small prize. We also had students sign the sticks and drew for a prize to make the Popsicle stick run even more exciting. The kids loved it, and most of them plowed around that cross-country route as fast as they could.

The unit had excited students about running. They had choices. They set their own goals; they ran while playing games that improved their cardiovascular performance; and they ran their own distance each day. That fourth year we had over 100 of our 280 students participate on our school cross-country team!

The Benefits of Individualized Programs

My experiences with the cross-country unit at Hugh Sutherland School and Bishop Kidd convinced me once and for all that giving kids choices in physical education instruction is the way to go if you want kids to buy into lifetime fitness. The benefits of individualized instruction are many. Here are some of them:

For the Student

• Students get to work at their own pace, which creates less stress. They are not forced to participate in activities well beyond their abilities, risking embarrassment through failure. Nor are they made to work at activities well below their skill level and become bored.

• Students make most of the decisions. This is an important benefit since decision making is an essential skill in our information-oriented society.

• Teamwork is fostered through helping other students achieve their goals in peer teaching situations and group work within the program.

• No one is excluded in the learning process, because everyone can be challenged and can succeed at their own level.

- Students get to work on skills they like. This increases on-task behavior and helps provide a more positive classroom atmosphere for both the students and teacher.

For the Teacher

- You act as a facilitator rather than as an instructor (i.e., "How can I help?" rather than, "Do this now!"). This makes peer-teacher relations more positive.

- You will find using individualized units reduces stress because students make the most of the decisions about how the skill practice segment of the lesson will run. This frees you from designing the drills and monitoring transitions, allowing you to focus on the role of facilitator.

- As a result, you have more time to spend helping those students who need it and praising those who deserve it.

- There are fewer discipline problems, because students are working at what they want to do, keeping them on task longer.

- If you are not strong at a certain skill, you can provide skills posters for the kids—and yourself!—to refer to.

- You can incorporate a variety of teaching styles in one lesson. Thus, you have a greater chance of reaching every student in the class at some point in your lesson.

Obstacles to Individualizing

With all these great benefits, why would anyone hesitate for a minute to institute individualized instruction and assessment? For lots of reasons! Here are some of the objections I've heard through the years, and my answers to them.

- **If you go this route, you give up class control.** I should hope not! A class that's out of control is a class where no one can learn. You remember Tom Urbanik, from chapter 1? Until I met Tom, I thought the only way to individualize was to go entirely with student choice of level. But Tom assigned all the levels himself, and for him, that worked perfectly well. Now I know it's important for you, as the teacher, to do whatever works best for you. How far you go in letting kids make choices is up to you. And the same thing goes with all the individualizing techniques

I share in this book. You can make many changes all at once or work into them gradually. You can adopt all these ideas or only a few of them. The main thing is to be sure you feel in control of each change and you pay attention to your students' reactions. If most of your kids aren't enjoying PE, acquiring skills related to sport or fitness, and enthusiastic about learning to be active for life, you owe it to yourself and them to keep trying different suggestions until you uncover those that work for you. If something works pretty well, try going a little farther with it. If it fails, back off and figure out why.

- **If you're not watching all the kids all the time, they won't stay on task.** My answer is that with individualized instruction you facilitate learning by using the teaching method that best fits the *student's learning style*. If a student needs to be directed to a given task, you tell him or her what to do. In a traditional class, for example, you might ask all the students to practice doing layups. You notice one youngster is fooling around or shooting three-point shots. You approach the student or call her over and redirect the behavior. It works the same way with individualized units. The student is given a task, for example, "Work on the skill and drill of your choice and have a partner act as the peer teacher." The teacher does not specify the exact skill or drill but does direct the task type. The student who is off task is given a task to complete from the contract he filled out earlier. The student who still doesn't respond is disciplined with a time-out. Classroom discipline does not change a whole lot—except that because students get to choose the skills they wish to work on, they are more likely to stay on task. Additional tips for classroom management are located throughout this chapter. Look for the boxes with the "Management Tip" title.

- **Given so much choice, kids will slack off.** In fact, the opposite is true, because students are involved in things they want to work at. For example, more gifted students can set up personal training programs, whereas students interested in activity for recreation might set up an active-living program that is specifically geared to their interests and abilities. In all the years I've let kids choose their own levels, I've had to intervene and tell a student he's got to move to a higher level only twice.

Management Tip

If you are running an individualized approach to instruction and see students practicing a drill that does not appear on your task sheets or posters, ask the students what they are doing before redirecting them, because they may have invented a drill that improves on what you have devised and helps them reach goals beyond your program.

Management Tip

During the part of the class when students are working on individual goals and you are acting as the "roaming facilitator," make sure you occasionally check up on what kids on the other side of the room are doing. Call out corrections or affirming statements from across the gym if you see misbehavior or exceptionally good work being done. This way, kids will know that even if you're not standing next to them, they're still being watched.

• **Unless I have all the class doing the same thing at the same time, I'll get really confused.** You'd be surprised how that doesn't happen if you just change the way you look at your role in the classroom. This is where learning to be a "facilitator" rather than a traditional teacher comes in. It doesn't mean at all that you surrender control of the classroom. It's very important for you to provide a general structure for each class. Each period should include a clear sequence of activity types that will ensure learning is occurring. Here's how I do it:

1. Every lesson begins with an introduction that connects it to the previous day's learning and outlines the goals for that day.

2. If the class is one in which kids will be physically active, I follow the introduction with a few minutes of student-led warm-up exercises.

3. Then I dismiss the kids to work on their individual goals. This is the bulk of the class period, and the time when I "roam," serving as a resource to kids as they work independently. For example, while I'm demonstrating drills to level A students, level B and C students might be playing in minipyramid tournaments. When I go to work with level B students, level C students continue their tournament while the level A group, who received the drill instruction, practice those drills, and so on. Throughout this stage of the class, I walk around whatever minilessons are going on, checking for comprehension, offering advice, posing questions, and correcting any incorrectly explained peer-teacher instructions. I include both formal and infor-

mal assessment as part of my instruction and make heavy use of peer instruction. You get the picture.

4. To track student performance, I use skill practice sheets such as the Volleyball Skills Test sheet, the first part of which is shown on page 32. Students are expected to record on these sheets the work they do every class. This helps them be accountable and helps me evaluate them. For other examples of practice sheets see Form E.2 on pages 221-222 in part II.

5. I finish every lesson by asking kids what they learned. I don't always do this the same way. Some of my techniques include the following:

   • Have a brief class discussion.
   • Hold an end-of-session class gathering for a few minutes during which each student retrieves and writes in his "learning journal."
   • Ask a group to demonstrate the practice drills they used during the skill practice portion of the lesson. The class is expected to be supportive of their fellow students during this demonstration.

Table 3.1 provides an example of how a typical individualized physical education class might look.

Individualizing Through Levels

When teachers level the material they teach, they provide a structured way to deal with the individual differences in their classes. Leveling

Volleyball Skills Test

Underhand serve	Not Present	Present
Opposite foot to serving hand is forward.		
Arm is straight on swing.		
Contact point is under ball.		
Steps through on contact and follows through to target.		

Accuracy test: Serve 10 times to your partner so he or she may contact, catch, or pass your serve after moving two steps or fewer. Number of successful trials out of 10: _____/10

Sidearm serve	Not Present	Present
Opposite foot to serving hand is forward.		
Arm swings on a plane near shoulder level.		
Arm is straight on swing.		
Contact point is just under the midline of the ball.		
Steps through on contact and follows through to target.		

Accuracy test: Serve 10 times to your partner so he or she may contact, catch, or pass your serve after moving two steps or fewer. Number of successful trials out of 10: _____/10

Adapted from a skills test developed by Raissa Adolphe.

does not mean putting everyone on the same level, leading to a situation in which some students are bored, others are frustrated and unable to achieve, and the lucky ones are working at a pace suited to their preparation and skills. Rather, it means creating different skill levels for the same subject matter, then placing students in the levels that are appropriate for them. In my experience, this was the most effective way of being sure that each student was challenged yet able to progress. Thus, my first task in creating a new unit is to create levels, gather or write materials appropriate for each of the levels, and assign students to appropriate levels.

Management Tip

Having trouble engaging your whole class in discussions or question-and-answer sessions? Ask all students to formulate an answer and raise their hand if they have some answer to the question before asking anyone in the room. You will not ask anyone until every hand is raised. If students are slow, let them know if they don't have a clue they can share a clean joke instead of an answer.

Table 3.1 Sample Individualized Physical Education Lesson

Time: 60 min.	Lesson phase and suggested instruction strategies	Action occurring
5 min.	**Warm up** • Peer-led activities • Teacher-facilitated activities	Include low-organization games and stretching. Games include large-muscle movements, such as running to help blood travel to the major muscle groups. Avoid overly strenuous activities to prevent muscle strain injuries.
3 min.	**Review** • Teacher-facilitated questioning	Review last day's progress. Ask students how they feel they are progressing and what they have learned. Also point out positive behaviors observed and express any general concerns.
22 min.	**Skill practice** • Reciprocal peer teaching • Practice style teaching • Group work	Students work on skill assessment worksheets. Within student groups, have partners teaching each other. Facilitate by being available for questions and assisting students as they work on perfecting their skill performances.
20 min.	**Culminating activity** • Teacher-facilitated	Design activities that integrate the skills the students have been working on in more authentic situations. Assess students' skill performances during these modified games.
5 min.	**Cool-down and closure** • Independent work • Peer-led activities • Teacher-directed activities	Provide closure during the cool-down stretch. Ask questions regarding how the students feel they are progressing. Celebrate the positive activities that took place during the lesson. The cool-down should include walking, then stretching, and can be student- or teacher-directed.

Developing Levels

The number of levels that works best for me depends on the unit, but it's usually three. So when I develop a unit, I start by thinking about appropriate student goals for each of three levels—beginners, recreational participants, and competitive participants. Following are the questions I ask myself as I flesh out the levels. Form 3.2 lists the results of this process as used with soccer.

1. **What are the basic skills needed to play the game?** You may already be an expert in the game or activity being taught in the unit. In this case, you should list the skills and then check with a published resource or another expert in the game. If you are not an expert, enlist the help

of someone who is or consult a published resource at the outset. If you have someone else assist you in coming up with the skills, be sure you check the final results against a published resource. You can see the answers that Neil O'Flaherty (a colleague) came up with for soccer in column one ("Skill") of form 3.2. If you can perform each of these skills, at least in a rudimentary fashion, you can play a real game of soccer, as long as it's with others who are also just learning the skills.

2. **What is the most basic version of each of these skills, the mastery of which would enable a person to get through an entire game without unnecessary pauses?** Again, if you are not an expert, consult with someone who is and rely on published resources. Generally sport

Skill	Level A	Level B	Level C
Passing	Begin with stationary ball. Be able to complete passes to partner standing 10 yards away. Partner can move 2 steps in any direction.	Be able to return a ball rolled or passed on the ground from 20 yards away using the instep without stopping the ball. Partner can move 2 steps in any direction.	Be able to chip a pass over or around a player standing between student and partner. Ball must land within 6 feet of partner (3 steps in any direction).
Trapping	Roll a pass along the ground to a partner 10 yards away. Trap with left foot 5 times; right foot 5 times.	Trap a ball thrown or kicked at least 10 feet into the air. Control, then pass it immediately back to your partner. Count number in *control*.	Trap the ball using another part of your body (e.g., chest, knee). Bring ball immediately under control using feet. Pass it back to partner immediately.
Heading	Using a self-toss, head 10 balls to a partner 5 yards away. Count number that cover 5 yards.	Head 10 balls kicked or thrown 20 feet in the air. Use the flat of the forehead to direct the ball back to partner. Partner can move 5 steps in any direction.	Head 10 balls kicked above shoulder height from the corner kick mark toward the net. Use flat or side of forehead to place the ball between the posts. Count how many go into the net.
Dribbling and footwork	Travel 40 yards while dribbling the ball (zig-zagging) without losing control of it. Successful is 10 points. Lose 2 points each time control is lost. Time limit: 20 seconds.	Using 12 cones, set up a zig-zagging course, extending 50 yards. As you dribble through the cones, use both insteps and outer sides of feet. Run as fast as you can. Successful is 10 points. Lose 2 points each time you lose control. Time limit: 30 seconds.	Juggle the ball, using your feet, head, knees, etc. Contact the ball 25 (or more) times before the ball hits ground. For every 5 contacts, score 2 points. If in between (e.g., 18 in a row), score highest level achieved (e.g., 15 contacts is 6 points).
Throw-ins	Feet shoulder-width apart, throw in 10 balls to partner 10 yards away, using proper technique. Partner may move one step in any direction and should practice trapping the ball.	Using a 1-2 step approach to sideline, attempt 5 throw-ins to a partner 20 yards away. Approach should give momentum to throw ball farther. Score 1 point for each throw that rolls to partner; score 2 points for each one partner must trap before it hits the ground.	Attempt 10 throw-ins with a 2-step approach to sideline. For each throw that rolls at least 25 yards, score 1 point; for each throw that rolls 35 yards or more, score 2 points. Use proper technique (key of the feet).
Shooting	Place 2 cones, 10 feet apart. Shoot stationary ball 10 shots at cones 20 yards away. Count number that pass between cones (on ground or in air).	Shoot 10 shots from penalty kick spot (12 yards from goal line) with your partner as goalie. Count goals made.	Have partner kick 10 attempts from corner kick spot. Without stopping the ball, use a "first-time" kick to shoot the ball at net (no goalie needed). Count "first-time" strikes that score.

         Individualized Teaching Techniques

From *Learning by Choice in Secondary Physical Education: Creating a Goal-Directed Program* by Kevin Kaardal, 2001, Champaign, IL: Human Kinetics.

governing bodies have resources you can use or can tell you where to get them. Column 2 ("Level A") of form 3.2 lists the beginner level soccer skills Neil and I developed using this procedure.

3. **What is the next level of mastery for each of the basic skills that would be necessary if a person wanted to play the sport during your school intramural activities or for the fun of playing with friends?** This level requires refining individual skills as well as introducing team skills beyond the rudimentary level. Keep in mind—and convey to the students—that recreational play may be enhanced by rule modification. For example, in recreational volleyball, teams may want to forbid spiking the ball. This modification emphasizes team skills of passing and allows students to get past the fear of being hit with a hard spike. Column 3 ("Level B") of form 3.2 describes the skills we decided are necessary to play soccer on the recreational level.

4. **What refinements of skills are crucial to being successful at a more difficult level, to using effective offensive or defensive strategies required of players on competitive teams, such as school teams or other elite nonprofessional leagues?** Preparing students for competitive play emphasizes refining team skills as well as becoming proficient at employing intelligent game strategies. This would include skills such as reading game situations correctly, reacting to them appropriately, and being able to employ good offensive and defensive strategies. Column 4 ("Level C") of form 3.2 shows the skills we believe are necessary for successful competitive soccer play after considering these issues.

Creating Activities for Learning the Levels

Once you have determined what skills are appropriate for each level, it's time to come up with activities that will enable the students to master the skills required for each level. You will probably need to begin with simple drills and then progress to a series of modified games that focus on the students applying skills and strategies appropriate to their skill level. For example, here are three activities that Leanne Timko and I came up with for soccer:

- Dribble Tag and Pirates: Level A students in soccer could play a modified game called Pirates, or Dribble Tag. About 10 players each have a ball within a coned rectangular field (pitch). (Set up coned courses and areas in advance.) The object of the game is to knock the other players' soccer balls out of the coned area while maintaining control of your ball, always dribbling inside the rectangle. A player whose ball travels outside the coned area is considered out and must practice juggling and dribbling. The pitch is made smaller and smaller as players are eliminated. The last one left is the winner. Modifications include having 2 players without balls who act as pirates and try to steal opponents' balls. If they steal them and maintain control, the victim stays in the game and acts as a pirate, and the pirate becomes a ball carrier and can win the game. Pirates can only win the game by being the last player in possession of a ball. A modification of this rule could be that if a pirate kicks the ball out of the pitch, the player whose ball travels outside the pitch is considered out and practices dribbling and juggling, and the pirate continues being a pirate.

- Fool Your Neighbor. Level B students might apply their game skills with this game. Fool Your Neighbor is set up by creating four teams of three players each. Each team has a goal (cone). The goals are placed one on each side of a small pitch. The object is to knock over your opponents' cones three times. Teams that are eliminated then play small-sided grid games working on dribbling and trapping (Keep-Away). To win, teams have to use deception, working with other teams for momentary advantages. Allegiances will be fleeting and serve a common goal of knocking over a cone not belonging to the teams that are attacking. Teams will use deception as well, pretending to go toward one cone working with a team but quickly changing direction and attacking a different team's goal. The pace in this game is fast and furious. It's a lot of fun!

- Six-on-Six. Level C students could work on game skills playing six against six soccer with goalies.

Don't feel like you're completely on your own to create these games and drills. There's plenty of material out there to help you with this part of your program. Chapters 2 to 4 of *Changing Kids' Games* by Morris and Stiehl and *Teaching Sport Concepts and Skills* by Griffin, Mitchell, and Oslin are two excellent resources. For complete information, see the bibliography on page 253.

Finally, as you are considering materials to use in your leveled unit, you must always keep safety issues in mind. If, for example, you are teaching road hockey, be sure to use a soft ball and have students wear helmets with Plexiglass visors. In gymnastics units, you must be sure that the number of spotters is adequate, you have enough mats and that they are in good condition, you use proper progressions, and you personally supervise any inverted skill. In soccer you modify rules about how close beginning and recreational players can shoot at a goalie from. A two-meter crease (no-player zone) might be a wise modification.

Management Tip

Ask students who are sure of their answer to raise their right hand. Ask those who feel they need the help of others to complete their answer to raise their left hand. Again do not request an answer from anyone until you have every hand raised. Then vary between asking those with their right hand and those with their left hand up.

Assigning Levels

The simplest way to assign levels is to allow students to choose their own. I did this by devoting a couple of classes at the beginning of each unit to letting the students experiment and find the level of skills they were challenged by but were also likely to succeed at. I also reserved the right to move students up or down a level depending on my judgment on whether their choice was appropriate. This moving of students would take place after meeting with the student and explaining how she could maximize her grade and performance by accepting my choice. Remarkably, in my 11 years of teaching using leveled units, I only had to have this discussion with students twice. Most students

want to be challenged and learn, because they are bored doing tasks they can easily complete.

Some teachers prefer to assign the levels themselves. A good way to do this is to have students play a game or do the activity involved in the unit in question. Observe the game or activity and note the names of the outstanding performers and the poor performers. The poor performers are your level A group, the outstanding performers are your level C group, and all the rest are your level B group.

It is a small step to move from having the teacher or student select one level at which the student must complete all skills to individualized instruction and evaluation in which each student can select skills from different levels if that seems appropriate. For example, in a basketball unit, a student could pick level C for passing and level A for dribbling. Once the student makes her selection of level or levels, she completes a contract that ensures everyone understands what is expected of her. The use of contracts is more fully discussed on pages 38 and 39.

Management Tip

When you call on a student in a class discussion, write a symbol by his or her name on your attendance grid and do not call on that student again until everyone else has had a chance to respond at least once. Play a game with the students where they get to pick the culminating activity if you ask a question of someone twice before asking every other student in the class.

A Brief Look at Individualized Instruction Techniques

For a leveled approach to work best, students must not only be started at appropriate levels but must also be taught in as many ways as it takes to ensure they are able to reach the desired goals if they invest reasonable effort. This approach will result in the delivery of the program so all students, regardless of ability, will achieve some measure of success as long as they are willing to take advantage of the opportunities they are given. Some approaches that may be used include

- intratask teaching,
- leveled task stations,
- peer teaching, and
- learning contracts.

Intratask Teaching

The most common strategy used is intratask teaching. In this approach, all students are given one task or skill drill that is challenging for the majority, and then modifications to this task are made by the individual or group who finds the task too easy or too challenging. For example, in a volleyball unit, students might be paired to receive a serve and then try to pass the ball to unoccupied space on their opponents' court. Students begin their serves from a spot on the court close to the net. As they achieve success, they attempt the skill from farther and farther away from the net until they are serving from the legal serving line. The students may start with the underhand serve and then work up to practicing the overhand floater or overhand spin serves. Students may only try the more difficult tasks when they have mastered the simpler tasks. In this way all learners can be accommodated. Each student is still practicing serves, and each student is more likely to be challenged using a skill progression appropriate for his ability. Beginning players may never move beyond the underhand serve, but they will master the skill well enough to be able to serve legally in a game. They will improve their skills while experiencing success at the easier progression levels. The skilled player will quickly achieve success and be challenged by practicing overhand spin serves or by serving to specific spots on the court.

All this individualized learning can occur within the same drill design, within the same class. Using intratask drills helps you get a quick impression of each student's skill level. Those students serving the ball underhand and close to the net are beginners, and you can group them accordingly to assist their play and learning. You can then easily modify other drills to accommodate their learning readiness. The students performing jump serves are expert or

Management Tip

To engage the introverted, use the think-pair-share questioning method. Have the students think of their answers on their own in silence, write it down, then share with a partner. Combine those answers after discussion and then pair with another group or two and share again. Finally, elect a spokesperson or ask for a volunteer to share each group's response with the class. To speed up the process, give them these rules for sharing:

1. You may talk for only 30 seconds (or some other appropriate length of time, depending on the nature of the expected answers).
2. You may not repeat anything said by another group.
3. After each group has had a chance to share for the specified time limit, you'll allow each group that wants to, to share again.

competitive performers, and their drills could be modified to include more game strategies rather than simple skill drills. The students in the middle (likely the majority of the students) are the students who dictated which types of skills were to be practiced on most of the courts.

Leveled Task Stations

In task station teaching, you must prepare posters or task cards in advance. To simplify the types of documents the students handle, the unit plan (see "Master Chart for Individualized Basketball" on page 90 for a sample unit plan) is posted on the gymnasium wall. Each skill listed on the master chart has a corresponding poster explaining it. The poster includes strategies or drills to practice or games to play that will help students learn that skill. Such a poster groups these strategies or games by skill level so each student, no matter what her initial skill or lack thereof, will be able to find activities that will help her learn or improve that skill. I will discuss task station teaching at length in this chapter's final section, which provides a step-by-step approach to teaching using task stations.

Peer Teaching

When a student has to teach a skill or strategy to peers or a small group, he is forced to internalize the information, analyze it, synthesize it, decide what is important, and paraphrase it back to his friends. He may not get the instruction exactly right every time, but as the roles reverse and he becomes the student while his peer teaches him, both kids will learn more than if they are passive recipients of a teacher's direct lectures to a large group.

Management Tip

Ask many questions, ensure humor is built into your lessons, and—most importantly—model what you want from your students. If you want your students to be positive, be positive and energetic yourself. If you want them to have fun, be sure you appear to be having fun. Model what you want. Follow what I call the "three tenets of integrity":

- Say what you mean.
- Mean what you say.
- Do what you say.

And if you follow these three tenets, of course, you will find that you must be very careful of what you say. Then students will learn to live up to your expectations.

How do you enable students to teach their peers? Obviously this is not done without careful thought and preparation. Clear criterion-referenced skill breakdowns, tasks or drills, or explanations of strategy can help the student teacher. I taught students the basic skills through once, discussed the whole-part-whole teaching method (see below), and gave the students some simplified background in basic skill analysis and biomechanics.

Learning Contracts

As you can no doubt tell from the number of times they've already been mentioned in this chapter, contracts are a great device for individualizing student learning. Contracts clearly establish the performance expectations and responsibilities for the student during a self-directed unit. The contract specifies the tasks the teacher and student agree will be mastered within a defined time period. Some contracts give the student an opportunity to select from a variety of skills, while others are more open-ended, and the conditions are developed by the student in consultation with the teacher. Contracts can be used both in the classroom setting and as a method of ensuring quality work outside the classroom for expanded opportunities. Depending on how it is written, a contract can help the student and teacher assess multiple goals. The Student Contract for Volleyball, on page 241, is a good example of a contract. The Student Progress Record Sheet

---

Management Tip

The whole-part-whole teaching method is a great way to introduce static skills to students. Here's how you do it:

1. Demonstrate the whole skill to the students, then demonstrate the key components of the skill, then demonstrate the whole again.
2. Ask the students to attempt the skill in its entirety. (They will usually not be very successful at this stage.)
3. Have them practice the key components using drill progressions.
4. Finally, have them attempt to perform the whole skill again. This time, they will usually be much more successful than in step 2!

Examples of static skills include golf swing or putting, basketball free throws, and volleyball service.

on page 95 illustrates another way of setting up a contract.

The number of skills a student will contract to complete depends on the time available for the unit and the student's grade and ability. She may choose any level she believes is a challenge yet allows her to be successful. She will be responsible for completing the tasks at the chosen level for each skill she has agreed to learn. As noted earlier, students may include work at several different levels at once. For example, a student who is a good shooter may be working at level C for shooting but be a poor dribbler and need to be working at level A for dribbling. A student could even circle more than one level of the same skill. In other words, if he is really good at shooting baskets but lousy at defense, a student could circle levels A, B, and C of several defensive skills, so he could bring his defensive game up to the level of his offensive game. In this case, each level would count for one "skill" in terms of how many skills you expect the student to complete.

If you are using contracts, begin by informing the students of the minimum number of skills you expect them to complete. You can hand out copies of the master chart for the unit (see page 90 and have them select the skills and levels to work on from that chart. (Other approaches to filling out the contract are discussed on page 38.) Tell them you reserve the right to ask them to try a more appropriate skill level on any given skill if you believe they are not being challenged or have chosen a skill that is too difficult. Go over the completed contract with each student to be sure that it appears appropriate and that he understands the obligations he is signing up for. Pages 28 and 241 offer examples of various kinds of contracts.

As the students progress through their skill practice and test their mastery, they may wish to change their contracts. You should impose a deadline for changes to their contracts. It worked best for me to specify that major changes to their goals had to be done early in the unit, as they discovered their goals were unachievable or not challenging, while minor changes—such as dropping a level in a given skill—could occur up to two-thirds of the way through the unit.

Management Tip

If you want students to listen when you talk, make sure you have systems of management that allow everyone to be heard. Some management techniques that work in elementary school still work in the high school, so don't be embarrassed to try them. For example, if someone wishes to speak, they raise their hand. If anyone sees someone with a raised hand, they look at that person and raise their hand. The process is repeated until everyone in the class has raised their hands and are quiet and ready to listen to the speaker. This usually is the teacher, but sometimes a brave student will ask a question for clarification that everyone else is thinking of, but afraid to ask. You may worry that the class attention-seeker will take advantage of this system, but students will pick appropriate times to use this power of free speech if you explain its appropriate use and model it.

Management Tip

Use low-level discipline techniques, starting with establishing simple-to-understand rules. I use what I call "The Five Ps of Perfect Performance":

- Be **p**repared for whatever activity is being taught.
- Be **p**unctual.
- Be **p**ositive, take risks, and encourage each other.
- **P**erform to the best of your ability each day.
- Be **p**olite, and respect each other.

These simple rules have helped me manage many classes so I can focus on teaching.

A Step-by-Step Approach to Leveled Task Card Programs

Because task card programs have worked so well for me as a means of individualizing instruction, I would like to share with you how I developed and conducted units using this technique. The steps I followed are

1. write your unit plan,
2. create your basic teaching and assessment tools,
3. assign levels,
4. have students write their contracts,
5. hold your learning and practice classes, and
6. continuously evaluate student progress.

Write Your Unit Plan

To write your task card unit plan, you must first analyze the activity to be sure you understand all the general skills that are necessary for successful participation. The steps for writing your plan are listed next. Reviewing "Developing Levels" (page 33) will help you approach these steps.

1. List the general classes of skills necessary for successful participation in the activity. See the major headings in the basketball master chart on page 90 as an example.

2. Analyze the general skills classifications. Break them down into the specific skills that will enable students to be successful in performing the general skills. Again, the master chart for basketball (page 90) provides an example: the general skills are the headings, such as "common skills," "individual offense," and "individual defense"; and the specific skills are what's listed under the general skills. Each of these specific skills will become the subject of a poster.

3. Analyze each specific skill. Make enough copies of the Skill, Drill, and Assessment Poster (page 89) so you have as many worksheets as the number of specific skills you have listed. Use one worksheet for each skill. Examine the "Skills analysis" sections of forms B.15 through B.22 to get you thinking about how to figure out what elements must be present for a skill to be successfully performed. Then fill in the "Skills analysis" section of the worksheet for the skill you are working on.

4. Complete the Skill, Drill, and Assessment Poster for the skill you are working on, then fill in the remaining blank forms, one for each specific skill. Examine the skills posters throughout part II for multiple examples of the kinds of information you need to think about to fill in "Concept," "Skill analysis," "Skill practice," "Skill

mastery," and "Modified games." Remember to take advantage of some of the resources in the bibliography (page 253) to help you come up with modified games and drills.

Management Tip

The teacher must be fair and consistent, taking action using escalating intervention when redirecting or disciplining students. Use low-level redirection techniques like redirective body language, a knowing look, a raised eyebrow, close proximity, or a nonjudgmental question such as, "Do you need some help?"

Create Your Basic Teaching and Assessment Tools

The basic tools of each unit will be the master chart, the task card posters, and the student progress record sheets. Create them now.

The Master Chart

Based on the work you did in the first two steps of writing your unit plan, create your master chart. The basketball master chart on page 90 will provide you with one good way to organize your chart. Color code each general skill classification ("Common Skills," "Individual Offense," and so on) and its subsidiary skills, one color for each skill group. The following are examples for basketball and soccer:

Basketball
  Red for Common Skills
  Blue for Individual Offense
  Green for Team Offense
  Yellow for Individual Defense
  Orange for Team Defense

Soccer
  Red for Ball Control
  Blue for Passing
  Green for Shooting
  Yellow for Passing
  Orange for Game Skills
  Purple for Suggested Modifications
  White for Key to Symbols

You can print each skill group with a different color of ink or marker, or mount each group on a different color background. However you choose to do it, the important thing is to make it obvious to the students which color goes with which skill group.

You should include one other category in the master chart: "Miscellaneous." It should include posters describing suggested modifications for students with physical and mental challenges, modified games, the offensive and defensive game rubrics, and the key to interpreting the symbols on the skills posters. Miscellaneous could be coded in purple.

Task Card Posters

Create your posters based on your notes on the Skill, Drill, and Assessment Posters you filled out when you were writing your unit plan. You may copy the format of the posters in part II of this book or come up with your own. The important thing is that you include all the information requested on Skill, Drill, and Assessment Posters for each skill. Matte your task card posters on colored paper or posterboard keyed to the colors on the master chart. This will help the students quickly find the poster they wish to use. For example, if students wish to practice dribbling, they can go to the master chart and see that dribbling posters will be blue. The students then need only examine the blue posters in the gym to find dribbling, rather than searching through each poster in the program. When you are doing this for the first time, referring frequently to the posters in this book will help you.

Student Progress Record Sheets and Rubrics

Make up task record sheets for each student. These sheets should include each skill in your program. They will serve as your record of student progress and can be used as contracts. Every skill offered in your unit and written on your master chart needs to be on this sheet so students can note whether it is part of their contract and whether they have attempted or mastered the skill. See form B.6 on page 95 for an example.

Create rubrics for each level. How to do this is discussed at length on pages 52-54.

Assign Levels

Start the unit by assessing the appropriate level for each student. As noted on page 36, you may

do this by allowing students to choose their own levels (subject to your approval) or by assigning them yourself as you observe short scrimmages.

If you allow students to choose their own levels, begin by giving each student an Individualized Program Exploration Sheet (page 86). Tell the class, "Look over the Master Chart and decide what skill you want to work on. Then find the appropriate posters, read them, and decide what level you are ready for. Choose whatever drills seem appropriate to you from one of the posters you want to work on, and try a drill listed at the level you have chosen to help you master the skill. If the drill is way too easy, move up a level. If it is so hard you feel like you'll never be able to do it, move down a level. Fill in the appropriate information on your Exploration Sheet. See how many drills and skills you can practice during this first class period."

Management Tip

Be approachable, friendly, and have a sense of humor. A classroom environment in which students feel comfortable is essential if students are to be educated risk-takers, peer-evaluators, and teachers as well as feel it's OK to work at a level of skill personally appropriate to them.

As the students work on their chosen skills, walk throughout the class and observe their ability to perform tasks independently and their skill levels. Focus on the obviously weak students and the very talented ones, as these will be your levels A and C students, respectively, and record this information in your attendance or evaluation book. This will help you guide students who have chosen an inappropriate skill level to a level that will allow success and challenge at the same time. This sheet should also help students choose an appropriate skill level by helping them reflect on their performance of a given task when they record their progress on the sheet.

If you decide to assign levels yourself based on observing students as they play short games, use the rubrics for offensive and defensive basketball play (pages 102 and 103) to assist you in making these assessments. After the students complete the task exploration sheet, or after you have evaluated them during a short scrimmage, explain how the unit will run. Begin by explaining the format of each lesson, since you would follow the same basic outline for each class (see table 3.1). Then go over the contract and point out that evaluation can occur any time a student has completed a task. Remind the students that independent work requires individual responsibility, and if students are having trouble at any point knowing what to do next, they should come to you for help. If you have students with physical or mental challenges in your class, remind everyone they should consult the suggested modifications poster (page 94) as appropriate.

Have Students Write Their Contracts

Students contract to complete the tasks for a certain number of skills at a given level on a contract. You may use a contract such as the one on page 28 or you may use a form such as the Student Progress Record Sheet on page 95. See the section on contracts on page 38 to remind you of how these are used.

Hold Your Learning and Practice Classes

After your class warm-up, move the students into the skill practice portion of the lesson. During this time, the students work independently or in groups of their choosing. As you were planning the unit, you should have walked in your imagination through all the games or drills likely to be used to see if they were simple enough for students to set up on their own or if they would require a quick demonstration. You should offer minilessons on any needing demonstration or on particular skills or aspects of the game. Invite students to attend the minilessons, but make their attendance voluntary. Those students not interested will continue working on their own. When not giving minilessons you should travel through the gym, monitoring student progress, offering encouragement, giving tips to individuals on how to execute a skill successfully, and responding to those students who need help or guidance. Refer to table 3.1 for a good summary of what might happen in your learning and practice classes.

Continuously Evaluate Student Progress

Students are responsible for tracking their progress each class on the Student Progress Record Sheet. You should either collect these at the end of each class or see that the students put them in a designated place before leaving. As you are monitoring the students as you rove while they practice, you should take notes on a class grid about what you observe about each student. If your observations don't match the progress a student has recorded on his Student Progress Record Sheet, you should give that student more individual attention. You should also encourage students to approach you for help if they believe they need it. The culmination of the unit can be skill testing or, if you evaluate skills throughout the unit, you can evaluate through a leveled jamboree-style tournament.

How do you run such a tournament? The best way to explain it is through an example. In basketball, for instance, you might choose

Management Tip

Pick teams in such a way so as to avoid the "left-out-student" scenario. In a situation in which you wish to have four equal teams, have your students form four single-file equal lines, facing in one direction. It is likely all the competitive students will end up in one line, and two lines will consist of friends, and one line will consist of students who experience greater social difficulty. Once your lines are formed, pick your teams by directing all the first players in line go to team one, the second players in line go to team two, and so on, repeating until the original four lines are gone. This gives you teams balanced by skill. If you want leveled teams, ask students to line up in groups according to the ability level in which they see themselves. Then number the students off in each leveled grouping to form teams within that group. You can also pick teams by dividing the students up by running shoes. Brand names X, Y, and Z are on these teams versus brand names A, B, and C. Whatever you do don't let captains pick teams: somebody always suffers the humiliation of getting picked last.

to do a two-on-two tournament. Divide the class into teams based on levels and assign or allow teams to pick their first opponent. The students play two on two at each basket in the gym. The first team to score a basket (or any number the teacher sets; keep it low to encourage movement and give the less-skilled students an opportunity to get lucky and win) wins. As soon as this happens, any team that has lost raises their hands, and the winners look for a team at another basket with their hands raised and move to that basket. The teams that lost start with first ball, and the game continues. Play stops and the tournament ends after a time limit. The goal is for a team to travel to as many baskets as possible. No one is ever eliminated from the tournament. Because the scores to win are low, every team has a legitimate chance at an upset. Students really enjoy this type of tournament, and it gives you plenty of time to evaluate each student. Game skills for basketball could also be evaluated during other appropriate culminating activities at the end of each class, based on the modified games poster on page 97.

A great deal more could be said about evaluation, but I will not do so here because the subject is of such importance that the next three chapters will be devoted to it.

CHAPTER 4
Creating Tools for Assessment

You may find it odd that so much of this book is devoted to assessing. But as I developed and taught individualized PE programs, I discovered firsthand the truth of Grant Wiggins' idea that good teaching can't happen apart from good assessing. Moreover, I have found that individualizing assessment is as a key to individualizing PE.

Who Should You Compare Kids To?

Most teachers compare students with each other to evaluate each one's standing in class. In academic courses, where the goal is for students to master a body of knowledge, that sort of attempt at objectivity is warranted. But this paradigm makes little sense for physical education classes. If the point of PE is to end up with people who engage in lifelong exercise for health, the criteria must be different. It makes much more sense to assess students keeping both their personal goals and innate abilities in mind. If a student works hard within those parameters and achieves a level of exercise that will promote her health, she should receive good marks, even if she's not an elite athlete.

By evaluating students within levels that are appropriate for them, we "level the playing field." An individual youngster might be gifted in one sport, such as basketball, but have a body type that prevents her from being outstanding at other endeavors, such as gymnastics or combative sports. Students in physical education classes have a wide variety of abilities, and these change from unit to unit. Using different criteria for each level ensures that no matter what unit we are engaged in, each student has a good chance to succeed and to be encouraged in her efforts to develop the exercise habit.

In real life people strive for *personal* bests. That is the only best each of us actually has control over. How fit we are, how good at a sport we are, will be limited by our own potential. We can't control how good the competition is, but we can control how we perform within a given set of circumstances. So it seems counterproductive to compare students with each other rather than to evaluate them against a set of criteria created for

Three Important Assessment Terms

To understand the assessment instruments (evaluation sheets and rubrics) presented in this book, you need to understand the following terms:

• **Diagnostic assessment**—Informal assessment of the student's level of understanding, attitudes, and interests (what the student would like to find out before the beginning of the unit). Use interest inventories, pretests, observations, brainstorming and the like. The student will consult with the teacher.

• **Formative assessment**—Ongoing assessment as the student works through the unit. Use checklists, assignments, quizzes, observation of work in progress, journal writing, demonstrations, conferences, peer evaluation, self-evaluation. The teacher or peer instructor uses this information to make suggestions to students about how they can improve.

• **Summative assessment**—An overall picture of the student's achievement when the unit is completed. The student will have completed the student self-evaluation sheet. This mark will be combined with the teacher's mark to come up with a final cumulative mark, also known as a "summative" mark.

levels that are appropriate for each. Youngsters see the fairness in measuring a performance against criteria of logical skill progressions. Individualizing evaluation takes learner readiness into account, assists students in progressing toward excellence, and gives them the opportunity to recognize their own gifts. In short, they can discover the reasons they enjoy being active.

As a teacher, you can track your students' progress based on their performance of observable criteria. You can justify your marks and repeat the assessments with a good degree of reliability. Furthermore, you can change the focus of your program from asking for excellence in sport to helping students achieve personal excellence in a variety of physical activities and sports. It helps both students and teachers focus on being active and fit for a lifetime instead of being gifted at a specific sport—or even very good at many of them. Instead of focusing on the few gifted athletes who are naturally good at every sport, you can focus on *all* your students. You can help them all

discover what activities interest them and what abilities they can develop. They can see and enjoy the benefits of sport and physical activity.

The programs I have been involved in have used performance-based standards, which current literature strongly recommends. Performance-based assessment requires students to demonstrate the ability to use appropriate knowledge and skills in real-life ("authentic") situations, and it uses observable criteria that are clear to both instructors and students. The strategies in this book reflect the content and performance standards designed by the National Association for Sport and Physical Education (NASPE), yet they are flexible enough to accommodate local or regional curriculum requirements and your own teaching philosophy.

Two common ways of achieving performance-based assessment are norm-referenced assessment and criterion-referenced assessment. Each approach has its strengths and weaknesses.

Required Changes in Assessment in Goal-Directed Physical Education

Changes from traditional assessment practices that will result from following the goal-directed model include changing from

- using a bell curve to everyone's achieving high expectations or some form of mastery;
- using class averages in reporting student progress to using individualized, specific reporting of a student's mark and percentage of the course completed;
- averaging a student's performances over a specific number of tests to come up with a report card mark to reporting specific final results on how well the student met his or her exit goals;
- emphasizing content to emphasizing skill development specified in exit goals;
- periodic monitoring and feedback to continuous and specific feedback in relation to the student's progress toward meeting a goal;
- single-discipline planning to interdisciplinary team planning of expanded opportunities to meet overlapping goals (in other words, credit across several courses for meeting goals that exist as an exit outcome in several disciplines, such as problem solving);
- using the same test for every student to giving students choices of how they are to be evaluated within a given unit, so the assessment more closely reflects progress toward their personal goals; and
- exclusively organizing learning based on available time to organizing learning based on mastery while offering extended and expanded opportunities, allowing students to progress at their own rates.

Norm-Referenced Assessment

Norm-referenced assessment requires a large sample of student performances on a measurable test. Youngsters' performances can then be measured against the norms represented in the curve and a rating or grade derived from where they compare to the statistics in the test. Table 4.1 shows an example of norm-referenced tests, the National Children and Youth Fitness Study I (NCYFS) norms for the one-mile walk-run (Safrit 1995).

One strength of these tests is that they enable youngsters to see where they fall in relation to the average performer. This can be interesting information especially for those students who are active because they enjoy competition. These types of tests also make it very easy for a teacher to arrive at a grade. It may seem odd that I'm recommending norm-referenced assessments at all, as they seem to compare kids against one standard, putting us back into the "comparing-every-kid-with-all-other-kids" mode. But norm-referenced assessments can easily be adapted to assessing within levels. The track and field assessment grid in form 4.1 demonstrates how norms tables can be broken down into performance levels and percentage grades.

Table 4.1 NCYFS I Norms by Age for the One-Mile Walk-Run

Boys	Age								
Percentile	10	11	12	13	14	15	16	17	18
99	6:55	6:21	6:21	5:59	5:43	5:40	5:31	5:14	5:33
90	8:13	7:25	7:13	6:48	6:27	6:23	6:13	6:08	6:10
80	8:35	7:52	7:41	7:07	6:58	6:43	6:31	6:31	6:33
75	8:48	8:02	7:53	7:14	7:08	6:52	6:39	6:40	6:42
70	9:02	8:12	8:03	7:24	7:18	7:00	6:50	6:46	6:57
60	9:26	8:38	8:23	7:46	7:34	7:13	7:07	7:10	7:15
50	9:52	9:03	8:48	8:04	7:51	7:30	7:27	7:31	7:35
40	10:15	9:25	9:17	8:26	8:14	7:50	7:48	7:59	7:53
30	10:44	10:17	9:57	8:54	8:46	8:18	8:04	8:24	8:12
25	11:00	10:32	10:13	9:06	9:10	8:30	8:18	8:37	8:34
20	11:25	10:55	10:38	9:20	9:28	8:50	8:34	8:55	9:10
10	12:27	12:07	11:48	10:38	10:34	10:13	9:36	10:43	10:50

Girls	Age								
Percentile	10	11	12	13	14	15	16	17	18
99	7:55	7:14	7:20	7:08	7:01	6:59	7:03	6:52	6:58
90	9:09	8:45	8:34	8:27	8:11	8:23	8:28	8:20	8:22
80	9:56	9:35	9:30	9:13	8:49	9:04	9:06	9:10	9:27
75	10:09	9:56	9:52	9:30	9:16	9:28	9:25	9:26	9:31
70	10:27	10:10	10:05	9:48	9:31	9:49	9:41	9:41	9:36
60	10:51	10:35	10:32	10:22	10:04	10:20	10:15	10:16	10:08
50	11:14	11:15	10:58	10:52	10:32	10:46	10:34	10:34	10:51
40	11:54	11:46	11:26	11:22	10:58	11:20	11:08	10:59	11:27
30	12:27	12:33	12:03	11:55	11:35	11:53	11:49	11:43	11:58
25	12:52	12:54	12:33	12:17	11:49	12:18	12:10	12:03	12:14
20	13:12	13:17	12:53	12:43	12:10	12:48	12:32	12:30	12:37
10	14:20	14:35	14:07	13:45	13:13	14:07	13:42	13:46	15:18

Reprinted, by permission, from M. Safrit, 1995, *Complete Guide to Youth Fitness Testing* (Champaign, IL: Human Kinetics), 123 and 124.

Form 4.1 Leveled Track and Field Evaluation Grid Sheet

Name:_____ Date:_____

Event	Mark	Level A	Level B	Level C
100m	90-100	13.6-14.0 s	13.0-13.3 s	12.5-13.1 s
	80-90	14.1-15.0 s	13.4-13.8 s	13.2-13.6 s
	70-80	15.1-16.0 s	13.9-14.5 s	13.7-14.3 s
	60-70	16.0-17.5 s	14.6-15.6 s	14.4-15.4 s
	<60	17.5+ s	15.6+ s	15.4+ s
Discus	90-100	20+ m	25+ m	30+ m
	80-90	15-19 m	20-24 m	25-29 m
	70-80	12-14 m	15-19 m	20-24 m
	60-70	10-12 m	12.14 m	15-19 m
	<60	<10 m	<12 m	<15 m
Shot put	90-100	9+ m	12+ m	15+ m
	80-90	7-8 m	9-11 m	12-14 m
	70-80	6-7 m	7-8 m	9-11 m
	60-70	5-6 m	6-7 m	7-8 m
	<60	<5 m	<6 m	<7 m
High jump	90-100	1.3+ m	1.5+ m	1.8+ m
	80-90	1.15-1.2 m	1.3-1.4 m	1.5-1.7 m
	70-80	1.1-1.14 m	1.2-1.25 m	1.4-1.45 m
	60-70	1.0-1.09 m	1.15-1.19 m	1.25-1.39 m
	<60	<1.0 m	<1.15 m	<1.25 m
50 m hurdles	90-100	7.5 s or less	7.3 s or less	7.0 s or less
	80-90	7.6-8.5 s	7.4-8.3 s	7.1-8.0 s
	70-80	8.6-9.5 s	8.4-9.3 s	8.1-9.0 s
	60-70	9.6-10.5 s	9.4-10.3 s	9.1-10.0 s
	<60	<10.5+ s	<10.3+ s	<10.0+ s
Long jump	90-100	4+ m	4.5+ m	5+ m
	80-90	3-4 m	3.5-4.4 m	4.0-4.9 m
	70-80	2.4-2.9 m	3.0-3.4 m	3.5-3.9 m
	60-70	2.0-2.4 m	2.5-2.9 m	3.0-3.4 m
	<60	<2.0 m	<2.5 m	<3.0 m
400 m run	90-100	1:10 or less	1:08 or less	1:06 or less
	80-90	1:11-1:15	1:09-1:13	1:07-1:11
	70-80	1:16-1:20	1:14-1:18	1:12-1:16
	60-70	1:21-1:25	1:19-1:23	1:17-1:21
	<60	1:25+	1:23+	1:21+
2000 m run	90-100	10:00 or less	9:20 or less	8:45 or less
	80-90	10:01-11:00	9:21-10:20	8:46-9:20
	70-80	11:01-13:00	10:21-12:05	9:21-10:20
	60-70	13:01-14:00	12:06-13:00	10:21-12:05
	<60	14:00+	13:00+	12:05+

Fill out your results on this summary grid:

Level: A B C	Event 1:	My performance =	My % =
Level: A B C	Event 2:	My performance =	My % =
Level: A B C	Event 3:	My performance =	My % =
Level: A B C	Event 4:	My performance =	My % =

Creating Tools for Assessment

From *Learning by Choice in Secondary Physical Education: Creating a Goal-Directed Program* by Kevin Kaardal, 2001, Champaign, IL: Human Kinetics.

Norm-referenced assessments do not have to be based on national standards. For example, to develop the track and field assessment grid in form 4.1, I typed in the T-scores from an old handwritten evaluation grid sheet left by the previous physical education teacher at my first teaching job. As a result of its mysterious origins, I could not attest to its validity or even if the scores indicated were based on a national norm or a locally developed one. I later discovered it had been developed by looking at the results from the county's track and field meet for the past 10 years. Where I have placed level A, B, and C, the former teacher had the rubric divided by age categories: junior (14 to 15 years old), intermediate (16 years old), and senior (17 to 18 years old). A strange event, "the 50-meter hurdles," was tested because the rural high school where these scores were originally used had only enough hurdles to cover 50 meters. Other adjustments to the timing and distance jumped or thrown criteria were made as this test was used at an inner-city junior high school (again with few hurdles), and the times and distances were adjusted based on city records.

The point is that although this example may not be reliable on a national scale, the norms used and the template itself were easy to adjust to fit the circumstances in which the test was used. To further improve this test's authenticity, students were marked on track and field for their performances in a culminating event—a modified track meet. Each student had to select at least three events, which had to include at least one running event and one event from either the throwing or jumping category. Their final performance mark was the average of their top three scores.

Norm-referenced assessment strategies are especially effective for those activities in physical education that involve muscular strength, speed, or endurance since these items are easy to quantify and measure. Keep in mind, however, there is not likely to be much improvement in strength or muscular or cardiovascular endurance over a 6 to 12 session unit: thus these skills should be assessed over the duration of the year and students should be given multiple opportunities to test their progress before a summative mark is assigned. It should also be noted that improving speed often requires training techniques such as plyometrics that are not appropriate and may even be dangerous for most students.

Criterion-Referenced Assessment

Criterion-referenced assessment, which allows students to compare their skill performances against preset criteria, is the type of assessment that should be used most often in the classroom, gym, and playing field. A grade is given based on how well the student's performance matches the criteria outlined. These criteria can be set for any type of skill or behavior that can be observed visually. All the rubrics given in this book are based on observable criteria. Form 4.2, for example, lists various observable criteria that may be applied to the right-handed golf swing.

There are many advantages to using criterion-referenced assessment techniques. Here are some of them:

• **It breaks the skill performance down into visible key points for students and provides them with clear descriptions of exactly what must be done to master each key point.** Having such unambiguous standards takes the mystery out of grading. It enables students to know exactly where they stand and enables teachers to be objective and fair in their grading. This makes for happier students and more relaxed teachers.

• **It facilitates students' working independently.** When I began using criterion-referenced assessment, I soon discovered that if I was busy assisting one group of students, others who were experiencing difficulty could refer to the criterion-referenced sheet, or "rubric," and use a mirror to self-check or have a peer check their performance (reciprocal teaching) to see if they were performing correctly. Thus, criterion-referenced assessment sheets turned out to be crucial to the effectiveness of individualized instruction. You can reinforce demonstrations or other instruction given by referring to the rubric, using these handouts as formative evaluation tools. For example, in form 4.2, the golf swing is broken down into its component parts. If a student is having difficulty with his grip and stance, you can refer him to the criteria outlined in the handout and have him work

Name: _____ Date: _____

Key points of the golf swing (right-handed golfer)	Present	Needs work (quick and jerky)	Good performance (smooth and relaxed)
Grip			
Both Vs point to right shoulder.			
Left hand: three bottom fingers maintain a firm and snug grip throughout swing.			
Right hand: grip is relaxed.			
Stance			
Upright, comfortable ready position.			
Left foot is pointing 45° from right foot toward target.			
Weight is a little more on right foot.			
Swing: Take-Away			
Smoothly draws the club head away from the ball.			
Keeps left arm extended fully.			
Pulls left knee inward.			
Turns hips so back faces target.			
Swing: Backswing			
Releases tension by take-away, shifting weight forward.			
Swings with tempo rhythm.			
Right hand drives club through ball.			
Keeps left arm extended, maintaining balance.			
Swing: Follow-Through			
Follows through toward target.			
Turns hips square to the target; finishes facing the target.			
Transfers weight to the left leg.			
Extends left leg.			
Arms follow through around left shoulder.			
Results			
Ball travels in air straight from golfer.			
Ball travels to target.			

From *Learning by Choice in Secondary Physical Education: Creating a Goal-Directed Program* by Kevin Kaardal, 2001, Champaign, IL: Human Kinetics.

independently while you assist other students. Thus, criterion-referenced assessment tools can also increase the on-task time of students in the class.

• **It can quickly demonstrate to a student that he is improving in his skill performance, even though his end result has not changed dramatically.** It takes the mystery out of how one can improve, demonstrates progress, and makes students who are novices feel better about their participation in physical activity. Most physical education programs do not provide a student enough time to improve skills dramatically. But think, for example, about a golf unit that involves criterion-based assessment tools. Using a rubric sheet enables a student to see when her stance and grip are right and—by adding mirrors or videos—when her backswing and follow-through are correct. Even if truly successful golf swings still require better tempo, better head position, or a thousand other factors, and will take hundreds of hours to perfect, through criterion-referenced assessment, the student can still feel good about her progress and will leave the class armed with the knowledge to improve. That knowledge is key to developing habits that lead to lifelong active living.

• **It encourages people to become physically active for life.** I have observed that the factors that most keep people from participating in a sport or athletic endeavor are

1. the experience of recurring failure ("I am no good at this game"),
2. the lack of progress after repeated trials, and
3. the frustration of not knowing why one is not succeeding.

Once people experience the encouragement of progress and, eventually, the exhilaration of mastery, they tend to get excited about physical activity. Then once they engage in healthy exercise long-term and experience the health and well-being benefits of doing so, they tend to embrace active living—certainly one of the primary goals of all physical education programs.

How to Write Rubrics

Rubrics are simply clearly written criteria for performance. "Rubric" can refer either to an entire sheet spelling out the details of various aspects of a category of performance or the individual criteria within each subcategory of the entire rubric. Having unambiguous rubrics is necessary for good assessment. How do you write such rubrics? You develop the ability to clearly analyze and describe basic skills and their components as well as different levels of skill. Let's look, then, at a couple of different kinds of rubrics and how you can learn to write them.

Rubrics for Teaching and Evaluating Skills

There are four basic kinds of information that must be in a rubric for students who are beginning or not very advanced in a particular skill:

1. **A clear identification of the skill.** You must identify the sport and be able to list the skills that are essential for successful participation in the sport.

2. **A list of the elements of each skill, with clear descriptions of each.** Unless you can break each essential skill down into the simplest components that go into its execution, students will be unable to learn the skill. For example, if you simply say "golf swing," "volleyball serve," or "baseball bat swing," the inexperienced student will be at a loss as to how to go about learning that skill. Rather, you must be able to break down the golf swing into

- the grip,
- the stance,
- the take-away stage,
- the backswing stage,
- the follow-through stage, and
- the result.

Furthermore, you must be able to explain how to achieve good results in each component. For example, you must know that to achieve a good grip for the golf swing, the player must have

- both "Vs" pointing to the right shoulder,
- the three bottom fingers of the left hand maintaining a firm and snug grip throughout the swing, and
- the right-hand grip relaxed.

Without such detailed directions, the novice will be unable to progress at all.

3. **A description of what the evaluator will observe when the goals being considered are achieved or not achieved.** This simply involves setting up a grid that accommodates what is being evaluated. For example, in form 4.2, only three levels are used:

- present,
- present, but needs work, and
- present with good performance.

In this instance, this is all the information the evaluator needs. In other instances, such as when the student is being evaluated for how well he performed on the level he chose for a particular unit, criteria for four levels should be used. See form A.2 on page 82 in part II for an example of a rubric that includes four categories of descriptors: minimal performance, acceptable performance, mastery performance, and going beyond.

4. **A way of recording performance against the criteria.** This simply involves setting up a grid with the appropriate information included and an appropriate number of spaces with

enough room in them for recording the requested information. See forms E.2 and G.2 on pages 221 and 242.

Rubrics for Evaluating Students on a Particular Level

Rubrics for evaluating students who have been working on a level for some time will be more general than those used to teach and evaluate students just beginning a level. Forms B.10 and B.11, the rubrics for defensive and offensive play in basketball (pages 102 and 103) are examples of this sort of rubric. These could both apply to students who are on either level B (recreational play) or level C (competitive play). Within the rubric, five different classes of descriptors are described:

1. Needs work
2. Below expectations
3. Meets expectations
4. Exceeds expectations
5. Extraordinary performance

Such a rubric gives players goals to aim for and provides evaluators with a tool. When using these rubrics for assessment, the evaluator will

Figure 4.2 An evaluator will use rubrics as a criterion-referenced assessment tool as he or she observes students participate in game. The rubric also helps students define their goals.

circle each statement that most consistently describes the player in each aspect of play on the appropriate rubric. Each item receives a numerical score that is equivalent to the number at the top of the column in which it appears, then all those numbers are added. If the student is working on level B, for example, her evaluation will be determined by where her total falls in the ranges for level B specified in the column heads. Let's say, for example, that in assessing defensive play for this student, you circle one item in "minimum expectations" (2 points), four items in the "acceptable performance" column (four times 3 points, or 12 points), and one item in the "mastery" column (4 points). Her total will be 2 plus 12 plus 4, or 18 points. Her total falls (barely) within the range for level B in the "mastery" column. If this student were working in level C, this same evaluation would result in her being barely in the "acceptable performance" column. (Note that in the offensive basketball rubric, items in the last column are worth 7 points each. That is because there are so many items in the fourth column that their total is almost as high as the total for the fifth column would be if each item in the fifth column received only 5 points. Thus, adjustments must be made to compensate for the higher number of items in the fourth column and the lower number of items in the fifth column.)

It is up to you to translate these general evaluations ("needs work," "minimal performance," and so on) into the grading system your school uses. For example, a reasonable "translation scale" might look something like this:

Needs work	F-D	0-49%
Minimum expectations	C	50-75%
Acceptable performance	B	76-90%
Mastery	A	91-96%
Going beyond	A+	97-100%

Whether specific numbers get pluses or minuses or where they fall in the percentage range would need to be specified for both levels. Any rubric that is created in the same format as these offensive and defensive basketball play rubrics can be adapted for this kind of use simply by assigning numbers and adding total score ranges to each column.

This method of assessment is excellent for evaluating whether a student exceeds the outcomes of the unit by being a gifted performer. The final statements in the last columns on the rubric are open-ended. The evaluator does not have a clear description of what that risk will be or how a player may create a situation where the defense or offense has an advantage. Thus, the athlete who pushes the boundaries of fundamental play in creative and unexpected ways will fulfill this criterion. When I was writing this rubric, I thought of watching Scottie Pippen and Michael Jordan playing defense. They continually challenged their opponents, took away what the opponents were comfortable with, and created opportunities for themselves or their teammates to pressure the other team into mistakes. They read each situation. Sometimes they fronted their opponents when they were in the post. Other times they anticipated where their opponents wished to go and beat them to those spots, forcing their opponents to make plays from positions where they felt insecure. It is this kind of imaginative playing that will win a student the "going beyond" grade.

Obtaining Good Information for Each Rubric

You may be saying to yourself now, "Oh, fine! So I have to be an analytical expert in every activity?" Don't worry. Just as in developing levels, you should not rely solely on your own experience: you should also take advantage of multiple resources. Read books and consult national or regional governing bodies of sports. Consult peers who have expertise on the sport in question, or talk with other experts to whom you have access. Always double-check your proposed rubric with an expert or against a published resource. And be creative about finding experts: if you are anywhere close to a university or college, for example, varsity players of various sports are often delighted with the chance to share their expertise with you and your classes.

Use the rubrics in this book to get a good start on building your goal-directed individualized program. You can use them as they are or as templates for creating rubrics customized for your approach to teaching. The important thing is to start in the area that seems most approachable for you personally, then build on each success.

CHAPTER 5

Individualizing Your Program With Peer and Self-Assessment

The idea of peer assessment and self-assessment makes some teachers nervous. They're afraid that such techniques will encourage kids to go easy on themselves or their friends and will become a way of "copping out" of vigorous physical activity. But in my experience, these approaches to assessment—if they're properly used—are great ways to facilitate student learning and to encourage enthusiastic participation. Before you even think about moving toward peer or self-assessment, however, be sure you understand and can use criterion-based assessment, as neither peer nor self-assessment can succeed without it. It is simple, clearly defined criteria that make assessment based on observation of repeatable phenomena possible.

Peer Assessment

Peer assessment is not only an effective tool for evaluation; it's also a wonderful means of teaching. This is because peer evaluation requires that students

- understand the key elements of a skill's performance,
- evaluate whether assigned partners have performed the skill as outlined by the criteria for correct performance, and
- tell their partners what they saw and what their partners need to work on to perfect the skill.

This process forces students to pay close attention to skills demonstrations, analyze and synthesize what they see, verbalize their understanding, and evaluate performance based on their comprehension and their observations.

Keeping Peer Groups on Task

A question I'm frequently asked is, "How do you keep students on task if they are working in peer groups?" The answer is simple, "You manage by walking around. You use proximity to students and awareness of what is going on, even to the point in the gym farthest away from you." Study the Management Tips in chapter 3 again. They apply to peer evaluation as well as individualized instruction.

Ensuring Fairness in Peer Evaluation

In my experience, students have no problem marking fairly when the terms identified in the peer evaluation sheet are defined well. Situations in which many students were marking the same group at the same time clearly bore this out: the range of marks given a single group of performers by the varied groups of markers was consistently small. The biggest problem I encountered in peer marking was that students can mark too harshly when they are evaluating groups at beginning levels. There are several things you can do to solve problems of fairness in peer evaluation when they do occur:

- When peers are evaluating a group performance, you also evaluate it. If the peer marks are too harsh, your mark stands.

- Walk around and observe the marks peers are giving. If they are too low, work with the peer assessor to help him understand how to use the criteria on the rubrics.

- Make sure students are aware that they may appeal the student or peer evaluation to you; then you will question or reevaluate any student you feel may have an inflated or deflated mark.

When students must help peers analyze their skill development progress, it helps them understand what they are expected to do themselves. And students who know what is supposed to happen and how to visualize it are more likely to perform a skill successfully than those who do not. When we involve students in the assessment process, we reinforce any demonstrations they have seen by forcing them to reconstruct these demonstrations in their minds. We immerse them in the learning process by having them evaluate and synthesize the information we have given them as they put the educator's descriptors into their own words and repeat the information to their peers. Furthermore, we state by our actions that we value the students' abilities and judgments and have trusted them to be leaders and help their peers. Allowing students to take ownership for their own learning in this way makes them more likely to be lifelong learners. Thus, having peers teach each other skills through ongoing peer evaluation may be the most effective way available to have students learn and retain material.

Preparing Kids to Assess Each Other

There are three things you must do as you prepare your students to assess one another: provide good examples of the skill's proper performance, teach students how to analyze the elements of the skill's proper performance, and teach students how to use the assessment tools.

• **Provide good examples of the skill's proper performance.** These good examples ("exemplars" in the jargon) may take many forms. The most common are demonstrations. These may

be live demonstrations with detailed instruction by the teacher or by a combination of the teacher and expert peers; videotapes by experts or produced by professional educational companies; or demonstrations by invited experts, such as college varsity players. The task sheets you provide are also exemplars. But they must not be used in place of demonstrations; rather, they are appropriate for reinforcing demonstrations.

• **Teach students how to analyze the elements of the skill's proper performance.** If you want students to help improve a peer's performance by suggesting changes, you must include some simple biomechanical hints during your demonstration of the skill. For example, a student seems to have the correct form when shooting a basketball but always comes up short. The two principles that may affect this performance are the principle of impulse and the principle of the summation of joint forces—the involvement of more body parts. In other words, the player needs to execute the skill more quickly and use more leg power to get the ball to the basket. If a peer teacher can analyze the skill in this way, she can help her partner be more successful. By teaching students basic biomechanical principles of each skill, you help them to recognize physical laws that will affect the performance of that sport. Just as you would not attempt to teach students about fitness without teaching them the phases of a workout, the different types of workouts, how to measure their heart rate and recovery rate, and how to determine their optimal or target heart rates, so you should not attempt to teach them sport skills without giving them some idea of what physical factors will affect the performance of that sport. The Canadian national coaching certification program technical manuals are great resources for teaching teachers what and how biomechanical principles apply to the skills they are teaching; their Web site is **www.coach.ca**.

• **Teach students how to use the assessment tools.** Go over the assessment tools you want students to use in the current lesson point by point before you turn students loose to evaluate one another. Emphasize that they should not try to observe every aspect of the skill every time it is performed: that is simply too much to be accurately noted at one time. Rather, the assessor should ask the "assessee" to perform the skill several times, focusing on one or two key points in each repetition. He should record what he has seen after each observation rather than waiting until he has observed all the points during several observed performances of the skill in question. Emphasize to students the importance of the results of observation. They must keep in mind that some students may have idiosyncrasies in how they perform the skill but still be quite effective. For example, Jim Furyk is a professional golfer with a very strange swing. It has a loop in the top that would not be recommended by any golf teacher as a skill to adopt. However, to say Jim Furyk has not therefore surpassed the "going beyond" phase as a golfer would be absurd! He has overcome his idiosyncrasy and can consistently strike the ball with a distance and accuracy that allow him fantastic success on the PGA tour: he is currently ranked 14th in world golf rankings. Thus,

if a student is consistently successful at sinking putts but does not have perfect form according to the rubric, he should not be penalized with a poorer mark. If something he's doing is working—even if it's not "by the rubric"—he should be congratulated and marked high.

And of course, no matter how much student-peer instruction preparation you do, the bottom line is that the kids can never take your place. Peer instruction cannot work unless you remain active, visible, and available throughout the class period. During the segment when students are instructing one another, you should be moving from group to group, checking out how things are going, offering your insights and corrections, encouraging and cheering on both peer instructors and peer learners. They cannot help one another adequately without strong input from you. But with it, students in a peer teaching situation can learn extremely well—and can usually have a pretty good time doing it.

Creating Tools for Peer or Self-Assessment

Once you have mastered the material in the last chapter about how to write rubrics, you will find that creating tools for peer or self-assessment of isolated skills is rather simple. This is because an assessment tool for this kind of skill is simply the rubric for the skill put into a form on which observations about each point of the rubric may be recorded. Applied or combined skills and game strategies are more difficult to write assessment forms for. But once you write a few forms for isolated skills, you will find that the more complex skills are easier to approach. For these, it will also be helpful to study some of the examples in this book.

Here is an example of how to write an assessment form for an isolated skill, in this case, golf putting. First, study your rubric for that skill, in this case, figure 5.1.

To create your peer or self-evaluation sheet, just use the rubric statements from the mastery descriptors in the four-point rubric in figure 5.1 as the key performance points for the peer assessment sheet. These statements are observable and break down the skill into six performance points and one results observation. Performance points for a skill should be kept

Golf Putting Rubric

Needs work (0 to 2.5)	Acceptable performance (2.5 to 3.5)	Mastery (4 to 4.5)	Going beyond (4.6 to 5)
Stance			
Feet shoulder-width apart; head over ball.	Feet shoulder-width apart; head "inside" ball.	Feet shoulder-width apart; head over ball.	Feet shoulder-width apart; head over ball.
Grip			
Not using 1 of 3 grips (overlap, Ventura, backhanded).	1 of 3 grips (overlap, Ventura, backhanded).	1 of 3 grips (overlap, Ventura, backhanded).	1 of 3 grips (overlap Ventura, backhanded).
Starting arm position			
Arms reach out from stance at angle in base-ball grip.	Arms drop comfortably from shoulders, forming "V."	Arms drop comfortably from shoulders, form-ing V.	Arms drop comfortably from shoulder, forming V.
Backswing			
V moves and unlocks.	V moves and unlocks.	V stays solid.	V stays solid.
Swing			
Movement is from shoulders, but wrists "break" when striking ball; consistently strikes ball outside of "sweet spot" of putter.	Movement is from shoulders, but wrists break when striking ball; strikes ball in sweet spot of putter.	Movement is from shoulders only; strikes ball in sweet spot of putter.	Movement is from shoulders only; strikes ball in sweet spot of putter *every* time.
Follow-through to target			
None observable; club de-celerates after contact.	Present, but club decelerates through ball.	Accelerates through ball.	Accelerates through ball; *is able to effec-tively read breaks in putting surface.*
Putting			
1 or 2 of 5 putts from 4 feet drop in hole.	3 of 5 puts from 4 feet drop in hole.	4 of 5 puts from 6 feet drop in hole.	4 of 5 puts from 12 feet drop in hole.

Figure 5.1 Use the rubric for golf putting to create an assessment form.

under seven because this is the average capacity of short-term memory, so students will be more likely to remember the key points. Study form 5.1 to see how the golf putting stroke worksheet has been created simply by placing the information from the golf putting rubric into a different format and adding spaces for record-ing observations. Take a few rubrics from this book (for example, the "stuntnastics" unit chart on page 251; the fitness rubric on page 218; and the softball unit chart on page 234) and try creating your own assessment forms based on them. You'll find that it isn't hard.

To create a rubric from one of the assessment forms in this book, merely reverse the process. Use the key performance points from the as-sessment form as the performance descriptors for the mastery column of a four-column rubric.

Form 5.1 Golf Putting Peer Assessment or Video Self-Assessment

Name: _____ Date: _____

Videotape yourself putting a ball and evaluate whether you performed the criteria outlined. Record the number of successful putts from two feet, four feet, and six feet versus the number of attempts, then calculate the percentage of attempts that were successful from each distance. Finally, answer the following questions:

What caused you to miss putts?

What improvement does your putting stroke need?

Design drills that might help you work on these skills. Be able to demonstrate them to your peers and teacher.

	Performed successfully	Needs improvement: What I saw
Stance: Feet shoulder-width apart. Head over ball.		
Grip: 1 of 3 grips (overlap, Ventura, backhanded)		
Starting arm position: Arms drop comfortably from shoulder, forming "V."		
Backswing: V stays solid.		
Swing: Movement is from shoulders only; strikes ball in "sweet spot" of putter.		
Follow-through to target: Accelerates through ball.		
Accuracy from 2 feet: "Sank" the ball what percent of attempts?		
Accuracy from 4 feet: "Sank" the ball what percent of attempts?		
Accuracy from 6 feet: "Sank" the ball what percent of attempts?		

From *Learning by Choice in Secondary Physical Education: Creating a Goal-Directed Program* by Kevin Kaardal, 2001, Champaign, IL: Human Kinetics.

Add an accuracy component to each of the descriptors by noting the number of successful performances versus the number of trials (usually four out of five correct performances) for the skill to be considered "present." To create the rubric columns of "needs work" and "acceptable performance," decide what common errors you see when observing students who are learning these skills, and adjust your rubric statements for each of those columns accordingly. To create a "going beyond" rubric descriptor, add creativity or being able to complete the skill with greater accuracy or in a more authentic or competitive situation than you used for the descriptors in the mastery column. Find more examples of reciprocal skills assessment sheets in the sample racket sports unit on pages 220-232 and in the dance unit on pages 246-252.

Remember that more than skills performance can be evaluated by peers. For example, in order to get input from the students on how each member contributed to the final product in a group performance or demonstration in a dance unit, the teacher could have each one fill out form H.7 (page 252). Note that this form combines self-assessment with peer assessment.

Self-Assessment

Self-assessment is great for taking the mystery out of assessment and the fear that something is being done to you—that you are being judged. For many students, it is the key to turning dread into eagerness and excitement in physical education.

Some Self-Assessment Options

Self-appraisal can be done using checklists and videotaped performances. This is particularly effective when using a stations teaching approach and teaching a relatively static skill like putting. Students are divided into groups that are given different tasks to complete at each station. At one station, they are self-evaluating putting on carpet using a self-check list and videotape. At a second station, they are involved in formative peer evaluation of their swing, striking Wiffle balls against the exterior gymnasium wall. At a third, they are playing a par three, three-holed minicourse using Wiffle balls and hula hoops and field marking flags as targets. At the final station, they are being videotaped for self-evaluation on their swing as they hit a ball into a golf practice net. The students

could watch the replay of their skill performance and use a checklist such as the one in form 5.1 to perform a self-appraisal.

Students do not need videotapes to score themselves on accuracy tests involving shooting, passing, or hitting an object toward a target because in these activities they can assess themselves for results rather than for form. Target-type self-assessments—whether basketball, golf, soccer, hockey shooting, football, baseball, or Frisbee throwing, or any racket sport where shuttle or ball placement is essential—can be made fun by turning them into timed obstacle courses testing various skills or shot types. You can also design Frisbee golf courses with targets that vary in distance from the thrower or have smaller target sizes or even defensive players involved.

Although affective items are harder to assess, even here you can use self-evaluation to a certain extent. The affective domain has three categories: leadership, cooperation, and effort. To evaluate herself, the student must be made aware of what observable behaviors constitute being a leader or cooperating or putting in effort. On-task time is a good example of an

Designing a Frisbee or Wiffle Golf Course

The simplest way to develop a course is to get a school map and shrink it so the school and the grounds fit on an 8.5-by-11 piece of paper. Diagram where you will place your cones (tee boxes) and where you will place your flags (football end zone marker sticks and flags or anything else you can think of, e.g., wooden stakes with flags stapled to them also work well). Try the course out and decide on a par. If you are playing Wiffle golf, you can use hula hoops as the hole or the green. Once the Wiffle ball is in the "green," the player puts a real ball on an artificial putting surface located by the green. You don't need to have an artificial putting strip, but it is more realistic to have to putt to finish a hole. If you don't have portable putting surfaces available, create flagpoles, put them in the center of the hula hoop, and tell the players they can consider the hole complete when their Wiffle ball strikes the flagpole.

observable behavior for putting in effort that peers can help students self-evaluate. For example, peers can note the number of minutes their partners are off task during the skill practice portion of a class. This information is then given to the student being evaluated, who then assesses her performance against a rubric that outlines expected behaviors and specifies how many "off-task" minutes in a certain amount of time constitute what mark. Form A.4 is an example of a rubric that defines affective behavior, which may be marked by an objective observer, and then given to the student to use as a basis for self-evaluation for cooperation.

It's true that we are judged by others every day, but students with high social and emotional needs or persons with an intellectual disability are particularly susceptible to damage from inappropriate evaluations. Often, these students will not participate in class because they fear failure or because they feel the tasks are too complicated. Self-assessment can be adjusted to become especially effective in working with such students. I found the questionnaire in form 5.2 to be a great motivator for these students and a useful tool for arriving at an appropriate mark for each of them.

How Students Self-Assessed a Fitness Unit

The easiest unit to evaluate using a self-assessment approach is fitness. This is because performance and progress can be measured objectively and there are hundreds of norm-referenced tests available to assist in the assessment process. Some examples of norm-referenced score tables are given in form D.3 (page 212). Based on these tables and on their own records of their performance throughout the unit, students can easily fill in worksheets such as the one in form D.1. There are some excellent books on fitness tests that include many norm-referenced score tables. The *Complete Guide to Fitness Testing* by Margaret J. Safrit (1995) is one such resource that provides many easy-to-use examples. Be sure to keep in mind the cautions and limits noted in chapter 4 about the use of norm-referenced as opposed to criterion-referenced assessment.

The Basic System

The objective of our fitness units was to teach students about fitness and show them that get-

Self-Assessing With Prewritten Programs

Calendars and fitness workout planning sheets or programs like the Canadian Active-Living Challenge developed by the Canadian Association for Health, Physical Education, Recreation and Dance help students plan to be active, while giving you a record of each student's progress.

The Canadian Active-Living Challenge teaches students to plan and record the heart healthy activities they do in and out of school. Students get 1 point for every 15 minutes of heart healthy activity they participate in. They get a maximum of 5 points per day and must get at least 210 points over 10 weeks. This program involves hundreds of activities that focus on attitudes, personal development, leisure, culture, health, environment, leadership, and active living for a lifetime.

Another example of a prewritten program is the Physical Best program of the American Alliance for Health, Physical Education, Recreation and Dance (AAHPERD). For more information, visit **www.aahperd.org/aahperd/programs-physbest.html**.

ting fit could be a lot of fun. We started them wherever they were and celebrated their personal progress. This is why we baseline tested. It was the surest way to show students that a little bit of effort every day does make a difference. Students who couldn't do 1 push-up at the beginning could often do 10 or 15 at a time by the end of a unit, because we had them practice techniques and do 20 push-ups every day, even if they could only do one at a time, spaced throughout the day. Half push-ups (push-ups done from the knees) were acceptable, too, as long as they progressed. The key was that each teacher had a positive cheerleader attitude. Statements like "Wow, you can do 1 push-up— that's a great start" and using personal records helped encourage students to keep progressing. A student who achieved a personal best by doing 4 push-ups in a row was celebrated the same way as a student who did 45 to set her personal best.

Name: _____ **Date:** _____

You receive the assigned point value for each question you can answer "yes" to. Your mark for this class will be out of 23 points. Your unit mark will be based on an average of all your class marks.

Positive statements	Yes	No
1. I was punctual. I came to class on time. (1 point)		
2. I was dressed in proper activewear and ready to participate in class. (1 point)		
3. I participated in the warm-up games and stretching today. (1 point)		
4. I exhibited a positive attitude and enjoyed today's lesson. (1-2 points)		
5. I was polite to my classmates and teacher today. (1-4 points)		
6. I was a good performer today. I stayed on task today. I did all that was asked of me. (1-4 points)		
7. I wrote in my journal today and brought it to class. (1-2 points)		
8. I got my heart rate into the target zone today. (1-4 points)		
Bonus: Points for good jokes, personal records, or cool fitness activities you did outside of school. (1-4 points; see the teacher)		
Total mark for today's lesson:	/23	

From *Learning by Choice in Secondary Physical Education: Creating a Goal-Directed Program* by Kevin Kaardal, 2001, Champaign, IL: Human Kinetics.

At the beginning of each fitness unit, we had each student set goals and then try to reach them. Throughout the unit, students performed the tests we specified, then recorded their own scores. To keep them honest, a teacher would review the scores, have peers assess one of the tests, or perform tests on randomly selected students during each class.

Grading Fitness Self-Assessed Units

When it came to translating the test scores into grades, we gave the students the choice of comparing themselves against the norm-referenced tables or of assessing themselves against their progress toward their personal fitness goals.

Self-Assessing With Software

It's easy to integrate computer technology into your fitness units. There is a great fitness tracking program that uses the Cooper points system called "E-Log." Information is available at **www.healthinvest.org/eloginfo.html**. Students record all their activities, including heart rate, intensity, and duration of the activity into this program and earn points, the number of which tells them how fit they are. It's an excellent, easy-to-use program and a great self-assessment tool, because it can produce all kinds of profiles and reports that help the students see how they are progressing.

If a student chose to assess her fitness by her progress rather than by how she compared with the norms, we would base her grade on whether she had reached the fitness goals she had established for herself at the beginning of the unit. If she met but did not surpass her goals, her grade would be a mastery performance mark—80 percent in the case of the school where I was teaching. This is because we wanted to teach students to set reasonable fitness goals to encourage them to remain active for a lifetime. The student would then set new goals and see if she could meet those goals and continue to improve her fitness. If she surpassed her goals, her grade would be over

80 percent, based on whatever system the instructor had established before the unit began. If the student did not meet her goals, she would receive a mark below 80 percent.

For example, the teacher might determine before the unit began that for a student whose goal was to run for 30 minutes continuously, every 5 minutes above and below his goal would be worth 2.5 percent. This means that if he was only able to achieve running for 20 minutes continuously, the teacher would note that he is 10 minutes below his goal. This is, of course, two 5-minute segments, each of which is worth 2.5 points. Thus 2 times 2.5 points (i.e., 5 points) would be subtracted from 80 percent, resulting in a final score of 75 percent. The key is to set measurable goals and arrive at some formula that allows for simple multiplication and division to arrive at a mark. Here are some ideas about how to do that:

• You might set up ahead of time with the student what personal goals would constitute a "C," and how much beyond those goals would merit a "B" or an "A."

• If a student is already on an elite level and there's not a lot of room for improvement, he might choose to be compared to national fitness norms, with his final percentile ranking constituting his mark.

• For students who would score at or below the national standards average, you could use a percentage of the goal achieved or exceeded to determine a grade. All these students could start with 65 percent as their starting grade. They perform baseline tests to measure their current fitness level in all areas of fitness that they wish to improve. They set their goals, and, based on 80 percent as the grade they will receive for reaching their goals, you determine what each level of achievement is worth for each student. For example,

• a student can do 10 push-ups as a baseline score, and she sets 20 push-ups as her fitness goal in the area of push-ups.

• Since she's starting with a score of 65 percent and her "target" score is 80 percent, she needs 15 percentage points (the difference between 65 percent and 80 percent) to reach her target score of 80 percent for her target of 20 push-ups.

- Since it will take 10 more push-ups to reach her target number of 20 push-ups, and if she reaches her target of 20 push-ups she should receive a total score of 80 percent, those 10 additional push-ups should be worth a total of 15 percent.

- To find out how much each individual additional push-up should be worth, then, you must divide the total number of points that all 10 are worth (15) by 10. 15 ÷ 10 = 1.5. Thus, each of the 10 additional push-ups the student must be able to do to reach her goal is worth 1.5 percent.

- It follows that if at the end of the unit she can do 16 push-ups, you would multiply those 6 new push-ups she can do by 1.5 percent for a total of 9 points to be added to her 65 percent base.

- Thus her mark will be 65 percent plus 9 percent, or 74 percent.

If she reaches her goal, her mark will be 80 percent (65 percent plus 15 percent). If she exceeds her goal and can do 30 push-ups, you will multiply those 20 extra push-ups she's added to her original 10 by 1.5 percent for a total of 30 percent, to be added to her original 65 percent base. Thus, her mark will be 65 percent plus 30 percent, or 95 percent. If, however, she did not work out at all and regressed so she could only do 5 push-ups after 10 weeks, you would multiply the 5 push-ups she can no longer do by 1.5 percent for a total of 7.5 percent, which you would subtract from her base score of 65 percent. This would give her a score for the push-ups aspect of her fitness grade of 65 percent minus 7.5 percent, or 57.5 percent.

Our heart health or active-living days, which were discussed in chapter 2, were excellent opportunities for fitness self-assessment. Students used both heart rate monitors and the tried and true pulse count as they engaged in their chosen activities. Using the chart on page 215, they tracked increases in heart rate to see if they hit their target zone and their three-minute recovery heart rate to see how close they could get it to their resting rate. Over time, this evaluation technique showed the students that their heart rate returned to its resting level more quickly as the fitness unit continued. It also showed that it took longer for them to reach their target zone—or they had to work out with

Preserving Self-Esteem

A student's state of fitness is related closely to his self-esteem and self-image. The physical education teacher must be extremely careful when evaluating fitness so as not to embarrass students. An obese student, for example, is painfully aware he is overweight. Every time he looks in a mirror, he sees an image that doesn't resemble the ideals constantly presented on TV, in magazines, and at the movies. Calling public attention to this fact can be devastating for a student and make him hate PE and—by association—exercise. This is why caliper testing for percent body fat was optional at our high school.

more intensity to reach the target zone as quickly as they became more fit. They discovered that the amount of activity we were doing in class was having a positive effect on their heart health. Such objective self-assessment is a powerful motivator for kids to adopt the exercise habit.

Combining Teacher, Peer, and Self-Assessments

It is important to consider how you will come up with students' grades when you are allowing the students to participate in the assessment process. A simple way of doing so is to tally the key points marked as "present" on each student's skills sheets and to note what percentage of the skills being assessed are present for that student. Or you can develop and post rubrics that specify what marks will be assigned for a given performance, based on the criterion-referenced assessment sheets and the conditions under which the skill was performed (from less authentic to more authentic).

In situations where groups are presenting demonstrations or performances for evaluation, I have had all the students not in the performing group evaluate that group. I would also mark each performance, then would average my and the students' marks. I found that students enjoyed the input and stayed focused and on task during each group's demonstration. They were also careful to be fair because they knew their

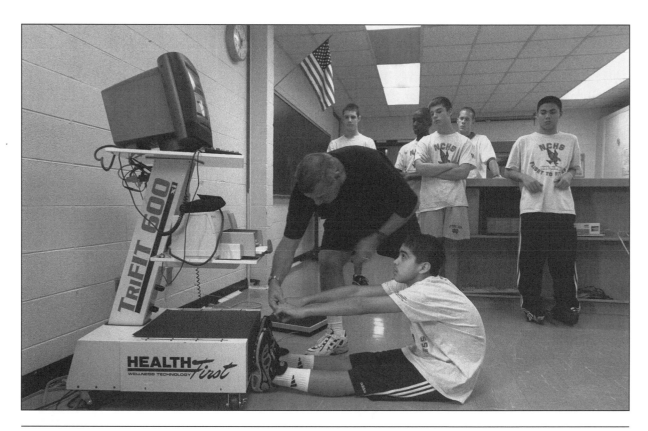

Baseline testing is a good start in teaching students that the road to physical fitness can be a lot of fun. As the students progress, the testing demonstates that a little effort every day makes a big difference.

own groups would soon perform and be marked by the students they were evaluating. In addition, they knew any mark could be appealed and that an unfair evaluation would be reflected negatively in their own group's knowledge mark, because it would show they did not have the ability to accurately assess skill performance.

Early in my career, I combined peer and teacher assessment when I was marking skill performance. For the peer assessment, I assigned values to each key performance point on criterion-referenced peer evaluation sheets. If there were five key points involved in the skill, I would assign a value of 20 percent to each key point for a possible total of 100 percent. If the student had noted that her peer had four out of the five key points present during his presentation of the skill, the performer would receive an 80 percent for the peer mark. The teacher assessment portion of the grade was based on a rubric I posted that outlined the performance goals for a skill during game play. I would evaluate the students during the modified game or culminating activity section of the lesson, using

the rubric as a guide to come up with a teacher-based mark. Finally, I would combine the two marks—usually 50/50—to arrive at a unit skill performance mark. I would then combine this mark with the evaluations of the cognitive and affective domains to arrive at a final mark.

The more experienced I became, the more I saw that maximizing students' involvement in assessment gave them a positive attitude toward physical activity and motivated them to work hard at improving their skills. I intensified the use of the techniques of self- and peer assessment discussed in this chapter, and my colleagues and I continually strove to develop ways for students to experience choice and control over their own marks. For example, we gave students bonus credits for setting personal performance records. Then we started taking Polaroid photos of them, noting their records on the photos, and posting the pictures on a "Stars of the Week" bulletin board in the gymnasium. When I saw a form my colleagues Wally Kozak and Raissa Adolphe had developed for students to use for selecting how their marks would be applied at Raissa's previous school, I recognized it would be far more effective than the one I'd written. So we adapted it to our goal-directed approach and began to use it at Bishop McNally as well (see form A.7 on page 87). Note that the form encourages working at a challenging level, demonstrations of knowledge, tournament and team play, and working on expanded opportunities. We found it to be a terrific motivator for our students. In fact, if you feel that you can implement nothing else, begin to make your program student-centered by using this form. It gave students who were not elite athletes a reason to be physically active, and it motivated

them to work; indeed, now that the form was adapted for use with levels, and students were no longer being measured against athletically gifted students, they had high chances of success. This, along with the personal benefits they began to see from physical activity, turned many of them into enthusiastic participants in class as well as in exercise outside of school.

Once you begin to try self- and peer assessment in your classes, you, too, will see a tremendous difference in how your students respond to physical education. You'll never consider limiting yourself to the traditional ways of marking again!

CHAPTER 6
Multifaceted Assessment

Effective assessment programs use a variety of assessment techniques. Multiple techniques are used because you will have multiple issues to address and varying situations in your school, including availability of personnel, resources, and time. Multiple techniques measure as many of the multiple intelligences as are possible for a given unit or course. Effective assessment programs measure performance in all three domains—psychomotor, cognitive, and affective—and involve students in the assessment process, maximizing student choice. They also include as much authentic assessment as is practical.

In this chapter, I discuss how to achieve effective assessment by making more of your assessment techniques authentic, by individualizing assessment through student choice, and by using multiple validations. A word of reminder, however: while using a variety of assessment techniques to ensure that we meet students' individual needs and differences, we must be sure alternative assessment performances are measured against consistent criteria so our evaluations have validity and reliability. Always use rubrics to make sure your criteria are consistent.

Using Authentic Assessment

Authentic assessment has a lot to offer physical education. What is it, precisely? According to Boschee and Baron (1993), "Authentic assessment consists of various performance-based methods of measuring and reporting the degree to which students demonstrate significant learning related to content and skills that are useful in real life."

Assessing skills in situations as close to real life as possible, as this quote suggests, adds meaning to learning. But if your assessment program is limited to authentic assessment, you may find you do not have the variety of assessment techniques demanded by your situation. I found that by combining authentic assessment with other valid assessment techniques to evaluate the psychomotor, cognitive, and effective domains of student achievement, I had a well-rounded and highly effective assessment program.

In many physical education programs, teachers assess skills progress with tests performed outside the context of playing the sport. Then they use a written test on rules and, finally, consider their impressions regarding the student's ability to get along with others in class and participate in activities without creating a disturbance. This approach is a good start. It addresses the psychomotor skills, basic knowledge of the rules of the sport, and whether the students are active in class and cooperating with each other. But authentic assessment demands that we think more deliberately about how we assess, considering the following.

• **Design skills tests to be more authentic.** In a typical volleyball skills test, one partner tosses the ball to another, and the receiving partner forearm-passes the ball back to the person tossing. The pass is considered successful if it meets certain criteria (see figure 3.1 Volleyball Skills Test on page 32). This is a good start to an authentic assessment of skill because it is useful as an assessment of how well students are acquiring the straightforward motor skill. But it does not take into account the many variables that can affect how the student may have to perform the skill during a game, so, by itself, it is not authentic. Game variables may require that while doing the forearm pass, the student will have to move to the ball, absorb and redirect the momentum of the opponent's serve, and/or square up to pass the ball to the setter. Thus, to be authentic, this skill assessment should require that the student demonstrate the applied skill of the forearm pass, using all three of these variations. If the criteria for a successful forearm pass were put in a checklist and the drill changed to include three students—one serving the ball away from the receiving player, forcing the receiving player to move to the ball and square up to pass to the setter—it would become more authentic. If this drill was successfully demonstrated, the teacher would know the students have acquired a skill they can use in a game situation. In the same way, all tests—skill, performance, or written—need to be designed to include tasks that are transferable to the students' real lives.

• **Include peer collaboration.** Another feature of authentic assessment is that students should be engaged in collaboration and cooperation to complete the tasks (Boschee and Baron 1993). As discussed in chapters 4 and 5, peer involvement in learning and assessment is a good way of achieving these goals.

• **Give more credit for skill demonstrations that more closely reflect real life.** Skills can be assessed by the teacher in a drill, modified game, or full game situation. It takes progressively greater skill to be successful in each of these situations—and that should be acknowledged in the assessment procedures. Teachers may develop rubrics in leveled assessment that distinguish whether the skill was performed in a drill, modified game, or full game situation. If, for example, a skill is demonstrated in a drill scenario, it may only receive a mark of 4 out of 5 on the rubric as a maximum. If a skill is performed in a modified game, where there are more external factors to consider, it might receive a 4.5 as a maximum mark on the rubric. However, if the skill is performed in a straightforward game situation, it can receive a maximum mark of 5 out of 5.

• **Use secured tasks.** Finally, secured tasks (recall "assessments of the individual student's performance under controlled conditions" [Boschee and Baron 1993]) should be included in effective assessment. Written tests, open book tests, fitness testing, or student performances in dance and gymnastics are all secured tasks. According to Boschee and Baron (1993) key characteristics of authentic secured tasks are that

1. assessment is administered under controlled conditions,
2. tasks are designed to assess specific content knowledge and skills,
3. scoring is completed by trained graders, including the teacher,
4. assessment of secured tasks matches learner goals,
5. students are provided feedback on task performance, and
6. students are permitted reassessments until they achieve acceptable skill performance standards.

More Authentic = Higher Grades

Giving higher marks for success in more "true-to-life" situations increases success while preserving meaningful grades. A level A student can still get 100 percent on his level one skill execution, for example, but to do so requires that the teacher observe it in a game situation with other level A students. If the student can only demonstrate the skill in a drill scenario, he remains in the lowest stage of skill development and therefore will not receive as high a mark as if he could perform equally well in a game. In this way, you can create discriminating marks within a leveled evaluation of skill performance. You don't judge based on comparing student performance to student performance but rather on the conditions under which a student performs the skill successfully. The following tennis evaluation (of the ready position of a student with level A skills) and its accompanying rubric are good examples of this principle. If the student performs the skill in a modified game of half court single on return of serve, she receives 4.5 points; if she performs the skill in a rally and returns to ready position after each stroke, she receives 5; if she cannot perform the skill consistently, she is asked to demonstrate the skill in a drill and may receive anywhere from 1 to 4 points.

Level A Skills

Skill: ready position	Present	Needs improvement and suggestions
Weight on balls of feet		
Knees relaxed		
Feet slightly apart		
Right hand relaxed on grip		
Left hand on racket throat		
Elbows slightly bent		
Racket in front of body		
Racket head higher than grip		

Rubric

1 2 3 4	4.5	5
Performed in a drill on command.	Performed during a modified game of half court single on return of serve.	Performed in a rally returning to ready position after each stroke.

Note that moving from simple drills to more authentic situations is built into teaching with levels. Generally level A will feature simple drills and modified games, while level C will feature games and drills with game-like conditions.

Individualizing Assessment Through Student Choice

Just as you can individualize instruction by giving students choices, you can also individu-alize assessment by giving students choices about weighting different categories of assessment and about how they will be assessed in each domain. You may either offer one choice or the other or combine the two.

Weighting the Domains

One effective way of offering students choice in assessment is to allow each student to select how the three domains—psychomotor (skills), cognitive (knowledge), and affective (atti-tudes)—will be weighted in arriving at the

---

An Effective Secured Task

An example of an effective secured task is the 30-minute walk-run test designed by the staff at Bishop McNally High School. Students begin continuously running around a set course. Because it is important that the teacher monitor whether each student is running continuously, the course must be small enough so the teacher can see all the students, all the time. The students must move around the course without stopping for 30 minutes. The students are awarded marks based on the following formula:

1. 5 percent for each minute they run up to the 12-minute mark
2. An additional 2 percent for each minute they run after the 12-minute mark
3. 2.5 percent for every minute they power-walk during the first 12 minutes
4. 1 percent for every minute they power-walk after the 12-minute mark
5. A 5 percent bonus if they continuously run or walk for the entire 30 minutes
6. 100 percent for running continuously

Thus, a student who runs continuously for 15 minutes and then power-walks for 15 minutes would receive a mark of 81 percent, because $(12 \times 5) + (3 \times 2) + 15 = 81$. In this way, the teacher is recognizing the aerobic, caloric-burn, and health value of walking as well as running.

Students perform the test until they have achieved mastery (80 percent or better) six times. Teachers act as the evaluators, and students run under controlled conditions. The advantages of this test are many. You don't have to measure the track the students will run on, as activity time is the factor you are measuring. It recognizes that continuous activity is the key to healthy living by giving credit to the health benefits of walking. At a basic level, it recognizes the benefits of increasing the intensity of exercise by rewarding students for running more than for walking. You can further emphasize exercise intensity by having the students set individual target heart rate and recovery heart rate goals. Finally, because students get to choose how long they run and walk within the 30-minute test, they feel they are in control.

If you wish to add more choices to this secured task, you can reward a student for the distance completed during the test. (To do this, of course, you do have to measure the course.) The student can choose the distance he will complete. You can further challenge the elite student by encouraging him to meet increasingly more demanding distance goals during the 30 minutes, heightening the intensity of his workouts as the unit progresses.

student's final grade. For example, students who are excellent at skill performance but poor performers on written tests could weight skill performance heavily and the written assignment lightly to maximize their overall mark. The activity is thus in more of a "real-life" setting than if the student had to perform to someone else's standards. This process produces a mark aligned with the student's own goals, producing a feeling of greater satisfaction than if the mark were based on goals someone else had chosen for her, thereby increasing the likelihood she will continue to use the skills she has acquired.

To ensure the student is evaluated in all the domains and all the community mandated goals (see chapter 2) are assessed for each unit, students must select at least one assessment category from each domain (psychomotor, cognitive, and affective) and be limited to a weighting range between 10 and 40 percent in each category. Students who start out as novices in a unit but feel they can demonstrate skill improvement with pre- and postskill testing can weight the psychomotor category heavily. Highly skilled performers who will see little or no improvement beyond subtle refinements of skill can weight the skill performance category highly. (Or they may choose to challenge the unit as discussed on pages 14 and 15.) Students who have histories of successful test taking or report writing may choose to weight the cognitive component higher than the psychomotor to maximize their marks. Students who typically demonstrate enthusiasm, high levels of on-task

time, and collaboration or leadership may choose to weight the affective domain more heavily. The assessment instrument used to combine the student's assessment, teacher's assessment, and the weighted scores from all of the assessment domains could look like the Physical Education Student Self-Evaluation (Adolphe and Kozak 1998) on page 87.

Frank Durante developed a method of allowing students to choose their assessment weightings by selecting one of four options for the weighting of each domain (Durante 1997). He found this very effective for junior high students, where maturity levels of students and the resources available somewhat limited the possibility of offering students choices. He called it the "PCAB" (psychomotor, cognitive, affective, balance) method of weighting. The chart in figure 6.1 explains the options. If your students are more mature and you wish to allow them to influence the weighting of different categories more individually, you can use a form such as the Physical Education Student Self-Evaluation (page 87) and have them fill out the "weighting" column at the beginning of the unit and add the final marks and their averages in each category as they become available.

Choosing Modes of Assessment

Another good way to individualize (and thus "authenticate") assessment is to give students choices about the ways in which various aspects of their performance will be assessed. For the cognitive domain, for example, students who are

PCAB Self-Evaluation Weighting Chart

	Option 1 Psychomotor	Option 2 Cognitive	Option 3 Affective	Option 4 Balance
Skill	40%	20%	20%	25%
Participation	20%	20%	45%	25%
Written	20%	45%	20%	25%
Fitness	20%	15%	15%	25%

Figure 6.1 Students can choose their own assessment weightings by using this PCAB Self-Evaluation Weighting Chart. Reprinted, by permission, from F. Durante, 1997, "Let Your Students Choose! The PCAB Method," *Runner* 35:3, a publication of the Alberta Teachers' Association.

not good at taking tests but who are good at research and working through question booklets may select written assignments or reports instead of tests. Or students may be encouraged to analyze or evaluate an article about the sport or activity they are involved in. (However, you must ensure the article is relevant and the review is researched and cites credible references; otherwise this assignment will demonstrate little more than the student's ability to summarize what he has read.) Open-ended questions or projects also make for exciting learning opportunities. Students can create a new game, do an Internet research project on the history of a sport, or identify all the recreational opportunities in the local community and categorize them by sport, cost, location, and so on. When students chose this last activity (from the Canadian Active-Living Challenge), they were always amazed to discover how many opportunities for fun they were missing. As another example, as a part of our leadership component, we have had students create low-organization games and teach them to the class. The opportunities for students to demonstrate cognitive understanding of physical education content are limited only by the teacher's and the students' imaginations.

Students who are not skilled at taking written rules tests or explaining a strategy on paper could demonstrate their understanding of the rules by playing a game and correctly self-officiating. They may also explain and rationalize some strategy they intend to employ against their opponent and then go out and try to execute that strategy. This helps the student who has difficulty expressing herself in writing and is often effective with students who are being taught in a language that is not their native tongue. These students often can demonstrate their understanding of rules, strategies, fair play, codes of conduct, and safety rules best by physically demonstrating them. Their kinesthetic knowledge and ability to play a sport or participate in an activity safely exceed the skill they have in communicating that knowledge through writing or speaking.

Alternative Validations

There is nothing wrong with using traditional ways of assessing students as long as your assessments are not restricted to these methods. Students need to be evaluated in multiple ways including the following:

- Activity checklists
- Culminating exhibitions and presentations
- Hands-on demonstrations
- Videotaping
- Contract fulfillment
- Written assignments and tests
- Oral interviews
- Reflective journals and learning logs
- Observations and anecdotal records on the affective domain
- Portfolios
- Allowing student challenges
- Authentic skills demonstrations
- Observable demonstrations of affective performance, that is, positive attitudes toward activity, leadership, collaboration, and sporting behavior

I have already discussed the use of contracts (pages 38 and 39), allowing student challenges (pages 14 and 15), and authentic skills demonstrations (page 68), as well as some alternative forms of written assignments (page 71). I will discuss the other items in the following sections.

Activity Checklists

Activity checklists (also called "performance checklists") are composed of the key performance points of a skill. For example, figure 3.1 on page 32 is a checklist that helps students and teachers assess some of the skills in volleyball. The observer watches the performer practice the skill and records whether the key performance points are present. This assessment tool can be used for prepractice and post-practice assessment. Observers use circles to indicate the prepractice skill performance and use check marks to record post-practice performance. The differences in performance demonstrate the skill improvement of the student. Review chapter 4 for tips on creating effective checklists.

Culminating Presentations and Exhibitions

Culminating presentations and exhibitions give students the opportunity to demonstrate their skill performance, knowledge of strategy, and ability to cooperate and perform with sporting behavior. Culminating presentations are often used in evaluating dance, gymnastics, or other activities that lend themselves to performance rather than to games or competitions. However, culminating performances can be used in team sports as well. Students can demonstrate a variety of skills necessary to execute an offensive strategy they have designed in basketball, flag football, soccer, lacrosse, or volleyball. Teachers are given a written explanation of the offense, including a diagram and a list of the skills the students expect to perform during their demonstration. This has the added benefits of involving students in their assessment and giving them a chance to write their own outcomes. See pages 248 and 251 for examples of dance routine and stuntnastics evaluation sheets.

One of the most effective examples of a culminating dance production I have witnessed was at Bishop Kidd Junior High. I have never seen an event that involved a higher percentage of a school's student body on a voluntary basis (over 70 percent!); that served as such an excellent public relations tool for the school and its physical education program; and—most importantly—that helped students believe in themselves as much as this event did. For this performance, students chose groups and choreographed dances with their physical education teacher's help. Students who wished to dance solo auditioned. The drama department came up with a theme with which scripted masters of ceremonies and actors could tie all the dances together. Students spent time in class, at lunch, and after school rehearsing for about a month. The art department prepared the sets, and when everything was ready, four performances were given: one to our feeder elementary schools, one to the students' peers, and two for family and friends in the evenings. The self-esteem that was built up was unbelievable. Students were evaluated by their teachers using open criteria, as each dance was unique, ranging from hip hop, jazz, classical, tap, folk, and square to ballroom dancing. All four performances were videotaped, allowing the teachers to mark the students' best performance. The fact that the evaluation took place during a performance before a live audience made the evaluation of this dance unit very authentic.

Hands-on Demonstrations

Hands-on demonstrations (also referred to as "skill tests" or "skill practice drills") are inherent in physical education assessment, as all physical education activities involve "doing." Hands-on demonstrations are a great way either to periodically evaluate a student's progress toward the unit outcomes or to assess his contract outcomes. They can be used to assess specific skill performance, performance and understanding of strategies involved in a game, or understanding of game rules in action. Having students demonstrate specific skills is a sound practice when the skill is assessed in an authentic situation.

Assessing students' understanding of strategy is easily done by conducting a quick oral interview with students who are playing a game, then observing what happens during play. For example, you may be marking two students involved in a squash match. You ask one student to quickly assess the strengths and weaknesses of her opponent and tell you what strategy she plans to employ. A typical response might be "My opponent has a weak backhand shot and cannot make kill shots from the corners of the court. I intend to keep playing the ball to the corners and to her backhand. This will give me ownership of the midcourt, and I will try kill shots to the opposite corner or drop shots off two walls to win points after she mishits her backhand." The teacher then observes the game and sees if the player is successful at her strategy, then repeats the process with the other student. You may also use such situations to note whether the students understand the rules of play—a more exciting way of being tested on the rules of squash than the traditional written test.

The main disadvantage of using skill demonstrations to assess students is that they can be time intensive. If you restrict the skill demonstrations to isolated skill drills, you will spend a significant amount of time observing a few students to assess their performance accurately. This obstacle can be overcome in several ways:

- Use peer assessment as discussed in chapter 5.
- During class, restrict skill demonstrations to game situations involving fairly large numbers of students, only rarely observing drills that involve only one or two students at a time.
- Videotape student skill performance so you can evaluate outside of instructional time.

Another potential difficulty with teacher-directed evaluation of student demonstrations is that while you are marking, the rest of the class can easily slip into unproductive behavior. But if you apply the techniques for individualizing instruction discussed in chapter 3, off-task behavior will not be a problem.

Videotaping

A skill or skill performance can also be videotaped and used for formative assessment and as a great teaching tool. Peers can critique each others' performance while the performer watches. You can point out to the performer key areas to concentrate on so that he may improve. When analyzing static skills like the golf swing, you can provide the student with a checklist and have him evaluate his own performance based on the videotaped evidence (see chapter 5, page 59).

Working with communications departments in the school will allow both classes to benefit from a student's expertise. The student in the communications class can get credit for videotaping outcomes, while you get the benefit of excellent taping of students' performances and the freedom to perform other tasks. An added advantage is you won't have to involve a member of your own class in videotaping, so every student may take advantage of the opportunity to be active and work toward fitness.

When they feel they are ready to take the test, students in an individualized environment may have their performance videotaped and turn the tape in to the teacher. This may be during the unit when you are busy assisting other students or even after the unit is finished if the students have taken advantage of extended opportunities (see pages 13 and 14).

You may be concerned that if you offer students the opportunity to present you with videotapes to assess, you are letting yourself in for a burdensome amount of work outside the classroom. In my experience, however, this has not been a problem. Since it is the student's responsibility to arrange for the videotaping of a performance—except in the case of group-culminating activities like stuntnastics or dance routines—a limited number of them take advantage of this opportunity. In fact, so rare is it for students to take the initiative and videotape on

their own that you may need to assign it as a project when video would be especially helpful for assessment. Expanded opportunities, for example, are easy to evaluate if the student provides you with tapes of her performance.

Written Assignments and Tests

Written tests and assignments are commonly used to evaluate students' summative knowledge of skills, strategies, rules, and safety practices. It is important and appropriate that we ask our students to demonstrate an understanding of the rules, strategies, safety issues, health benefits, and etiquette involved in each activity we teach them.

Oral Interviews

Oral interviews are a terrific way to assess whether students understand the current lesson and its connection to previous lessons. For example, at a natural break in a badminton game, such as after the shuttlecock has been grounded, you can ask a student to describe and rationalize her strategy before play resumes. The student's answer will tell you whether she has understood the concept or strategy well enough to apply it to an authentic situation. Oral interviews can be very open-ended and can provide you with a wealth of information on student progress as well as on whether they are enjoying the learning process. This information can alert you to necessary changes to the unit delivery to accommodate student needs. It is an effective assessment strategy because it emphasizes the formative rather than the summative aspect of assessment: you are able to provide feedback to the student and the student can refine his strategy. It also has the potential of improving teacher-student relations as students come to recognize that their progress and opinions have value within the classroom.

Reflective Journals and Learning Logs

Another opportunity for formative assessment is to have students write about their experiences in physical education classes in reflective journals, an activity that can take as little as five minutes at the end of a class. These journals would not receive marks for content. You can have students write about what they have learned, record questions about what they did not understand, and reflect on their feelings about participating in the activity. In addition, completed skills tests, written exams, and assignments may all be kept in journals. This allows both teacher and student to get an overall picture of the student's progress throughout the year without referring to formal marks.

Journaling can be used in a number of ways. Here's what has worked best for me: require each student to bring in a three-hole binder. All blank journal pages, skills tests, written exams, and assignments should be on three-hole punched paper so they can easily be placed in the notebooks, which are kept in students' PE lockers or a filing cabinet or shelf in the physical education office. Use tabbed pages to separate the categories of papers from one another, and as students add pages, they should be placed in the back of the appropriate section. This gives you a chronological record of each category you wish to track. These can include

- journal pages,
- skills test evaluations,
- written exams,
- written assignments,
- research projects, and
- student feedback on what they like and what changes they would like to see in the program.

Require that the journal be brought to each class like a physical education textbook. A journal page might look like the example on page 81, and the rubric on page 82 can again be used to help evaluate the journals.

Observations and Anecdotal Records on the Affective Domain

Observations and anecdotal records of students can be kept quickly and easily by the teacher on a grid sheet such as the Attitude and Effort Assessment Criteria chart on page 83. You take very brief notes to record notable observed behaviors during class, and after class you transfer this information—adding point values—to a class grid sheet. By using codes such as the ones noted at the bottom of figure 6.2, this can be done very quickly (one to five

minutes total per class), depending on what happened that day. The grade or class record of these anecdotal records would look something like the example in figure 6.2, which illustrates what your marking grid might look like after a short unit during which you recorded notable behaviors.

This method of assessment is easy, as you record only the remarkable (either good or bad) behaviors you observe, and assume later that students with no notable behaviors recorded should receive an average mark. For example, Fred and Sally have done enough extra notable behaviors to receive a mark of 20 out of 20. In Sally's case she had a class where she achieved a personal best. Fred demonstrated a positive attitude (pa +4) by setting up and putting away equipment and by leading the warm-up stretch (ps +2). Ralph had a couple of bad days where he decided not to participate (np –11) and was off task and had to be timed-out (ot –6), but recovered marks throughout the rest of the unit by working extremely hard in class and staying on task (pe +4) and leading the warm-up and stretch (ps +2).

If you ask students to help you not to miss any positive behaviors that are worthy of noting, most of them will be eager to point out their positive behaviors. This helps the students focus on the behaviors you hope to see. When they are given the Attitude and Effort Assessment Criteria (form A.3 on page 83), they can understand what kind of concrete actions are evidence of having a positive attitude about participating in class.

It is amazing how having clearly defined criteria for the affective domain improved the learning environment in my classes. Junior high students competed to take on leadership roles in the class and took pride in themselves as they shared their personal bests with me. Even students who experienced difficulty in class early in the unit knew they had an opportunity to improve their grade with improved behavior. It was easy to demonstrate that their attitude marks were based on observed behaviors, not on whether I liked them. Soon the students began to discipline themselves. If students made a bad decision that required a time-out and resulted in a deduction of marks, they knew that with some planning they could earn those marks back. I would often find

Anecdotal Record Example Class Roster

Unit: Badminton Class: Grade 10 PE	03/ 12	04/ 12	05/ 12	06/ 12	07/ 12	08/ 12	09/ 12	10/ 12	Total att./effort
Fred	pa +4		ps +2						20
Sally							pr +1 0		20
Luis	ot −4			imp −4		pr +1 0			16
Gorgette									14
Kodjovi					ps +2				16
Bruno									14
Nanda									14
Amit	np −11		imp −4			ps +2	pvg +2	pun +2	5
Brad									14
Billy		pr +1							15
Heather				np −2					12
Jon									14
Amisha									14
Ralph	ot −6	np −11	pe +6	ps +2	pe +4		pe +4		17

Codes

imp = impolite
ot = off-task
np = not participating
pa = positive attitude
pe = performance, effort excellent

ps = polite, set up equipment
pr = set personal record
pvg = performance, effort very good
pun = punctual, first person changed

Figure 6.2 Codes are used to note observed behavior in this Anecdotal Record Example Class Roster.

students who had recently been off task pointing out some cooperative or leadership action they had just completed. The rules and consequences were clear and easily understood so students could turn a negative into a positive by making simple behavior changes. This system was also a powerful tool at parent-teacher interviews as I was able to point out to parents specific positive and negative behaviors and the dates on which they occurred.

Portfolios

Portfolios, which comprise a collection of the student's best work, are essential to effective assessment of a student's improvement and performance. If you use the leveled approach to instruction, delivery, and assessment, portfolios make it easy for you to keep track of a student's performance and improvement as he advances through his program.

Why Use Portfolios?

Portfolios provide tangible evidence of a student's knowledge, abilities, and skill performance or academic improvement. Boschee and Baron (1993) outline the primary purposes for using portfolios as

- assessing the students' accomplishments of learner goals and community-mandated goals;
- assessing the quality of the students' sustained work;
- allowing students to showcase their unique interests and abilities;
- encouraging pride in the quality of workmanship, the ability to self-evaluate, and the ability to accomplish meaningful tasks; and
- documenting improvement of students' work.

The portfolio can also be used to track a student's progress over several years. In a leveled program that offers individualized units with hundreds of skill choices, it is impossible for students to master all the skills within a unit in one year. Thus, the portfolio may be used to track a student's performance in badminton for the two or three years that this unit is offered in high school. Portfolio assessment does not have to result in a grade. It is an authentic way of showing growth and displaying the best the student has had to offer. It is an ideal tool for assessing for celebration, information on what the student feels she has done best, and demonstration of growth.

Portfolios can be kept in a filing cabinet in alphabetical order. At the beginning of each academic year, you would collect your students' portfolios from the cabinet when you received your class lists. This would give you a quick introduction to the students in class. By examining examples of their best work, you will have an idea what students were capable of before you met them. Although you have to be careful not to let this picture cloud future evaluations, it could prove useful in helping motivate students to improve on the previous year's personal best results. You could use examples of the students' best work to help motivate them to continue to meet that standard in each unit.

The portfolio can also serve as a terrific public relations tool. Teachers and students can use the portfolio to communicate more effectively with parents what they are doing and how well they are accomplishing it. Imagine, for example, popping in a video of a child's performance from her portfolio during parent-teacher interviews to help explain how her grade was determined. Students may also use their portfolios during culminating presentations to classmates. Rather than "This is what I did over the summer," the presentation becomes "This is what I learned this year."

Video in Portfolios

Video livens up a portfolio and allows your assessment to expand beyond the walls of the gymnasium: by using videotapes, students can include in their portfolios skills learned outside the classroom through expanded opportunities. Video can be coupled with computer presentation software like Power Point to create a multimedia project to include in the portfolio. Project topics could include a history of the development of a group's dance or stuntnastics presentation or a biomechanical skill analysis of a peer or one's self-performing a sport skill. Both can have music, stop motion, and other special effects added to serve as excellent and fun projects.

What Should Be Included in a Portfolio?

It is important to understand that students have a major role to play in what should go into their portfolios: selecting their best work. To get a picture of the student's progress from teacher to teacher and year to year, make sure students include

- leveled skill tests, peer or self-evaluated (the criteria outlined on them serve as a good review, and the evaluations allow you to ensure students progress to higher levels as soon as they are ready);

- their best cognitive work;
- journal entries of the students' best days;
- work done as a result of challenging a unit (pages 14 and 15);
- their fitness goals and results to be used in planning their next years' goals, emphasizing that fitness is an ongoing venture that is never finished;
- fitness goals they set for over the summer, which again extends physical education beyond the classroom or even school year and into their everyday lives; and
- completed questionnaires on what they enjoyed about courses and suggestions on how courses could be improved.

All this information is invaluable in helping you plan for the following year. Depending on what the questionnaires reveal, they can also sometimes serve as a nice pat on the back for you. After all, teachers as well as students need encouragement!

Summing Up

I hope I've persuaded you by now that offering kids the opportunity of learning by choice in secondary PE is worth doing. If you have any doubts left about how well this approach works, perhaps this story will convince you: My brother was visiting me from out of province, and we went to run some errands at the local strip mall. Many of my students stopped us and made positive comments to me. One young man whom

I had taught in grade 8 (he had long since graduated) recognized me and made a point of introducing me to his wife and children as the best teacher he ever had. My brother asked after the shopping trip if I was some kind of local hero! But I knew it was simply that I gave students choice, took the mystery out of marking, was excited by what I did, and—most importantly—treated each student with dignity and respect.

For me, confirmation of the rightness of offering students choice came every day in my classes as I saw the excitement and pleasure so many youngsters exhibited at the chance to engage in physical activity. I was especially touched by the comments of students with special needs on how much they enjoyed physical education because they could succeed. Moreover, at every school where I taught, my colleagues' teaching practices changed to include more student- and choice-centered methods of assessment and instruction than they had used before. These teachers were convinced by what they saw in my classes, too.

This is a method that works. Try it yourself, instituting changes as you feel comfortable. Start small, and you'll see benefits that will make you want to expand your use of student- and choice-centered instruction and assessment until you, too, have many previously sedentary students who are now turned on to physical activity for life. And when you think of all those benefits of physical activity we talked about in chapter 1, you'll know that whether anyone else recognizes it, you really are a hero.

PART II
Reproducibles to Help Build Your Program

When I started teaching physical education, Larry Auger, a teacher I was replacing while he was on an educational leave for one year, left me all of his files. Those files were a treasure trove. They included handouts, tests, posters, task sheets—everything Larry had used to deliver a fantastic physical education program. Not being Larry, I used his skill posters for slightly different purposes than he had, adjusted his handouts where necessary, and made changes to his tests to meet the goals I had for my program. Larry's generous gift saved me so much time, and I can never repay him, so I determined that I would do as he had done and share my materials with others every chance I got. The units in part II are the result of that sharing. First I shared; then the people who used them made adjustments and improved them, and shared their ideas with me. You can use these sheets as they are or as starting points for collegial professional discussions and planning.

The Basketball and Soccer Units

The basketball and soccer sample units are not meant to be recipe books. Instead, they are designed to be used as a starting point for teachers interested in giving students the opportunity to learn basketball or soccer skills at their own rate and at a level that challenges them yet allows them to experience success. If students discover or develop drills that are more appropriate to their development than those offered here, or if your professional judgment and experience indicate that a different direction should be taken, make adjustments. These units are meant to be flexible—individualized to meet the students' needs and the teacher's style. The first modification you may wish to make is to copy the task card posters onto 11 × 17-inch paper at 129% to enable kids to read the posters better when they are posted on the gym wall.

The basketball and soccer units have been slightly modified in size to fit this book. I hope that you and your students will find these modified basketball and soccer units helpful and enjoyable.

Other Sections in Part II

The other sections in part II provide examples of various kinds of useful planning and assessment forms that you may wish to create for other units. These examples can be used as they are, or they may be modified as you like and used as models for creating more complete materials for any physical education unit. In the unusual cases when more than one form appears on a page, you will no doubt wish to copy them onto separate pages before using them with students.

Part II includes A forms (planning); B (basketball); C (soccer); D (fitness), E (racket sports); F (softball); G (volleyball); and H (dance and stuntnastics). The planning section contains sample forms that are useful for assessments and for your own and students' planning. Though the basketball unit has been scaled down from what I used in my programs, it is complete enough to be used as it is. Of course, you may wish to adapt or supplement it with your own materials. Soccer includes a master chart and enough task card posters to present a unit. To have all the forms necessary for a complete soccer unit, you will probably want to create additional forms using the basketball unit as a model. The remaining sections include samples of all the other forms discussed in part I. These forms are presented in a variety of sports to help you create the forms you will need to build and run any unit you wish to offer.

As you move toward goal-directed physical education, remember that for most people (including myself) making this change is a gradual process. Begin with the units that you are already most confident teaching, and change your materials and methods at a pace that works for you. This is a long-term project that will reap a lifetime of benefits for both you and your students.

Form A.1 Journal Work Sheet

Name: _____ **Class:** _____

Date: _____ **Journal entry number:** _____

Happenings: Today in physical education class we . . .

_____

_____

_____

_____

Something new I learned today was . . .

_____

_____

_____

_____

Today I felt . . .

_____

_____

_____

Today I enjoyed . . .

_____

_____

_____

I rate my pyschomotor performance . . .

_____

_____

_____

Next class my goals are . . .

_____

_____

_____

Teacher's response . . .

_____

_____

_____

From *Learning by Choice in Secondary Physical Education: Creating a Goal-Directed Program* by Kevin Kaardal, 2001, Champaign, IL: Human Kinetics.

Rubric
Levels of Performance
(To be used in planning unit outcomes)

	Minimal Reassessment required	**Acceptable** Reassessment recommended	**Mastery** Reassessment not required	**Going Beyond** Reassessment not required
Outcome	Describes happenings in class accurately; reflects part of lesson plan as executed.	Describes happenings in class accurately; reflects most of plan as executed.	Describes happenings in class accurately; reflects lesson plan as executed.	Describes happenings in class accurately; reflects lesson plan as executed.
Outcome	The student does not comment.	Student shares relearning something during the lesson.	Student discovers and shares learning something new during lesson.	Student discovers and shares learning something new during the lesson, adding comments from coaches, articles, or other information sources that enhance what was taught.
Outcome	Student does not comment.	Student mentions feelings and some enjoyable part of lesson without explanations.	Student mentions and explains feelings and enjoyable part of lesson, matching teacher observations.	Student mentions and explains feelings and enjoyable part of lesson, matching teacher observations. Student also comments on most effective part of lesson and offers suggestions to improve learning.
Outcome	Student does not set any goals.	Student sets one to three inappropriate (too easy or too hard) short-term goals for next class.	Student sets one to three appropriate short-term goals for next class.	Student sets four appropriate short-term goals for next class.
Descriptive scale:	1	2 3	4	5

Descriptive scale: Ranges from minimal (1) to going beyond (5). Each outcome is described in detail in the appropriate box.

Indicators: Answer the questions "How do you know?" and "What do you see?" in ongoing monitoring and observations.

From *Learning by Choice in Secondary Physical Education: Creating a Goal-Directed Program* by Kevin Kaardal, 2001, Champaign, IL: Human Kinetics.

Your attitude mark starts at 70% or 14 of 20 points for each unit. You can earn or lose marks from this starting point by engaging in the behaviors listed below. If you lose points during one class by engaging in negative behaviors, you can gain them back during the same class or in a future class by engaging in positive behaviors: **politeness, preparedness, punctuality, performance,** and **positive attitude**.

Positive Behaviors	Negative Behaviors
Politeness	**Impolitness**
• First student to put hand up to answer a question. +2% • Is cooperative with teacher, as demonstrated by helping set up or take down the equipment. +2% • Treats all people with respect by being kind, sharing equipment, and generally being polite and helpful to others. +4%	• Treats others disrespectfully in any way. Acts in an unsporting way (e.g., bad language, rude body language, put-downs, and the like). −4%
Preparedness	**Unpreparedness**
• Comes to class prepared to be involved in physical activity. If injured or unable to participate in the assigned activity, student is willing to offer or accept suggestions on how the class goals and objectives can be modified to allow participation and learning. +1%	• Comes to class unwilling to participate. Student has no active wear and no journal to write in and is not willing to consider any suggestions on how the goals of the class might be modified to accommodate learning. No points are deducted. This is considered a discipline problem. Student must call home and explain the choice not to participate to a parent. If not corrected, it could result in suspension from class and a score of null or zero on the unit.
Punctuality	**Lateness**
• Is the first student changed and ready to participate; leads warm-up game. +1% • Proper clothing and readiness to participate is expected of all students.	• Sent to office for a late slip. No points deducted, but student could have to make up missed time.
Performance	**Nonperformance (off-task behavior)**
• Is on task and working hard. +2% • Sets a personal performance record. +10% • Demonstrates a skill or drill for the class. +2% • Leads the class stretch, a low-organization game, or warm-up. +2% • Reciprocally teaches a classmate voluntarily during a skill drill. +2%	• Once −2% • Twice and timed out −4% • Sent out and unable to return as a result of extreme inappropriate behavior. Up to −10%
Positive attitude	**Negative attitude**
• While on task, student is demonstrating joy in the activity by smiling, laughing, or cheering. +4% • Compliments classmates on their efforts. +2%	• Student complains about the activity without offering any constructive suggestions. −2% • Puts down classmates for any reason. −4%

From *Learning by Choice in Secondary Physical Education: Creating a Goal-Directed Program* by Kevin Kaardal, 2001, Champaign, IL: Human Kinetics.

Form A.4 Affective Evaluation Chart

Rating	Student Self-Evaluation Criteria for Cooperation, Sporting Behavior, and Effort Points
8.6 to 10 Superior	• Always concentrates on activities at hand • Works well and is polite and positive with all members of the group • Always puts forth 100% effort • Works at a challenging level • Always uses good judgment; always displays honesty • Responsible and cooperative beyond teacher expectations • Always comes prepared • Sets personal performance records
8 to 8.5 Mastery	• Almost always concentrates on activities at hand • Usually polite and positive; works well with most members of the group • Puts forth 100% effort most of time • Works at a challenging level most of time • Always uses good judgment; always displays honesty • Displays cooperative and responsible behavior consistent with teacher expectations • Almost always comes prepared
6.5 to 7.9 Acceptable	• Concentrates on activities at hand most of time • Attempts to be postive and polite and to work with most members of the group if externally motivated • Displays constructive and honest behavior when supervised • Occasionally requires follow-up on preparation, duties, and responsibilities
2.5 to 6.4 Unacceptable	• Often fails to concentrate on task at hand, unless closely supervised • Frequently does not attempt to work well with others • Does not put forth a reasonable effort • Does not work at a challenging level • Never sets personal records • Tends to show poor judgment when not under direct supervision • Not generally cooperative; avoids responsibility
1 to 2.4 Very poor, nonexistent	• Never concentrates on activities at hand • Continually displays undesirable group behavior; rude to other members of group • Consistently makes little or no effort • Frequently displays destructive behavior and dishonesty • Frequently displays irresponsible and uncooperative behavior

From *Learning by Choice in Secondary Physical Education: Creating a Goal-Directed Program* by Kevin Kaardal, 2001, Champaign, IL: Human Kinetics.

Calendar Time	Tasks to Be Completed and Accountable	Resources

Read the posters and practice the skills outlined. Record the skill level, poster color, the skill you practiced, and a brief description of the drill below. Then rate your performance by circling a number under "Quality of Performance" column.

Personal challenge: How many drills and skills can you experience in a class period?

Skill#	Poster Color	Skill Attempted and Drill Used	Quality of Performance 1 = Needs work 5 = Mastered				
1.			1	2	3	4	5
2.			1	2	3	4	5
3.			1	2	3	4	5
4.			1	2	3	4	5
5.			1	2	3	4	5
6.			1	2	3	4	5
7.			1	2	3	4	5
8.			1	2	3	4	5
9.			1	2	3	4	5
10.			1	2	3	4	5
11.			1	2	3	4	5
12.			1	2	3	4	5
13.			1	2	3	4	5
14.			1	2	3	4	5
15.			1	2	3	4	5
16.			1	2	3	4	5
17.			1	2	3	4	5
18.			1	2	3	4	5
19.			1	2	3	4	5
20.			1	2	3	4	5

From *Learning by Choice in Secondary Physical Education: Creating a Goal-Directed Program* by Kevin Kaardal, 2001, Champaign, IL: Human Kinetics.

Form A.7 Physical Education Student Self-Evaluation

Name: _____ Class: _____ Level: A B C D

Unit: _____ Teacher: _____

Evaluation Domains Student choice of assessment categories from each domain	Weighting Total possible marks equaling 100	Student Mark Student rating of how well unit goals were met	Teacher Assessment Based on test results and how well teacher assesses student attainment of unit goals	Unit Mark Average of student and teacher marks
Psychomotor				
Skill performance				
Skill improvement				
Fitness				
Tournament play/ team play				
Expanded opportunity bonus				
Cognitive				
Article review				
Written assignments				
Demonstration of knowledge through play				
Quizzes				
Affective				
Leadership				
Cooperation and sporting behavior				
Working at a challenging level/effort				
Totals	100%	/100	/100	%

Student comments:

Teacher comments:

Reprinted, by permission, from R. Adolphe and W. Kozak, 1996, "Student Self-Evaluation in Physical Education," *Runner* 34:1, a publication of the Alberta Teachers' Association.

From *Learning by Choice in Secondary Physical Education: Creating a Goal-Directed Program* by Kevin Kaardal, 2001, Champaign, IL: Human Kinetics.

Instructions: Brainstorm and write which skills, drills and progressions, modified games, and assessment outcomes and strategies are appropriate for each level.

Unit: _____ **Level:** _____

Skills	Drills and Progressions	Modified Games	Assessment Outcomes and Strategies

From *Learning by Choice in Secondary Physical Education: Creating a Goal-Directed Program* by Kevin Kaardal, 2001, Champaign, IL: Human Kinetics.

Instructions: Get specific and describe the skill, practice drills, and how they will be assessed for each level.

Topic: _____

Skill: _____

Concept: _____

Insert a picture of the skill being performed here.

Skill Analysis:

_____

_____

_____

_____

_____

Skill Practice:

Level A _____

Level B _____

Level C _____

Level D _____

Skill Mastery:

Level A _____

Level B _____

Level C _____

Level D _____

Suggested Modified Games:

_____

_____

_____

_____

_____

_____

From *Learning by Choice in Secondary Physical Education: Creating a Goal-Directed Program* by Kevin Kaardal, 2001, Champaign, IL: Human Kinetics.

Basic Information	Low Control Dribbling
Terminology	Speed Dribbling
Simplified Rules and Definitions	Hesitation Dribbling
Key to Symbols	Crossover Dribbling
	Spin Dribbling
Miscellaneous	Offensive Rebounding
Suggested Modifications	Perimeter One-on-One: Three Moves
Student Progress Record Sheet	Low Post One-on-One: Three Moves
Modified Games	
Creating Your Own Individualized Units	**Team Offense**
Basketball Program Exploration Sheet	Passing, General
Defensive Play Rubric	One-Handed Push Pass
Offensive Play Rubric	Chest Pass
	Shovel Pass
Common Skills	Overhead Snap
Footwork, General	Baseball Pass
Optimal Maneuvering Speed	Bounce Pass
Ready Position	Fast Breaks
Triple Threat Position	Two-on-Two
Running Backward	Three-on-Three: Screen-Away
Stride Stop	Five-on-Five: STAR Principles
Jump Stop	
Shuffle Step	**Individual Defense**
Pivoting	Defensive Stance
Change-of-Direction Step	Defensive Shuffle Step
L- and V-Cuts	Drop-Step and Recover
Sealing	Ball-Challenging
Faking: Head and Shoulder Fakes, Ball or Hand Fakes, Look-Away Fakes, Jab Step	Taking the Charge
Refereeing	Defensive Rebounding
Individual Offense	**Team Defense**
Shooting: BEEF	Half-Fronting
Set Shot	Full-Fronting
Layups: Power and Running	Defending Screens
Jump Shot	Help Side and Recovering
Hook Shots: Jump and Running	Defending Fast Breaks
Ball Handling Drills	Double-Teaming
Dribbling, General	Five-on-Five: Disrupting STAR

From *Learning by Choice in Secondary Physical Education: Creating a Goal-Directed Program* by Kevin Kaardal, 2001, Champaign, IL: Human Kinetics.

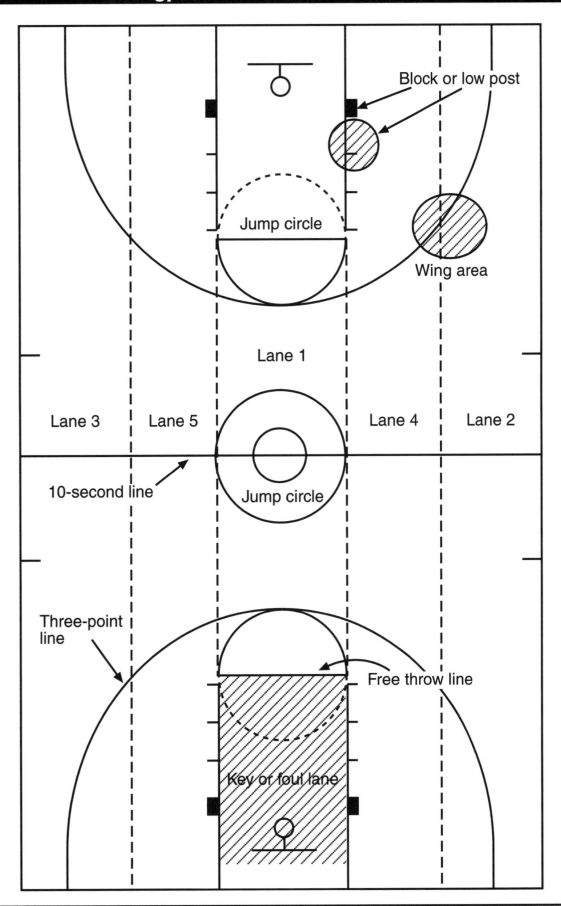

Block or low post

Jump circle

Wing area

Lane 1

Lane 3   Lane 5   Lane 4   Lane 2

10-second line

Jump circle

Three-point
line

Free throw line

Key or foul lane

Form B.3 Simplified Rules and Definitions

For complete rules, refer to the Official Basketball Rules of the International Basketball Federation. Their website is **www.fiba.com**.

A-1 and B-1—Any player of Team A or B, respectively. A-2 is a teammate of A-1. A-6 is an entering substitute for Team A.

player—A member of a team who is on the court and is entitled to play.

substitute—A squad member who is not a player; a squad member who is sitting on the bench or waiting to enter the game.

opponent's basket—The basket at which a team shoots.

playing time—The game is made up of four 10-minute periods with 2 minutes between each, and with *normally* a break of 10 minutes between halves.

interval of play—The period of time beginning with an official's arrival on the playing floor and until the game starts; the time during the halftime interval (10 minutes); during an interval before an extra period (2 minutes).

player foul—A foul, personal or technical, committed by a player.

personal foul—A player foul that involves contact with an opponent, regardless of whether the contact occurs during a live or dead ball.

technical foul—Any act by a player, coach, assistant coach, substitute, or team follower considered unsporting and not in the spirit of the game.

team control foul—A player foul, which is neither technical nor intentional, committed by a player while his or her team is in control of the ball.

team fouls—Player fouls are also recorded as team fouls; when a team has accumulated four team fouls, any subsequent player fouls carry a two-shot penalty. (Exception: a player control foul results in the ball being awarded to the defending team on the nearest sideline.)

penalty shots—After a team has accumulated four fouls in one period, the fifth foul and every subsequent foul results in the fouled player being awarded two free throws.

intentional foul—A personal foul committed by a player, which, in the opinion of the official, was deliberate.

double foul—A situation in which two opponents commit fouls against each other at about the same time.

multiple foul—A situation in which two or more teammates commit personal fouls against the same opponent at about the same time.

disqualifying foul—Any flagrantly unsporting infraction (technical foul by player or personal foul).

violations—Errors that cause the ball to become dead. Examples are traveling, double-dribbling, and sending the ball out of bounds; violations do not involve contact or unsporting conduct.

dribbling—The act of bouncing the ball as a player moves along the floor.

fumble—The accidental loss of player control by unintentionally dropping the ball or having it slip from the player's grasp.

From *Learning by Choice in Secondary Physical Education: Creating a Goal-Directed Program* by Kevin Kaardal, 2001, Champaign, IL: Human Kinetics.

pivot foot—The foot that remains in contact with the floor as a player holding the ball pivots, or turns.

traveling—Illegal movement of the pivot foot.

held ball—A situation in which a player on the court is holding the ball and is being guarded by an opponent. "Guarding" is either attempting to gain control of the ball or attempting to prevent a pass or shot.

jump ball—A means of determining which team is to gain control; the ball is tossed between two opponents within one of the three jump circles.

out of bounds—The area beyond the sidelines and end lines; also, the back of a backboard and the supports holding the backboard; *but* the side edges of a backboard are *not* out of bounds.

throw-in—Returning the ball to play by passing it onto the court from out of bounds.

free throw lane—That area beneath the basket at which a team is shooting. Its boundaries are the free throw line, the end line, and two sidelines. Often it is painted in a solid color.

free throw line—The line from which a player attempts a free throw; the farthest edge of a free throw lane.

three-point field goal areas—Areas on the court from where a successful shot for goal counts as three points. Stepping on the three-point line as player tries the shot makes it a two-point try.

rebound—A ball that has bounced off a backboard as a result of a try for goal.

control of the ball—A *player* is in control of the ball when he or she is holding a live ball or dribbling it or when the ball is his or hers for a throw-in. A *team* is in control when a player of that team is in control of the ball and also while a live ball is being passed between teammates. Team control continues until a shot for goal, or an opponent secures control, or the ball becomes dead. Team control continues until the ball is in flight during a shot for goal.

act of shooting—When, in an official's judgment, the player starts to try to score by throwing, dunking, or tapping the ball, continuing until the ball has left the player's hand(s).

continuous motion—Normal movement that comes before a shot for goal, including any body, foot, or arm motion normally used in shooting for a goal. It ends when the ball leaves the hand(s) on a shot. Whenever a foul is called on an opponent of a player who has started to shoot for goal, the shooter is permitted to complete customary arm movement and, in pivoting or stepping when the shooter or a teammate is fouled, customary foot or body movement may be completed as long as the shooter is still holding the ball. If the ball is dropped to dribble, the "continuous motion" ends immediately.

shot for goal—Starts when a player begins the motion that normally comes before the release of the ball. Shot ends when the throw is successful, when it's certain the throw will be unsuccessful, when the thrown ball is touched by any player after the expiration of time at the end of any half or extra period, or when the ball becomes dead. A "shot for goal" would also include a "tap" for the purpose of committing offensive or defensive interference.

ball goes into play—When (a) an official enters the circle to administer a jump ball, (b) an official enters the free throw lane with or without the ball to administer a free throw, or (c) in an out-of-bounds situation, the ball is with the player who is at the point of the throw-in.

play phase—The period of time when a team in control of the ball plays it and scores a field goal, or loses it through an interception by opponents, or until the ball becomes dead because of a violation or a foul. The moment the ball is again in play, a new play phase begins.

From *Learning by Choice in Secondary Physical Education: Creating a Goal-Directed Program* by Kevin Kaardal, 2001, Champaign, IL: Human Kinetics.

Form B.4 Key to Symbols

Offensive player	①②③④⑤ ⒶⒷ
Defensive player	X_1 X_2 X_3 X_4 X_5
The ball	●
Dribbler's path	∿∿∿∿➤
Cutter's path	⟶
Screen	⌐
A pass	- - - - - - - -➤
A shot	⌒➤
Faking	⥮
A roll to the basket	↶

Form B.5 Suggested Modifications of Drills for Persons With Physical Challenges

For students who have difficulty standing or supporting their weight

- Have them sit down for passing drills.

- Those in wheelchairs can use wheelchair basketball rules. Allow two pushes between each dribble, and ensure the athlete is positioned in the chair so that the shooting arm is not obstructed by the chair's armrests. Also be sure that positioning allows free breathing and facilitates speech.

For students who have visual impairments or muscle control challenges

- Use a larger ball for dribbling drills to help students gain control.

- Use colorful balls and large target goals such as large squares taped on the backboard. Hitting the area inside the tape is worth one point; scoring a basket is worth two.

- Lower the basket height and use a smaller ball for shooting games.

For students with mental challenges

- Focus on the simple shooting and passing games such as 21, Horse, No-Dribble Basketball, and Keep-Away.

Basketball

From *Learning by Choice in Secondary Physical Education: Creating a Goal-Directed Program* by Kevin Kaardal, 2001, Champaign, IL: Human Kinetics.

Form B.6 Student Progress Record Sheet

Name: _____ Class: _____ Date: _____

Contract completion due date: _____

Instructions

1. Look through the posters, then circle the skills you wish to work on under the "Topic" column. This will serve as your unit contract. My **goal** is to master _____ skills during this unit.
2. Beside skill, circle difficulty you are working at (A, B, or C) under the "Level" column.
3. At end of each class under the "Attempted" column, mark the box next to the skills you have practiced. Place an "M" in box next to skill if you have mastered some part of the skills identified in poster.
4. Have the teacher or a peer evaluator initial in the "Mastered" column after you have completed skill mastery requirements for a given level and skill.
5. Ask the teacher or peer evaluator to write a percentage mark beside the skills you have mastered under the "Mark" column.

Topic	Level	Attempted									Mastered	Mark
Common Skills												
Footwork, General	A B C											
Optimal Maneuvering Speed	A B											
Ready Position	A B											
Triple Threat Position	A B C											
Running Backward	A B C											
Stride Stop	A B C											
Jump Stop	A B C											
Shuffle Step	A B											
Pivoting	A B C											
Change-of-Direction Step	A B C											
L- and V-Cuts	A B C											
Sealing	A B C											
Head and Shoulder Fakes	A B C											
Ball and Hand Fakes	A B C											
Look-Away Fakes	A B C											
Jab Step	A B C											
Individual Offense												
Shooting: BEEF	A B											
Set Shot	A B C											
Layups	A B C											
Jump Shot	A B C											
Hook Shots	A B C											
Ball-Handling Drills	A B C											
Dribbling, General	A B C											
Low Control Dribbling	A B C											
Speed Dribbling	A B C											

(continued)

From *Learning by Choice in Secondary Physical Education: Creating a Goal-Directed Program* by Kevin Kaardal, 2001, Champaign, IL: Human Kinetics.

Topic	Level	Attempted									Mastered	Mark
Individual Offense (continued)												
Hesitation Dribbling	A B C											
Crossover Dribbling	A B C											
Spin Dribbling	A B C											
Offensive Rebounding	A B C											
Perimeter One-on-One	A B C											
Low Post One-on-One	A B C											
Team Offense												
Passing, General	A B C											
One-Handed Push Pass	A B C											
Chest Pass	A B C											
Shovel Pass	A B C											
Overhead Snap	A B C											
Baseball Pass	A B C											
Bounce Pass	A B C											
Fast Breaks	A B C											
Two-on-Two	A B C											
Three-on-Three	A B C											
Five-on-Five: STAR Principles	A B C											
Individual Defense												
Defensive Stance	A B C											
Defensive Shuffle Step	A B C											
Drop-Step and Recover	A B C											
Ball-Challenging	A B C											
Taking the Charge	A B C											
Defensive Rebounding	A B C											
Team Defense												
Half-Fronting	A B C											
Full-Fronting	A B C											
Defending Screens	A B C											
Help Side and Recovering	A B C											
Defending Fast Breaks	A B C											
Double-Teaming	A B C											
Five-on-Five: Disrupting STAR	A B C											
Rules												
Simplified Rules	A B C											

I achieved my goal of mastering _____ skills during this unit (circle): **Yes   No**

On the back of this form, write comments regarding your effort and how much you feel you improved during this unit. Also write down what you enjoyed about this unit and what you feel could be improved.

From *Learning by Choice in Secondary Physical Education: Creating a Goal-Directed Program* by Kevin Kaardal, 2001, Champaign, IL: Human Kinetics.

Tag-Type Games: One person is "It" and runs after other players, trying to tag them by touching them with a hand. A person tagged becomes "It," and the game continues. Modify this game by having the "It" people join hands as they are tagged and chase after other players in a chain, splitting the chain after it grows to eight people (Amoeba Tag), having the tagged person freeze until a free player ducks under the tagged person's arms (Frozen Tag), or having the players try to run from one safe zone at one end of the gym to another safe zone at the other end of the gym—after the "It" people call, "British Bulldog!" (British Bulldog Tag).

Dribble Tag: One person is "It." All students dribble. If you are tagged you become "It." Students may only move if they are dribbling the ball. Try to do legal jump or stride stops if you stop and pick up your dribble. You may stop and pick up your dribble and then continue dribbling. You may be tagged "It" at any time, including when you are stopped. However, students may wish to adjust the rules; they may look at performing a legal stop as a way of preventing being tagged.

Elimination Dribble: Every person is "It." They must all dribble the ball within the same confined space, such as a volleyball court. The object of the game is to force your opponent's ball outside the confined space, or cause your opponents to lose control of the dribble, or cause your opponents to pick up the dribble. Once a player is forced to do any of these, they are eliminated from the game and must go practice layups, jogging clockwise around the gym from basket to basket. The game continues until only one dribbler is left in the confined space and is declared the winner. It is best to reduce the space size as the number of players is reduced until the final two players are dribbling in half of a jump circle.

21: You need two players. One player shoots a free throw, and the other waits to rebound. If the shooter scores, the shooter continues to shoot until the game is finished or the shooter misses. When the shooter misses a free throw, the other player rebounds the missed shot. The rebounder must shoot a field goal from the place on the floor where control of the rebound was gained. If the rebounder scores the shot, the rebounder goes to the foul line and becomes the free throw shooter. The first shooter now becomes the rebounder. If the new shooter misses the field goal attempt, the new rebounder rebounds the ball and shoots a field goal. This continues until one person scores a field goal and earns the right to shoot free throws. Field goals are worth 1 point and free throws are worth 2 points. The object of the game is to score exactly 21 points before your opponent. Players may not go over 21 points or they restart at 0. For example, a player has 20 points and is shooting free throws. The shooter must intentionally miss the free throw by striking the rim with the ball, allowing the opponent to rebound the miss. The shooter must wait until the opponent misses a shot attempt and rebound the miss to be able to attempt a field goal and score 1 point to win the game. If the shooter were to score the free throw, the shooter would have 22 points and have to start over at zero. If the intentional miss does not strike the rim, the rebounder may take the field goal from any position near the basket.

51: You need two people. One player starts as the shooter. The shooter may shoot anywhere from outside the free throw line (about 15 feet from the basket). Shots scored from inside the three-point line are worth two points. Shots scored from outside the three-point line are worth three points. The shooter continues to shoot until reaching a score of 51 and the game is won, or until a missed shot is rebounded, shot, and scored while in the air by the opponent. If the opponent is able to rebound the shooter's miss, shoot, and score all before landing, the players switch roles and the game continues.

Bump: Play with any number of players. Start with all the players forming a single-file line, starting at the foul line. The first two players in the line each have a basketball. The object of the game is to bump the player ahead of you in line by scoring a basket before he or she does. The first player in line shoots the ball. The second player may not shoot until the ball has left the first shooter's hand. If both shooters are successful they both retrieve their basketballs and pass them to the next two

(continued)

From *Learning by Choice in Secondary Physical Education: Creating a Goal-Directed Program* by Kevin Kaardal, 2001, Champaign, IL: Human Kinetics.

shooters in line. The first two shooters then run to the end of the line, and the next shooters begin. If the first shooter misses, the shooter retrieves the ball and attempts any type of field goal he or she wishes. A layup is the most common second shot used to score off a rebound. If the second shooter scores before the first shooter, the first shooter is eliminated, or "bumped," out of the game. The first shooter must still pass the ball to the next shooter in line before leaving the game. The second shooter retrieves the shot and passes it to the shooter behind the next person in line. The second shooter then goes to the end of the line to wait until the line moves up and gets an opportunity to bump the player ahead of her or him. The game continues until only one shooter remains and is the winner. (The teacher should organize an inclusive activity for eliminated players to improve free throw shooting. Eliminated players can go to another basket and try to set personal records for the most made baskets in a row.)

One-on-One: Play one against one (as outlined on the One-on-One skill posters B.39.a-c and B.40.a-c), in games of up to 7 or 11 points, focusing on the skill they are practicing (e.g., speed dribbling, power layups, jump shots, and so on). Change the rules to help you get more trials of the skill you are practicing (e.g., limiting the number of dribbles to two will help you develop believable initial fakes). Call your own fouls and violations.

Two-on-Two: Same as One-on-One, except play two against two (as outlined on the Two-on-Two skill posters B.49, B.49.a, and B.49.b). You can also effectively practice passing, L-cuts, and running layups.

Three-on-Three: Same as One-on-One and Two-on-Two, except play three against three (as outlined on the Three-on-Three skill poster B.50). You can also effectively practice sealing, defending screens, and hook shots.

Four-on-Four: Same as One-on-One, Two-on-Two, and Three-on-Three, except play four against four.

No-Dribble Basketball: May add this change to any full- or half-court game. Do not dribble the ball, except when performing a move to goal, and then the limit is one dribble. This helps you pass and receive the ball as well as move without the ball. It will also speed up a game and force players to involve more of their teammates per play.

Keep-Away: Practice creating space for passing and using pivots, target hands, and seals with two to four players. Two players assume offensive positions, facing each other, 15 to 20 feet apart. In the three-person game, one defender defends the ball handler. The defender tries to deflect the pass between the two offensive players. If the pass is deflected, forcing the pass receiver to move past a legal pivot, the passer switches roles with the defender. Try to stay on offense as much as possible. Every time a player ends up as a defender, he or she gets a point. Time the game for 5 to 10 minutes; after the time limit is up, the player with the fewest points wins. To play with four players, add another defender and allow the first receiver to L- or V-cut toward the ball.

Horse: Include two to as many players as desired. (But more than five players may be boring.) The players line up and decide on first shooter, second shooter, and so on. The first shooter has the lead and shots of his or her choosing. If the shot is successful, all the shooters must try to duplicate the shot. If a shooter misses, he or she earns a letter "H." After all have shot, the leader shoots a different shot. If successful, the process repeats. If the leader misses, the lead is passed to the next shooter, who then tries a shot of choice. If the shot is successful, each shooter must attempt the shot, as before. Every shooter receives a letter to spell "horse" for every shot he or she misses. When a shooter misses five times, the shooter will have spelled "horse" and is eliminated from the game. The object of the game is to be the last shooter left. Eliminated shooters practice shots while out and can start new games of Horse with their classmates who are also eliminated.

Fox and Hound: This game requires two players and one ball. One player (the "fox") stands at the free throw line extended. The other player (the "hound") stands on the baseline with the ball. The hound throws a pass ahead of the fox. The fox then speed-dribbles to the basket on the far end

From *Learning by Choice in Secondary Physical Education: Creating a Goal-Directed Program* by Kevin Kaardal, 2001, Champaign, IL: Human Kinetics.

of the court. The hound pursues and tries to stop the fox from scoring a layup without fouling. For every layup prevented, the hound scores 2 points. The fox earns 1 point for every successful layup. The players switch roles after each chase. The game ends once one player has scored 21 points.

Up-and-Over: Practice rebounding with two or more people. Players stand on either side of the basket, facing the backboard. Player A shoots a shot over the rim off the backboard to Player B. Player B leaps, receives the shot, and shoots it back to Player A while still in the air. Player A repeats Player B's feat. The object of the game is to see how many times in a row the team of Players A and B can keep the ball rebounding up and over the basket. Players can play for personal records or against other teams. To involve more than two players, form lines behind Player A and Player B and have the next person in line replace the player who successfully rebounded the ball and shot it back to the other line. The rebounder goes to the end of the line and is replaced by the next person in line and so on.

Hamburger: An offensive rebounding game for up to eight players, the object of the game is to rebound the ball and score three baskets before the rest of the players. It is every player for themselves. Each player tries to stop the others from rebounding and scoring. The game starts when one player shoots the ball toward goal. Then all players try to rebound the ball and score a basket. The play stops only when a basket is scored. Play is restarted when the scorer shoots the ball back toward goal. Baskets only count if scored immediately after a rebound.

Box-Out: In teams of two to five, compete to box out and keep the opponent away from the ball after a missed shot until it bounces on the floor. The defenders get 1 point per bounce, and the offensive players get 1 point per offensive rebound, 2 points per score, and switch to defense if they score. The game ends at 21 points.

Relay Races: Teams race through an obstacle course of cones set in a zigzag pattern on the floor, one or two players at a time. When they complete the course, they use a shovel pass or short pass of any type to hand off to the next player or group of players in their line. The team that is first to have all its players complete the course wins.

King's Court: In its simplest form, three people play One-on-One. The offensive player who scores a basket is "king (or queen) of the court," and the defender leaves to be replaced by another. If a defender gets the ball, he or she goes on offense, and the king of the court defends. The defender, or king, only leaves the court when scored on. The game goes up to as many baskets as the players decide (7 or 11 is usual). This game can also be played tournament-style: One-on-One, Two-on-Two, Three-on-Three, half-court. Declare one half-court the king's court, and the teams play up to a specified number of baskets. The winners move clockwise toward the king's court, the nonwinners move counterclockwise toward a nonwinners' court. The winners on the king's court stay and challenge the winners from the adjacent court. The team that loses on the nonwinners' court stays to challenge the team that loses on their adjacent court. The goal is to remain on the king's court.

One-Man Short: Three players shoot for first ball. The player winning first ball takes it at the top of the key and tries to score on the other two. The game is every player for themselves. If a shot is missed, the rebounder is instantly on offense, trying to score on the other two players. Once someone has scored a field goal, the scorer gets to shoot two free throws. If successful, the scorer takes the ball at the top of the key and the process starts over. If the shooter misses a free throw the ball is live, and the rebounder is instantly on offense. The game goes to 21 points. Free throws are worth 1 and field goals are worth 2. If you go over 21 points you start over.

Weave Races: Weave races are races that can become relay races. As a relay race you would have teams of six players. Three players line up facing the same direction, down court, equal distances from each other (five to eight feet apart). The ball starts in with the middle player and the players begin by passing the ball to each other—catch and receive without traveling while running down the court. The weave develops when the passer must run behind the receiver. The pattern of passes creates a weave. When these three players complete their two lengths they pass the ball to their teammates who are waiting to begin and so on.

Basketball 99

From *Learning by Choice in Secondary Physical Education: Creating a Goal-Directed Program* by Kevin Kaardal, 2001, Champaign, IL: Human Kinetics.

Step 1

Divide your program into stations, based on the skills used in the activity or sport.

Step 2

Divide these skills into three or more levels based on difficulty.

Step 3

Make up posters of each skill in your program, outlining the key points required to accomplish these skills. Include drill progressions for learning these skills.

Step 4

Make up and hand out task record sheets that include each skill in your program. These will serve as your record of student progress and be used as contract sheets.

Step 5

Set your expectations, then plan your lessons to accommodate these.

Step 6

Teach the progressions for the basic skills, then begin your program.

Step 7

Evaluation

- Give an attitude mark, based on classroom observations and the number of tasks completed as written on the student contract sheets.
- On the task record sheets, record your skill performance marks based on student performance of the contracted skills.
- Give a written test, mark the student's log book entries, or mark a demonstration of knowledge evident in his or her play or ability to teach or referee his or her peers.

Now you have evaluated all three domains. You decide the weighting!

From *Learning by Choice in Secondary Physical Education: Creating a Goal-Directed Program* by Kevin Kaardal, 2001, Champaign, IL: Human Kinetics.

Read the posters and practice the skills outlined. Below, record the skill level, poster color, the skill you practiced, and a brief description of the drill. Then rate your performance by circling a number in the "Quality of Performance" column. Personal challenge: How many drills and skills can you do in a class period?

Skill#	Level	Poster Color	Skill Attempted and Drill Used	Quality of Performance 1 = Needs Work 5 = Mastered				
1.				1	2	3	4	5
2.				1	2	3	4	5
3.				1	2	3	4	5
4.				1	2	3	4	5
5.				1	2	3	4	5
6.				1	2	3	4	5
7.				1	2	3	4	5
8.				1	2	3	4	5
9.				1	2	3	4	5
10.				1	2	3	4	5
11.				1	2	3	4	5
12.				1	2	3	4	5
13.				1	2	3	4	5
14.				1	2	3	4	5
15.				1	2	3	4	5
16.				1	2	3	4	5
17.				1	2	3	4	5
18.				1	2	3	4	5
19.				1	2	3	4	5
20.				1	2	3	4	5
21.				1	2	3	4	5
22.				1	2	3	4	5
23.				1	2	3	4	5
24.				1	2	3	4	5
25.				1	2	3	4	5

From *Learning by Choice in Secondary Physical Education: Creating a Goal-Directed Program* by Kevin Kaardal, 2001, Champaign, IL: Human Kinetics.

Use this rubric in the evaluation process.

1 Needs Work	2 Below Expectations	3 Meets Expectations	4 Exceeds Expectations	5 Extraordinary Performance
Level B total: 6 or lower	Level B total: 7-10	Level B total: 11-18	Level B total: 19-23	Level B total: Should move up level
Level C total: 9 or lower	Level C total: 10-15	Level C total: 16-19	Level C total: 20-24	Level C total: 25-50
Player does not play defense. Tries to block every shot. Goes for every fake. Doesn't get back on offense's fast break. Never blocks out. Gets rebound only if it happens to drop in his/her hands.	Player not consistently in good defensive stance. Not consistently in position on strong or weak side. Usually too close. Reacts to all/most offensive fakes. Offense breaks down defense & gets 2-on-1 situations.	Player usually in good defensive position when defending person on ball side. Denies passing lanes on strong side. Occasionally beat on weak side or back-door cuts. Too close to check on side. Occasionally reacts to offensive fakes. Boxes out 3 of 5 shots.	Player consistently in good defensive position whether on ball or away from ball. Pushes players to weaknesses by denying passing lanes & forcing offensive players to weak side & out of position they wish to establish. Does not take risks to steal ball. Never (or rarely) reacts to offensive fakes. Boxes out 4 of 5 shots.	Consistently reads & reacts to offensive players' weaknesses. Creates situations, giving defense advantage or resulting in steals. Takes risks outside normal way of playing; able to recover if unsuccessful (e.g., shoots passing lanes, overplays in posts, fakes traps & defensive moves, double-teams other players when they look away [still knows where check is]; able to recover, maintain defense if maneuver fails). Gets rebounds when needed. Fakes offense.

From *Learning by Choice in Secondary Physical Education: Creating a Goal-Directed Program* by Kevin Kaardal, 2001, Champaign, IL: Human Kinetics.

Use this rubric in the evaluation process.

1 Needs Work	2 Below Expectations	3 Meets Expectations	4 Exceeds Expectations	5 Extraordinary Performance
Level B total: 5 or lower Level C total: 9 or lower	Level B total: 6-10 Level C total: 10-15	Level B total: 11-25 Level C total: 16-32	Level B total: 26-32 Level C total: 33-46	Level B total: Should move up level Level C total: 47-76
Shows no sense of spacing. Not in triple threat position when has ball. Does not set screens. Always dribbles on getting ball. Passes only under duress.	In good offensive position (about 12 feet from any teammate in 1/4 court & facing basket) every 2 of 5 possessions. Not in triple threat position when has ball. Sets screens away from ball & on ball handler's defender but doesn't roll or fade after screen. Fakes to cause defense to move out of good defensive position. Passes only when dribble is stopped.	In good offensive position 3 of 5 possessions. In triple threat position 3 of 5 times when has ball. Sets screens away from ball & rolls to basket or fades to open spaces after screening. Fakes to cause defense to move out of good defensive position. Makes perimeter passes only, no penetrating passes.	Consistently in good offensive position. Always in triple threat position when has ball. Moves without ball well. Cuts to basket with strong ball side position in relation to defensive player. Sets screens away from ball & rolls to basket or fades to open spaces after screening. Reads defense well; reacts positively to opportunities. Fakes to make defense move out of good defensive position. Cuts backdoor when defense is overplaying, denying defense wing entry pass. Reads & makes successful backdoor passes.	Always exhibits all behaviors; consistently reads & reacts with/out ball to defensive players' weaknesses & *creates* situations, giving offense 2-on-1 advantage, resulting in scores or good shots. Reads development of play; successfully passes, resulting in uncontested on-balance shots by teammates. Uses variety of offensive fakes to get offensive rebounds. Scores high percentage of put-back shots after offensive rebounding.

From *Learning by Choice in Secondary Physical Education: Creating a Goal-Directed Program* by Kevin Kaardal, 2001, Champaign, IL: Human Kinetics.

Form B.12 Footwork, General

Common Skills—Footwork

Concept

Space is limited on the basketball court, especially near the basket. Here the game truly becomes a game of inches. A mastery of footwork skills can help you get away from a defender on offense to an open space, giving you an easy shot.

On defense, footwork can help you close open spaces and prevent players from moving the ball close to the basket for an easier shot.

There are several footwork skills used in basketball, including the stride and jump stops, pivoting, the change-of-direction step, shuffling, and running backward.

Form B.13 Optimal Maneuvering Speed

Common Skills—Body Control

Concept

The limited space on the basketball court and the fast-paced nature of the sport make basketball a finesse game. Therefore, as spaces open and close on the floor, you must be able to move quickly, change direction, and stop suddenly, taking advantage of opportunities to penetrate toward the basket, stop the ball, or transition from offense to defense or vice versa quickly.

Skill Analysis

Practice moving under control. The faster you can move under control, the better player you will become. Move as quickly as you can during each drill.

Skill Practice

Level A: Run around the gym, changing direction on the colored line of your choice (or when needed to avoid colliding with other players). Change your running speed as you run. Start on the command "Go!" for 60 seconds, stopping on every whistle.

Level B: Practice all skills as quickly as you can.

Skill Mastery

Level A: Complete drills for one minute without losing your balance or colliding with other people.

Level B: Work in all drills at the fastest controlled speed. When done at your quickest controlled speed, you have mastered body control.

Modified Games

Any tag-type game (e.g., Dribble Tag), No-Dribble Basketball, One-on-One, Two-on-Two, Three-on-Three

From *Learning by Choice in Secondary Physical Education: Creating a Goal-Directed Program* by Kevin Kaardal, 2001, Champaign, IL: Human Kinetics.

Common Skills—Body Control

Concept

The ready position allows you to move quickly in any direction.

Skill Analysis

1. Keep head up, eyes forward.
2. Keep back straight.
3. Flex hips.
4. Bend knees.
5. Place feet shoulder-width apart.
6. Balance weight on balls of feet.

Skill Practice

Level A: Practice moving into the ready position on command.

Level B: Finish in ready position while practicing stride and jump stops.

Skill Mastery

Level A: Demonstrate the ready position on command, using correct form.

Level B: Finish 9 of 10 stops in the correct ready position.

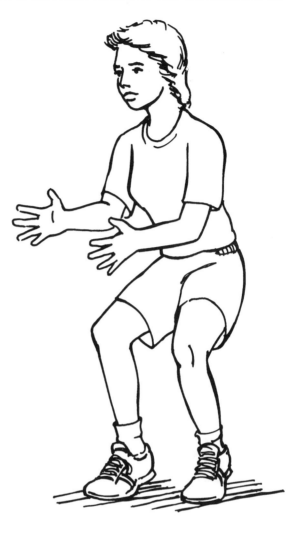

From *Learning by Choice in Secondary Physical Education: Creating a Goal-Directed Program* by Kevin Kaardal, 2001, Champaign, IL: Human Kinetics.

Common Skills—Body Control

Concept

This is the ready position when you have the ball. It allows you to dribble, pass, or shoot quickly from the same starting position.

Skill Analysis

1. Body position is the same as the ready position.
2. Square shoulders to the basket.
3. Hold the ball with both hands at chest level, with the shooting arm's elbow behind the ball.

Skill Practice

Level A: Practice moving into triple threat position on command.

Level B: Receive 20 passes and assume the triple threat position upon reception.

Level C: During game situations, assume the triple threat position each time you receive the ball.

Skill Mastery

Level A: Demonstrate the triple threat position on command, using correct form.

Levels B & C: Finish 9 of 10 stops in triple threat position.

From *Learning by Choice in Secondary Physical Education: Creating a Goal-Directed Program* by Kevin Kaardal, 2001, Champaign, IL: Human Kinetics.

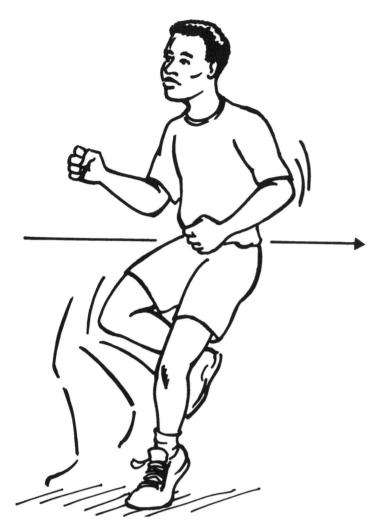

Common Skills—Footwork

Concept

During transition from offensive play to defensive play, you may run backward to see your opponents and the ball under the following conditions: if the ball is in front of you and if you are between your check and the basket.

Skill Analysis

1. Run backward on the balls of the feet.
2. Maintain balance by maintaining optimal maneuvering speed.
3. Watch your check and the ball.

Skill Practice

Level A: Run five lengths of the gym backward.

Level B: Run five lengths of the gym backward, staying in front of a dribbling partner.

Level C: Run backward in transition, during a full-court modified game when appropriate (as defined in the "Concept" statement above).

Skill Mastery

Level A: Complete five of five successful court lengths, maintaining your balance.

Level B: Complete four of five court lengths, staying between your opponent and the back of the court.

Level C: Run backward during full-court game at appropriate times, four of five times.

Modified Games

Relay Race

From *Learning by Choice in Secondary Physical Education: Creating a Goal-Directed Program* by Kevin Kaardal, 2001, Champaign, IL: Human Kinetics.

Common Skills—Footwork

Concept

This controlled stop involves planting the pivot foot then stepping once to stop yourself.

Skill Analysis

1. Lower your center of gravity.
2. Lean back slightly.
3. Plant the lead leg.
4. Step through with the trail leg.
5. Plant the trail leg.
6. If ball handler, finish square to the target and in triple threat position.

Skill Practice

Level A: Execute 5 stops without the ball.

Level B: Execute 10 stops with the ball.

Level C: Play Three-on-Three, allowing only two dribbles per player per possession. Practice stride stops.

Skill Mastery

Level A: Finish stopping in ready position, 8 of 10 trials.

Level B: Finish stopping in triple threat position, 8 of 10 trials.

Level C: During the game, stop under control without traveling, 8 of 10 trials.

Modified Games

One-on-One, Two-on-Two, Three-on-Three

From *Learning by Choice in Secondary Physical Education: Creating a Goal-Directed Program* by Kevin Kaardal, 2001, Champaign, IL: Human Kinetics.

Common Skills—Footwork

Concept

This quick stop allows you to quickly transfer forward momentum to upward momentum (often used in the jump shot). It also allows ball handlers to choose either foot as the pivot foot.

Skill Analysis

1. Lower your center of gravity.
2. Hop into the stop.
3. Lean back slightly during the hop.
4. Land with both feet at the same time.

Skill Practice

Level A: Execute 5 stops without the ball.

Level B: Execute 10 stops with the ball.

Level C: (1) Execute 10 jump stops that transfer into jump shots. (2) Play Three-on-Three, allowing only two dribbles per player per possession. Practice jump stops.

Skill Mastery

Level A: Finish by stopping in ready position, 4 of 5 trials.

Level B: Finish by stopping in triple threat position, 8 of 10 trials.

Level C: (1) Perform 8 of 10 successful transitions from a jump stop into a jump shot. (2) During the game, stop under control without traveling, 8 of 10 trials.

Modified Games

One-on-One, Two-on-Two, Three-on-Three

Basketball

From *Learning by Choice in Secondary Physical Education: Creating a Goal-Directed Program* by Kevin Kaardal, 2001, Champaign, IL: Human Kinetics.

Common Skills—Footwork

Concept

Use the shuffle step primarily on defense to quickly move laterally (sideways) while maintaining balance. You may use the shuffle step on offense as well, most often when moving laterally to create a passing lane to receive a pass or when sliding from a high post position on the free throw line to a low post position above the block in the foul lane.

Skill Analysis

1. Start in ready position.
2. Shuffle feet sideways by sliding the foot closest to travel direction and, after planting this lead foot, sliding the trail foot almost to it. Repeat this action over and over as quickly as you can while maintaining your balance.
3. Don't let your feet touch or cross over.

Skill Practice

Level A: Shuffle-step the length of the key 10 times.

Level B: Shuffle-step around the court in a figure eight pattern.

Skill Mastery

Level A: Shuffle-step 8 of 10 key lengths, maintaining ready position.

Level B: Complete two laps, maintaining a ready position without crossing feet over.

From *Learning by Choice in Secondary Physical Education: Creating a Goal-Directed Program* by Kevin Kaardal, 2001, Champaign, IL: Human Kinetics.

Common Skills—Footwork

Concept

Pivoting allows you to adjust your body orientation on the court without traveling when you have the ball. You may also use the pivot to establish a position on the court against an opponent. This is called "sealing," or "posting up."

Forward pivot

Skill Analysis

Forward Pivot When Using a Stride Stop

Plant the lead foot and step forward around it, staying in the ready position.

Backward Pivot When Using a Stride Stop

Plant the lead foot and step backward around it, staying in the ready position.

Note: After a jump shot, you may choose either foot as your pivot foot.

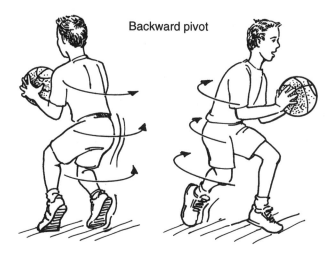

Backward pivot

Skill Practice

For Both Pivot Directions

Level A: Execute five forward and five backward pivots without the ball.

Level B: Execute five forward and five backward pivots with the ball while being defended.

Level C: Execute five forward and five backward pivots during a modified game situation, such as Two-on-Two, Three-on-Three, or No-Dribble Basketball.

Skill Mastery

Level A: Demonstrate four of five pivots forward and backward while maintaining a ready position.

Level B: Demonstrate four of five pivots forward and backward without traveling and while staying in the ready position.

Level C: In a modified game situation, demonstrate four of five pivots forward and backward without traveling and while maintaining a ready position.

Modified Games

Keep-Away, No-Dribble Basketball, One-on-One, Two-on-Two, Three-on-Three

From *Learning by Choice in Secondary Physical Education: Creating a Goal-Directed Program* by Kevin Kaardal, 2001, Champaign, IL: Human Kinetics.

Common Skills—Footwork

Concept

This step allows you to change direction quickly while maintaining body control. Players often use it to get away from a defender. Use it in the back- or midcourt during fast breaks or in the half-court. Two specific skills that use the change-of-direction step are the L-cut and the V-cut. The change-of-direction step allows an offensive player to move from spaces closed by defenders to open spaces on the court; to move using feints or changes of direction to elude defenders and thus create open spaces where he or she can receive the ball; to move away from the ball to create space for a teammate to play one-on-one; or to screen a teammate's defender.

Skill Analysis

1. Lower your center of gravity.
2. Plant the lead foot.
3. Drive off the planted foot by turning the upper body and swinging the trail leg in the new direction.

Skill Practice

Level A: Place chairs or cones five feet apart in a zigzag pattern. Run the course five times, changing direction at each chair.

Level B: Play a game of British Bulldog or Dribble Tag (both under Tag-Type Games, form B.7).

Level C: Have a partner defend aggressively while practicing crossover dribbling to change direction and protect the ball while moving down court. Do five court lengths.

Skill Mastery

Level A: Successfully navigate the zigzag obstacle course, five of five trials.

Level B: Play three tag games demonstrating the ability to change direction, to feint an opponent and move about the court without a basketball.

Level C: Complete four of five court lengths without losing control of your dribbling.

Modified Games

Any tag-type game, One-on-One, Two-on-Two, Three-on-Three

From *Learning by Choice in Secondary Physical Education: Creating a Goal-Directed Program* by Kevin Kaardal, 2001, Champaign, IL: Human Kinetics.

Common Skills—Footwork

Concept

To get away from the defender to an open space and within shooting range, use a change-of-direction step. Run in an "L" or "V" pattern.

Skill Analysis

The L-Cut

1. From the low block, run up the key to the foul line.
2. Do a change-of-direction step and shuffle-step out to the open wing.
3. While, or immediately after the change-of-direction step is initiated, extend the arm/hand farthest away from the defender as a target hand.
4. Trap the pass into triple threat position and back-pivot to face the basket.

The V-Cut

1. From outside the low block, run one step into the foul lane.
2. Do a change-of-direction step and shuffle-step out to the open wing.
3. While, or immediately after making the change-of-direction step, extend the arm/hand farthest away from the defender to act as a target hand.
4. Trap the pass into triple threat position and back-pivot to face the basket.

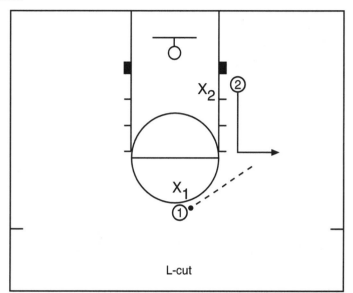

L-cut

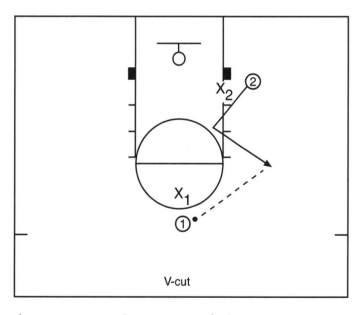

V-cut

Skill Performance

Level A: Place a cone at the point where the change-of-direction step will occur. With a passive defender, run the L-cut and V-cut patterns 10 times each.

Level B: Still using the cones but with an active defender, perform 10 L-cuts and 10 V-cuts. Receive a pass each time.

Level C: During a game of Two-on-Two, do 5 L-cuts and 5 V-cuts.

Skill Mastery

Level A: Get open 8 of every 10 attempts, per type of cut.

Level B: Successfully receive the ball within your shooting range, 8 of 10 times per cut.

Level C: During the game, successfully receive the pass within your shooting range, 4 of 5 times each cut.

Modified Games

Two-on-Two, Three-on-Three

From *Learning by Choice in Secondary Physical Education: Creating a Goal-Directed Program* by Kevin Kaardal, 2001, Champaign, IL: Human Kinetics.

Common Skills—Footwork

Concept

Sealing creates open space for an offensive player to receive a pass in the low or high post positions.

Skill Analysis

1. While standing in an exaggerated ready position, back to the defender, back-pivot and "sit" on the defender's leg. (Make contact with the defender's leg and lower your center of gravity.) This effectively seals the defender behind you.
2. Extend the arm/hand farthest away from the defender as a target hand to receive a pass.

Skill Practice

Level A: Practice sealing 10 times with a passive defender and receive a pass after each seal.

Level B: Practice sealing 10 times with an active defender and receive a pass after each seal.

Level C: Practice sealing in Two-on-Two or Three-on-Three and receive a pass after each seal.

Skill Mastery

Levels A & B: Seal correctly and receive, 8 of 10 passes.

Level C: Seal correctly during a game and receive, 9 of 10 passes successfully.

Modified Games

One-on-One, Two-on-Two, Three-on-Three

Common Skills—Body Control

Concept

Uses of Fakes

1. On offense, use fakes to create an open space by making the opponent move in the opposite direction.

2. On defense, use fakes to get the offensive player to commit to a course of action that will benefit the defense.

Characteristics of All Fakes

1. They are short and quick.

2. They must mimic the real action without making you lose your balance.

Types of Fakes

Head and shoulder, ball or hand, look-away, and the jab step

Skill Analysis

Head and Shoulder Fakes

1. Drop your head and shoulders as if to start dribbling to move the defender back in that direction. (Often used in combination with the jab step.)

2. Arch your back and move your head and shoulders up as if to shoot to make the defender jump.

3. As a defender, drop your head and shoulders toward the dribbler, as if to jump in front of the dribbler, to make the dribbler pick up the ball and stop advancing.

Head and shoulder fakes

(continued)

From *Learning by Choice in Secondary Physical Education: Creating a Goal-Directed Program* by Kevin Kaardal, 2001, Champaign, IL: Human Kinetics.

Ball or Hand Fakes

Move the ball or your hands in the opposite direction from the direction you intend to move yourself or the ball.

Ball or hand fakes

Look-Away Fakes

Look away from the play you are going to make for a "look-away pass" (e.g., as the ball handler, look away from the teammate you plan to pass to).

Look-away fakes

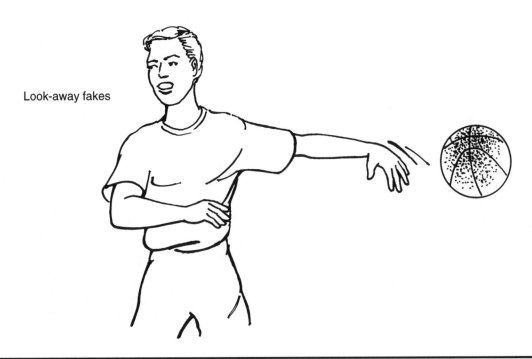

Basketball

From *Learning by Choice in Secondary Physical Education: Creating a Goal-Directed Program* by Kevin Kaardal, 2001, Champaign, IL: Human Kinetics.

Jab Step

Step forward to get your opponent to move back in that direction. Keeping the pivot foot planted (back foot), rock back to a stable position to create space between yourself (the faker) and your opponent. On defense, you may step into a penetrating offensive player's path to get the player to stop, change direction, or pick up the dribble and then step back to their own check.

Jab step

Skill Practice

Level A: Execute each type of fake, trying to get a teammate to move.

Level B: Execute fakes along with the following skills during practice: passing, shooting, before dribbling, and helping recover on defense.

Level C: Practice faking when appropriate during modified games.

Skill Mastery

Level A: Be able to demonstrate each type of fake on command.

Level B: Fake before half of all practice trials of passing, shooting, before dribbling, and helping recover on defense.

Level C: Successfully fake, causing a change in the movement pattern of the player you're faking, three of every five trials.

Modified Games

One-on-One, Two-on-Two, Three-on-Three

Basketball

From *Learning by Choice in Secondary Physical Education: Creating a Goal-Directed Program* by Kevin Kaardal, 2001, Champaign, IL: Human Kinetics.

Basketball Rules

Concept

The rules of basketball are designed to ensure no player or team gains an unfair advantage during play. The rules also help keep the game flowing quickly. Referees are in charge of enforcing the rules. Referees are to be fair, impartial, understand the rules, and behave calmly while enforcing the rules.

Skill Analysis

See the B.3 Simplified Rules and Definitions poster.

Skill Practice

Level A: Call your own fouls and violations during games of One-on-One, Two-on-Two, or Three-on-Three.

Level B: Referee Three-on-Three.

Level C: Referee a full-team scrimmage.

Skill Mastery

Levels A, B, & C: Players must conduct themselves with a sense of fair play and sporting behavior. The teacher will assess your knowledge of the simplified rules by watching you referee or by giving you a written test.

From *Learning by Choice in Secondary Physical Education: Creating a Goal-Directed Program* by Kevin Kaardal, 2001, Champaign, IL: Human Kinetics.

Offense—Individual

Concept

Shooting is how basketball players make the ball pass through the hoop, scoring points. Shots made during the flow of the game are worth two points if made from areas on or inside the three-point line and three points if made from beyond the three-point line. Free throws, or foul shots, are taken from the free throw line and are worth one point if made; these are awarded primarily to a shooter fouled in the act of shooting.

Skill Analysis

Common Components of All Shots: BEEF.

1. **B**alance: Start from triple threat position, face the basket with the shooting leg and arm in line with the basket.
2. **E**lbow under the ball, ball resting on finger pads.
3. **E**yes on target while aiming for the middle of the basket.
4. **F**ollow through toward target with the body and shooting arm and snap the wrist upon fully extending the shooting arm. (The guide hand leaves the ball just before release.)

- Balance

- All shots are one motion from start to finish

- Thumbs form a "7"

- Eyes on target
- Elbow under the ball

- Follow through

(continued)

From *Learning by Choice in Secondary Physical Education: Creating a Goal-Directed Program* by Kevin Kaardal, 2001, Champaign, IL: Human Kinetics.

Skill Practice

Level A: While sitting, shoot the ball into the air, 20 times.

Level B: From a triple threat position, shoot the ball to a point on the wall 14 feet above the ground, 20 times.

Skill Mastery

Level A: Catch the ball without moving, after the ball bounces off the floor, 16 of 20 trials.

Level B: Hit the target point on the wall, 16 of 20 trials.

From *Learning by Choice in Secondary Physical Education: Creating a Goal-Directed Program* by Kevin Kaardal, 2001, Champaign, IL: Human Kinetics.

Offense—Individual

Concept

Use the set shot when you are open. Also use it when shooting foul shots, or free throws. The set shot allows you to repeat the same movement patterns easily because variables, such as a vertical jump, are not part of it, making this a consistently high-percentage shot when taken inside a shooter's range. "Range" is the distance from the basket you can shoot with a high degree of success.

Skill Analysis

1. Refer to BEEF (see form B.26).
2. Do not let your feet leave the ground.

Skill Practice

Level A: Take 20 shots from 5 to 8 feet from the basket. Take the shots from various positions on the floor by using five spots along an imaginary arc in front of the basket.

Level B: Take 10 shots from 10 to 12 feet from the basket. Take the shots from various positions on the floor by using five spots along an imaginary arc in front of the basket.

Level C: (1) Take 10 shots from 15 to 22 feet from the basket.

(2) Take the shots from various positions on the floor by using five spots along an imaginary arc in front of the basket.

Skill Mastery

Level A: Score 8 of 10 attempts from A distance.

Level B: Score 6 of 10 attempts from B distance.

Level C: (1) Score 5 of 10 attempts from C distance.

(2) Score 4 or 5 of every 10 shots.

Modified Games

Horse, 21, 51, Bump, One-on-One, Two-on-Two, Three-on-Three

From *Learning by Choice in Secondary Physical Education: Creating a Goal-Directed Program* by Kevin Kaardal, 2001, Champaign, IL: Human Kinetics.

Form B.28 Layups: Power and Running

Offense—Individual

Concept

Layups are shots taken very near the basket. There are two types: power and running. Usually, take power layups when you are guarded closely. Use running layups when you are driving to the basket and outrunning the defender, either in a full-court fast break or a half-court drive.

Power layup

Skill Analysis

Power Layup

1. Start the same as jump shot.
2. Go up strong.
3. Bank your shot off the backboard, just above the basket.

Running layup

Running Layup

1. Refer to BEEF (see form B.26).
2. Lower the center of gravity.
3. Start running, then plant the lead leg.
4. Drive off the trail leg.
5. Drive the shooting leg and shooting arm (along with the guide hand) upward toward the basket.
6. Release the ball at the top of your jump, banking the shot off the backboard, just above the basket.

From *Learning by Choice in Secondary Physical Education: Creating a Goal-Directed Program* by Kevin Kaardal, 2001, Champaign, IL: Human Kinetics.

Skill Practice

For Both Layups

Level A: Practice 20 layups from one step away, shooting with the right hand from the right side of the basket and the left hand from the left side.

Level B: Practice 20 layups from two and three steps away. Dribble to avoid traveling.

Level C: (1) Practice 20 running layups without a defender. (2) Practice 10 layups with a defender. Choose the layup appropriate to the position of the defender as explained in the Concept section.

Skill Mastery

Levels A & B: Complete 8 of 10 attempts successfully with each hand.

Level C: Complete 7 of 10 attempts successfully with each hand.

Modified Games

Horse, Bump, 51, Fox and Hound, One-on-One, Two-on-Two, Three-on-Three

From *Learning by Choice in Secondary Physical Education: Creating a Goal-Directed Program* by Kevin Kaardal, 2001, Champaign, IL: Human Kinetics.

Offense—Individual

Concept

Use the jump shot to shoot quickly over opponents. Jump by quickly transitioning from forward movement to upward movement (that is, stop quickly and transfer forward momentum into the natural upward momentum of the shot, making you leave the floor).

Skill Analysis

1. Refer to BEEF (see form B.26).
2. To jump, quickly flex and extend your legs, back, and stomach muscles.
3. Release the ball on the way to the top of the jump where it feels natural.

Skill Practice

Level A: Take 20 shots from 5 to 12 feet from the basket, using five spots along an imaginary arc in front of the basket.

Level B: With defenders who must keep their hands at shoulder height, take 10 shots from 10 to 12 feet from the basket, using five spots along an imaginary arc in front of the basket.

Level C: Same as Level B, but shoot from 15 to 22 feet from the basket with defenders playing live defense.

Skill Mastery

Level A: Score 7 of 10 attempts.

Level B: Score 5 of 10 attempts.

Level C: Score 4 of 10 attempts.

Modified Games

Horse, Bump, 51, One-on-One, Two-on-Two, Three-on-Three

From *Learning by Choice in Secondary Physical Education: Creating a Goal-Directed Program* by Kevin Kaardal, 2001, Champaign, IL: Human Kinetics.

Offense—Individual

Concept

Use the hook shot to shoot over a defender when near the basket and closely guarded. The running hook shot and jump hook shot allow you to keep your body between the defender and the ball while shooting.

Skill Analysis

1. Refer to BEEF (see form B.26).
2. Step toward the basket, away from the defender.
3. Keep your shoulders in line with the basket.
4. Push the ball up and release, turning to square your shoulders to the basket.
5. For a running hook shot, use a one-footed takeoff, as in the running layup.
6. Use a jump stop and two-footed takeoff for a jump hook shot.

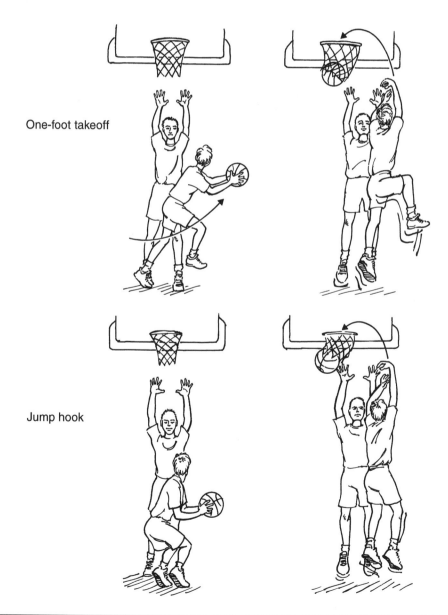

One-foot takeoff

Jump hook

(continued)

From *Learning by Choice in Secondary Physical Education: Creating a Goal-Directed Program* by Kevin Kaardal, 2001, Champaign, IL: Human Kinetics.

Skill Practice

Level A: Practice 10 shots with each hand, shooting at a point on the wall 12 to 14 feet above the floor.

Level B: Practice 10 shots with each hand, 4 to 8 feet from the basket.

Level C: While being defended, practice 10 shots with each hand 4 to 8 feet from the basket.

Skill Mastery

Level A: Hit the point on the wall 8 of 10 trials.

Level B: Score 7 of 10 shots with each hand.

Level C: Score 5 of 10 shots with each hand.

Modified Games

Horse, One-on-One, Two-on-Two, Three-on-Three

From *Learning by Choice in Secondary Physical Education: Creating a Goal-Directed Program* by Kevin Kaardal, 2001, Champaign, IL: Human Kinetics.

Common Practice for All Dribbling Methods

Concept

These ball handling drills help to build motor patterns that will help you better handle the ball while dribbling, passing, or receiving a pass. Practice the same movement patterns you will use in a variety of dribbling and passing methods to help you better perform fundamental skills during a game. Top tip: don't look at the ball.

Skill Analysis

See ball handling diagrams.

Skill Practice

Body Circles

Level A: Move the ball around your body, passing it from hand to hand in circles as quickly as you can.

Level B: Start at your ankles and work up to circling your head.

Level C: Dribble in circles around your body, switching hands while dribbling.

Fingertip Toss

Level A: Toss the ball from hand to hand, using only fingertips to contact the ball. Do this as quickly as you can.

Level B: Add body circles while doing the fingertip toss.

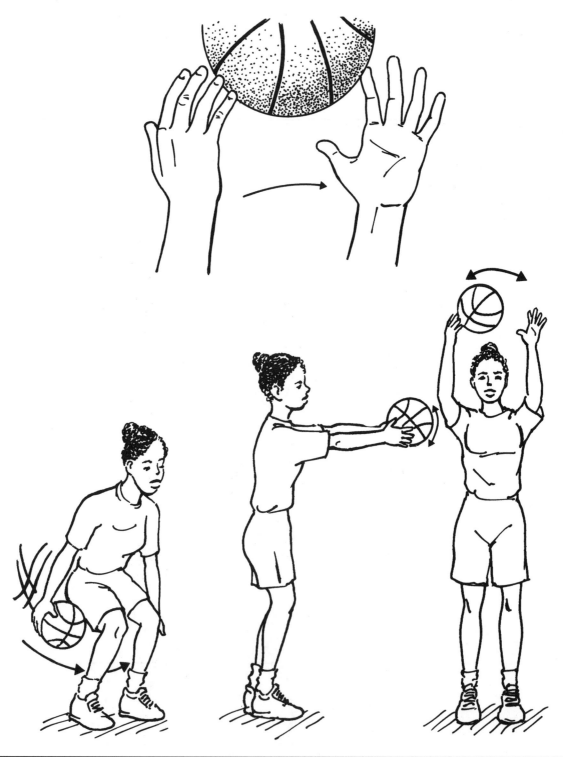

From *Learning by Choice in Secondary Physical Education: Creating a Goal-Directed Program* by Kevin Kaardal, 2001, Champaign, IL: Human Kinetics.

Figure Eight Dribbling

Level A: Move the ball through and around the legs so that the movement path of the ball makes an "8."

Level B: Do Level A more quickly.

Inventing Your Own Drills

Level C: Invent drills that will help you handle the ball better.

Suggestions:

1. Drills using two basketballs
2. Challenge drills, such as Follow the Leader
3. Two-person, two-ball passing drills, trying to keep two or more basketballs on the go at the same time

Figure eight dribbling

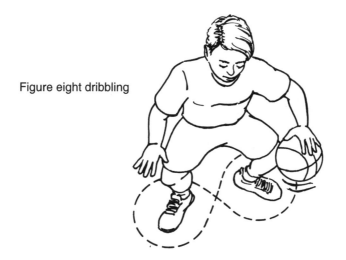

Inventing your own drills

From *Learning by Choice in Secondary Physical Education: Creating a Goal-Directed Program* by Kevin Kaardal, 2001, Champaign, IL: Human Kinetics.

Offense—Individual

Concept

Dribble to move the ball down court when no one is open for a pass ahead of you. Also dribble to drive past your own defender and break down the defense.

Preparation

Delivery

Skill Analysis

Preparation

1. Start in triple threat position.
2. Place weak hand on the side of the ball.
3. Flex wrist and elbow of strong hand and place behind ball.

Delivery

Extend arm, wrist, and hand, sending ball to the floor.

Reception

Reading

Reception

Move arm, wrist, and hand with the ball. This cushions the ball's return flight.

Reading

Always keep your head up, watching for open spaces or open teammates.

Dribbling Types

1. Low control
2. Speed
3. Hesitation—behind legs or behind back
4. Crossover
5. Spin

From *Learning by Choice in Secondary Physical Education: Creating a Goal-Directed Program* by Kevin Kaardal, 2001, Champaign, IL: Human Kinetics.

Offense—Individual

Concept

Use the low control dribble to keep the ball low and away from the defender, allowing you to contact the ball more times per second and improving ball control.

Skill Analysis

1. Refer to Dribbling, General (form B.32).
2. Do the low control dribble in an exaggerated ready position.
3. Dribble at about knee height.
4. Position your nondribbling arm between the defender and the ball to guard it.

Skill Practice

Level A: Be able to dribble standing still with the right or left hand for 30 seconds on command.

Level B: Using your right and left hands on alternating laps, dribble 10 laps of the gym. Don't look at the ball.

Level C: (1) Dribble for 30 seconds inside a confined space (e.g., jump circle) without losing control of the ball while a partner tries to check it away. (2) Dribble six lengths of the gym while being aggressively defended by a partner, three lengths using your right hand and three using your left.

Skill Mastery

Level A: Demonstrate the skill perfectly.

Level B: Complete the 10 laps without losing control of the ball or looking down at it.

Level C: (1) Dribble without losing control of the ball the entire 30 seconds. (2) Complete four of five court lengths without losing control of the ball.

Modified Games

Dribble Tag, Elimination Dribble, Two-on-Two, Three-on-Three

From *Learning by Choice in Secondary Physical Education: Creating a Goal-Directed Program* by Kevin Kaardal, 2001, Champaign, IL: Human Kinetics.

Offense—Individual

Concept

Speed-dribble to move the ball up court quickly when you are unguarded and have no open player ahead of you to receive a pass.

Skill Analysis

1. Refer to Dribbling, General (form B.32).
2. Push the ball well out in front of yourself.
3. Run "onto" the ball, receiving it at waist level. (Push the ball several walking strides ahead of your starting position and then run to catch up to the ball, receiving it at the apex of its bounce.)

Skill Practice

Level A: Using your strong hand, speed-dribble the length of the gym, dribbling fewer than 7 times. Repeat 5 times, dribbling 35 times or fewer, total. Do not travel.

Level B: Alternating between your weak and strong hands, speed-dribble length of gym, dribbling 5 times or fewer. Repeat 5 times, dribbling 25 times or fewer, total. Do not travel.

Level C: Alternating between your weak and strong hands, speed-dribble the length of the gym, dribbling 4 times or fewer. Repeat 5 times, dribbling 20 times or fewer, total. Do not travel.

Skill Mastery

Levels A & B: Maintain control of the ball four of five lengths, without traveling.

Level C: (1) Same as for Levels A & B. (2) Score four of five layups.

Modified Games

Fox and Hound, Dribble Tag, Elimination Dribble, One-on-One, Two-on-Two, Three-on-Three

From *Learning by Choice in Secondary Physical Education: Creating a Goal-Directed Program* by Kevin Kaardal, 2001, Champaign, IL: Human Kinetics.

Offense—Individual

Concept

Use this change-of-speed dribble to create space between a defender and yourself. It also helps you beat a defender. You hesitate, or slow, your forward motion, causing the defender to stop moving so that you can speed up again and dribble past the defender before he or she can react.

Skill Analysis

1. Run while dribbling, then jump-stop or stride-stop.
2. While stopping your forward momentum, transition into a low control dribble (you might also take a rocker step or jab step back).
3. When the defender stops, immediately start to speed-dribble again, running past the defender.

Skill Practice

Level A: Without a defender, run 10 lengths of the gym hesitation dribbling, five with each hand.

Level B: Add a passive defender to Level A practice.

Level C: Add an aggressive defender to Level A practice.

Skill Mastery

Levels A, B, & C: Complete 8 of 10 court lengths without losing control of the ball.

Modified Game

Dribble Tag, Elimination Dribble, One-on-One, Two-on-Two, Three-on-Three

From *Learning by Choice in Secondary Physical Education: Creating a Goal-Directed Program* by Kevin Kaardal, 2001, Champaign, IL: Human Kinetics.

Offense—Individual

Concept

Crossover dribble to move the ball away from a defender to your free hand. Players often combine the crossover dribble with a change-of-direction step (see form B.21).

Skill Analysis

1. Refer to Dribbling, General (form B.32).
2. When dribbling forward, lower your center of gravity as in the change-of-direction step.
3. Then bounce-pass the ball to your free hand.

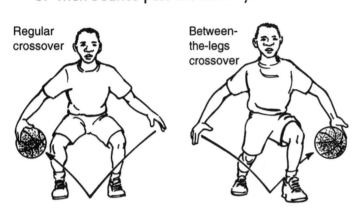

Regular crossover

Between-the-legs crossover

Variation A: Between-the-Legs Crossover

Add a bounce pass to the free hand between the legs to the crossover dribble. This is easier to do from the inside of the leg to the outside.

Variation B: Behind-the-Back Crossover

1. Start with a pull dribble to move the ball behind your back. (As you are dribbling the ball in front of your body, pull the ball back so you are dribbling beside your leg or slightly behind your leg. This is accomplished by sliding the hand slightly forward on the ball and pulling the ball back toward your body.

2. Step forward with the leg opposite your dribbling hand, pushing the ball behind your back to your free hand.

Behind-the-back crossover

Skill Practice

For Both Variations

Level A: Dribble 20 times while stationary, 10 times right hand to left hand and 10 times left hand to right.

Level B: Set up an obstacle course in a zigzag pattern, using cones. Complete the course 10 times, 5 times right to left and 5 left to right.

Level C: With an aggressive defender, crossover-dribble, running five court lengths.

Skill Mastery

Level A: Complete 20 of 20 attempts successfully.

Level B: Complete the obstacle course 8 of 10 times without losing control of ball.

Level C: Complete four of five court lengths without losing control of ball.

Modified Games

Elimination Dribble, Dribble Tag, One-on-One, Two-on-Two, Three-on-Three

From *Learning by Choice in Secondary Physical Education: Creating a Goal-Directed Program* by Kevin Kaardal, 2001, Champaign, IL: Human Kinetics.

Offense—Individual

Concept

Spin-dribble to get away from a defender who has closed the space directly ahead of you in the open court.

Skill Analysis

1. From a low control dribble, plant your lead foot between the defender's legs.
2. Reverse-pivot off the planted lead leg.
3. Pull-dribble the ball as you pivot past the defender. (As you are dribbling the ball in front of your body, pull the ball back so you are dribbling beside your leg or slightly behind your leg. This is accomplished by sliding the hand slightly forward on the ball and pulling the ball back toward your body.)
4. Switch hands and continue down court.

Skill Practice

Level A: Practice 20 trials of the pull dribble.

Level B: Practice 10 trials of the pull dribble, pivoting while dribbling around a cone.

Level C: Practice 10 trials of the spin dribble against an active defender.

Skill Mastery

Levels A, B, & C: Complete 9 of 10 trials successfully (without losing control of ball).

Modified Games

Dribble Tag, Elimination Dribble, One-on-One, Two-on-Two, Three-on-Three

From *Learning by Choice in Secondary Physical Education: Creating a Goal-Directed Program* by Kevin Kaardal, 2001, Champaign, IL: Human Kinetics.

Offense—Individual

Concept

Rebounding is the skill that keeps your team in possession of the ball after a missed shot. Offensive rebounds often result in second shot opportunities, increasing scoring potential for a given offensive sequence.

The attack

Skill Analysis

The Attack

1. Keep your eyes on the ball.
2. Fake, pivot, or run past your defender.
3. Using a two-footed takeoff, jump aggressively at the ball.
4. Catch the ball at the top of your jump.
5. Land in a balanced triple threat position.

Land and Shoot

1. From the triple threat position, shoot a jump shot or, if you are close enough, a power layup.
2. If you are defended well, fake, then shoot or pass to an open teammate.

Skill Practice

Level A: (1) Toss the ball off the wall at a height of 10 feet. Use a two-footed takeoff and catch the ball at the top of the jump, 20 times. (2) Fake, then run past or pivot off an opponent who is trying to block you out and prevent you from getting to a stationary ball placed behind the defender, 10 times.

Level B: (1) Without a defender, rebound 10 shots from each distance of 5, 10, and 15 feet. (2) Land in triple threat position. Upon landing, shoot jump shots or power layups, depending on your distance from the basket (when you catch the rebound).

Land and shoot

Level C: Add an aggressive defender to Level B drills.

Skill Mastery

Level A: Catch 16 of 20 rebounds at the top of your jump.

Level B: (1) Retrieve 8 of 10 rebounds at each distance. (2) Score six of eight shot attempts.

Level C: Retrieve 4 of 10 rebounds at each distance. Score three of four shot attempts.

Modified Games

Hamburger, Up-and-Over, 51

From *Learning by Choice in Secondary Physical Education: Creating a Goal-Directed Program* by Kevin Kaardal, 2001, Champaign, IL: Human Kinetics.

Offense—Individual

Concept

Before dribbling, fake in many ways to make the defender move away from potential open spaces, to create opportunities for open (undefended) shots. There are three general fake combinations used by most offensive players when facing the basket: the fake and shoot; the fake and drive to the basket; and the fake, crossover-step, and drive, finishing with either a jump shot or layup. Usually, you should include a jab step combined with a ball fake and a head and shoulder fake. The fake works when the defender jumps in any direction, the defender's legs straighten, or the defender appears to be off balance.

Skill Analysis

1. Fake and Shoot
2. Fake and Drive
3. Fake, Crossover-Step, and Drive to a Jump Shot or Layup

Skill Practice

Level A: Without a defender, practice each move 10 times from three perimeter spots (top of the key and 45 degrees from the basket on the wings, free throw line extended on each side of the offensive court).

Level B: With a defender who must react to all believable fakes but make no attempt to steal the ball, practice as in Level A.

Level C: Play five games of One-on-One, using the three fake combinations. Start from a position inside the offensive player's shooting range at different spots on the floor.

Skill Mastery

Level A: Score 5 of 10 shots after completing a fake.

Levels B & C: Successfully fake out a defender 7 of 10 attempts. Score 6 of 10 shots.

Modified Games

One-on-One, Two-on-Two, Three-on-Three, King's Court, One-Man Short

From *Learning by Choice in Secondary Physical Education: Creating a Goal-Directed Program* by Kevin Kaardal, 2001, Champaign, IL: Human Kinetics.

Skill Analysis

1. From inside your shooting range, without dribbling, use a combination of fakes to move the defender away from yourself.

2. Move the defender far enough away that you have time to take an undefended balanced set or jump shot.

3. Key skill points to remember are (a) make the fakes look believable, (b) make them short and quick, and (c) stay on balance in triple threat position so you can quickly transition from faking to shooting.

From *Learning by Choice in Secondary Physical Education: Creating a Goal-Directed Program* by Kevin Kaardal, 2001, Champaign, IL: Human Kinetics.

Skill Analysis

1. Combine fakes to move the defender off a direct path to the basket.

2. Speed-dribble to the basket, if there are no help side defenders (see Team Defense forms B.58-B.64), or quick, low control-dribble, if help side defense reacts to stop the drive.

3. Another way to use the fake and drive is to jab-step then fake as you are going to shoot as in the fake and shoot. As the defender moves closer to attempt to guard the shot, drive by him or her. The defender will not be able to change direction quickly enough to stop the drive.

4. If you place your foot even with the defender's foot on the first step, drive to the basket. End with a layup.

From *Learning by Choice in Secondary Physical Education: Creating a Goal-Directed Program* by Kevin Kaardal, 2001, Champaign, IL: Human Kinetics.

Skill Analysis

1. Jab-step and combine fakes to make the defender step back.
2. Fake, taking the shot.
3. As the defender moves forward to defend the shot, front-pivot, crossing in front of the defender's body.
4. Drive into the open space beside the defender. Remember to dribble before picking up your pivot foot.
5. If no help side defenders are between you and the basket, drive to the basket. If help side defenders are waiting, pull up and perform a jump shot in the open space you just entered.

Basketball

Offense—Individual

Concept

You are more likely to score on a shot taken close to the basket than from a long distance. This is why the objective of most offensive plays is to get the ball into the *low post area* in a *one-on-one* situation. Here, you will most often be facing away from the basket and contending with one or more help side defenders. So you need specialized moves to take advantage of the ball's movement this close to the basket. Once you receive the pass, time and space are limited because the defenders in help side positions are close by and space to move in the key or near the baseline is limited. Therefore, any fakes and the motion into the shot must be quick so that help side defenders can't double-team you as the shooter.

If you hope to receive a ball in the low post, you must first seal the defender and establish a stable ready position so that the pass into the post can be made safely and effectively. On receiving the ball, you have three basic moves that will allow you to quickly deliver the shot: drop-step to the baseline, finishing in a power layup (Move A), fake and drop-step to the middle with a jump hook shot (Move B), and back-pivot to face the defender and shoot a jump shot (Move C).

Skill Analysis

Also see specific Skill Analyses and diagrams for Low Post One-on-One.

Common Components of All Low Post Moves (A-C)

1. Seal the defender and put out a target hand away from the defender to receive the pass, *trapping* it.
2. Check where the defender is once you have received the ball by feeling the defender with the body contact that exists as a result of a proper seal.
3. Set up the defender by quickly faking in the direction opposite from the one you intend to go.
4. As the defensive player reacts to the fake, move quickly into the selected shot.

Skill Practice

For All Low Post One-On-One Moves (A-C)

Level A: Without a defender, practice receiving the ball and then performing each move 10 times.

Level B: (1) With a half-speed defender in denial position from the baseline side of you, practice Move A 10 times. (2) With a half-speed defender in denial position from the side of you nearest the foul line, practice Move B 10 times. (3) With a half-speed defender directly behind you, practice Move C 10 times. (4) With a half-speed defender, read what type of post defense is being played and react accordingly. The defender may choose any of the defensive strategies noted in One-on-One or Two-on-Two.

Level C: (1) Repeat all Level B drills with the defender playing full-speed defense. (2) Play five games of One-on-One or Two-on-Two from the low post up to seven baskets. Possession of the ball changes after each score.

Skill Mastery

For All Low Post One-on-One Moves (A-C)

Level A: Demonstrate each move correctly to the teacher and, when practicing, score 7 of every 10 attempts.

Level B: (1) Beat the defender on 8 of 10 attempts. (2) Score 7 of every 10 successful attempts.

Level C: (1) Beat the defender on 8 of 10 attempts. (2) Score 7 of every 10 successful attempts.

Modified Games

One-on-One, Two-on-Two, Three-on-Three, and Four-on-Four

From *Learning by Choice in Secondary Physical Education: Creating a Goal-Directed Program* by Kevin Kaardal, 2001, Champaign, IL: Human Kinetics.

Specific Skill Analysis for Move A

After receiving the pass, if the defender is sealed away from the basket, then do the following:

1. Quickly drop-step toward the basket, putting the defender behind you (a "drop step" is a reverse pivot made toward the basket or the center of the key that starts a move in a given direction).

2. While drop-stepping, quickly low control-dribble, keeping the ball in the center of your body.

3. Stride-stop or jump-stop.

4. Finish with a power layup.

From *Learning by Choice in Secondary Physical Education: Creating a Goal-Directed Program* by Kevin Kaardal, 2001, Champaign, IL: Human Kinetics.

Specific Skill Analysis for Move B

After receiving the pass, if the defender is sealed on the side of your body nearest the basket and baseline, then do the following:

1. Ball- and shoulder-fake toward the baseline and the basket to get the defender moving in that direction.
2. Drop-step toward the center of the key.
3. Quickly low control-dribble, keeping the ball in the center of your body.
4. Stride-stop or jump-stop.
5. Finish with a jump hook shot.

From *Learning by Choice in Secondary Physical Education: Creating a Goal-Directed Program* by Kevin Kaardal, 2001, Champaign, IL: Human Kinetics.

Specific Skill Analysis for Move C

After receiving the pass, if the defender is directly behind you, then do the following:

1. Reverse-pivot to face the basket.
2. If the defender is more than an arm's length away, shoot a quick set or jump shot.
3. If the defender is less than an arm's length away, head- and shoulder-fake and drive past the defender with a quick low control dribble.
4. Jump-stop and perform a jump shot or a power layup.

From *Learning by Choice in Secondary Physical Education: Creating a Goal-Directed Program* by Kevin Kaardal, 2001, Champaign, IL: Human Kinetics.

Offense—Team

Concept

Several types of passes will help you move the ball quickly to open players on the floor, including the chest pass, overhead pass, baseball pass, shovel pass, and one-handed push pass. You can also modify these passes by bouncing the ball off the floor for a "bounce pass."

Skill Analysis

Common Components of All Passes

1. Pivot away from your defender to create space for the pass to travel.
2. Keep your head up, looking for targets.
3. Keep hands and feet behind the ball.
4. Step into the pass for more power.
5. Aim for your teammate's target hand.
6. "Lead the receiver" (that is, pass the ball ahead of a moving teammate so that he or she runs "onto" the ball).
7. Snap wrists upon releasing the ball.

Pass Receptions: The Trap Method

1. Move away from your defender to create a passing lane.
2. Hold out a target hand.
3. Move toward the pass.
4. Watch the ball.
5. When the ball hits your target hand, trap it by quickly directing the ball to the other hand.

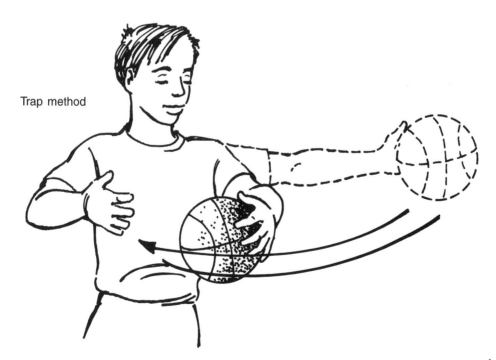

Trap method

(continued)

Basketball

Pass Receptions: The Funneling Method

1. Move away from your defender to create a passing lane.
2. Extend both hands toward the ball to act as a target.
3. Watch the ball.
4. Move toward the pass.
5. As the ball hits your hands, cushion it by flexing your arms back toward your body.

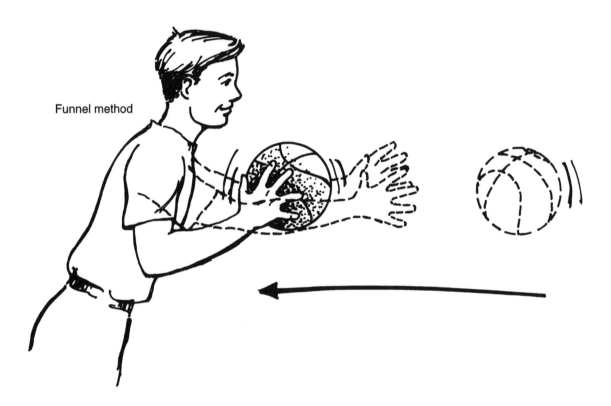

Funnel method

Skill Practice

Level A: Practice passing to a partner without a defender. Pass to the target hand, leading the receiver. Receivers move toward the ball and funnel it 10 times, using a two-handed target, and trap it 10 times, using a one-handed target.

Level B: Add one or more cones or nonaggressive defenders to Level A instructions, leading the receiver by passing away from the defender or cone.

Level C: Receive a pass while moving and transfer to dribbling without traveling.

Skill Mastery

Levels A, B, & C: Complete 8 of 10 successful passes and receptions.

Modified Games

Keep-Away, No-Dribble Basketball, Two-on-Two, Three-on-Three

From *Learning by Choice in Secondary Physical Education: Creating a Goal-Directed Program* by Kevin Kaardal, 2001, Champaign, IL: Human Kinetics.

Offense—Team

Concept

This is the most commonly used pass in basketball, used for trying to pass while closely guarded. One arm and hand deliver the pass while the arm closest to the defender guards the ball.

Skill Analysis

1. Refer to Common Components of All Passes (see form B.41).
2. Pass with the arm and hand farthest away from the defense.
3. Guide and guard the pass with the arm and hand nearest the defender, keeping the defender away from the ball.
4. Take the guide hand off the ball right before releasing the ball.
5. Follow through toward the target.

Skill Practice

Level A: From each distance of 5, 10, and 15 feet, pass 10 times to a wall target with each hand.

Level B: (1) With a defender, pass to a moving receiver from 10 to 15 feet, 10 times with each hand. (2) Pass to a defended teammate who is moving to the ball, using L-cuts or V-cuts, 10 times with each hand.

Level C: During Two-on-Two games, pass 20 times to a partner who is practicing L-cuts, V-cuts, steals, and screen-and-rolls.

Skill Mastery

Levels A, B, & C: Perform each task successfully 8 of every 10 trials.

Modified Games

Keep-Away, No-Dribble Basketball, Two-on-Two, and Three-on-Three

From *Learning by Choice in Secondary Physical Education: Creating a Goal-Directed Program* by Kevin Kaardal, 2001, Champaign, IL: Human Kinetics.

Offense—Team

Concept

Chest-pass to advance the ball to a teammate when you are undefended. This pass is often helpful on fast breaks.

Skill Analysis

1. Refer to Common Components of All Passes (see form B.41).
2. With both hands behind the ball, push the ball toward your intended target.

Skill Practice

Level A: From each distance of 5, 10, and 15 feet, pass 10 times to a wall target.

Level B: Pass to a partner while moving down court, five court lengths.

Level C: Pass to a partner who is being defended while moving down court, five court lengths.

Skill Mastery

Level A: Perform 8 of every 10 trials successfully.

Levels B & C: Advance down court successfully completing every pass, four of five lengths.

Modified Games

Weave Races, Two-on-Two, and Three-on-Three

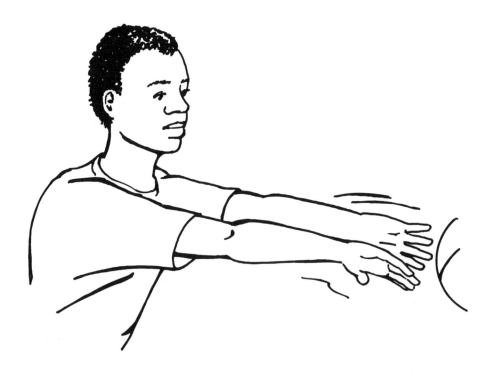

From *Learning by Choice in Secondary Physical Education: Creating a Goal-Directed Program* by Kevin Kaardal, 2001, Champaign, IL: Human Kinetics.

Offense—Team

Concept

Shovel-pass when, while dribbling, you beat your defender and draw another teammate's defender. Then shovel, or "dish," the ball to your now-unguarded teammate by redirecting the ball with one or both hands.

Skill Analysis

1. Drive to the basket after getting past your defender.
2. When your teammate's defender switches to guard you, redirect your dribbling into a pass by shifting your hand behind the ball and pushing the ball in the direction of your open teammate.
3. You may also shovel-pass by wrapping the ball behind your back or faking a shot and dumping the ball off to the open teammate.

Skill Practice

Level A: While stationary, dribble alongside a chest-high wall target and perform 20 shovel passes.

Level B: (1) Dribble along the wall. When you move near the target, have a defender step out and force you to shovel-pass to the target, 20 times. (2) In groups of three (one dribbler/passer, one defender, and one receiver), have the dribbler drive to the basket and then dish to the receiver as the defender steps out to stop the dribbler, 20 times.

Level C: Playing Two-on-Two, penetrate to the basket, driving past the defender and drawing your teammate's (the receiver's) defender. Then shovel-pass to the receiver. Try 10 times.

Skill Mastery

Levels A, B, & C: Perform each task successfully 8 of every 10 trials.

Modified Games

Two-on-Two, Three-on-Three

Basketball

From *Learning by Choice in Secondary Physical Education: Creating a Goal-Directed Program* by Kevin Kaardal, 2001, Champaign, IL: Human Kinetics.

Offense—Team

Concept

Use the overhead snap pass to send the ball over the defense quickly. This pass is especially effective when used to pass over help side defenders.

Skill Analysis

1. Hold the ball overhead.
2. Cock your wrists back.
3. Refer to the Common Components of All Passes (see form B.41).
4. Follow through toward the target.

Skill Practice

Level A: From each distance of 10, 15, and 18 feet, pass the ball 20 times to a wall target.

Level B: (1) With a defender on the passer, pass the ball to a stationary target, 20 times. (2) With a defender on the passer and another positioned halfway between the receiver and the ball, pass to a moving receiver, 20 times.

Level C: Playing Three-on-Three, pass the ball, using the overhead snap pass, 20 times.

Skill Mastery

Levels A, B, & C: Perform each task 8 of every 10 trials successfully.

Modified Games

Keep-Away, No-Dribble Basketball, Two-on-Two, and Three-on-Three

From *Learning by Choice in Secondary Physical Education: Creating a Goal-Directed Program* by Kevin Kaardal, 2001, Champaign, IL: Human Kinetics.

Offense—Team

Concept

Baseball-pass to advance the ball down court quickly to open teammates, 30 or more feet away.

Skill Analysis

1. Refer to the Common Components of All Passes (see form B.41).
2. Throw the ball overhanded and one-handed like a baseball.
3. Lead your target by a few steps if your teammate is moving.

Skill Practice

Level A: Pass to a stationary partner 30 feet away, 20 times.

Level B: Pass to a moving partner 45 feet away, 20 times.

Level C: Pass to a moving partner 45 to 85 feet away so that the partner can catch the ball in stride without stopping, 20 times.

Skill Mastery

Levels A, B, & C: Perform 16 of 20 trials successfully.

Modified Games

Fox and Hound

From *Learning by Choice in Secondary Physical Education: Creating a Goal-Directed Program* by Kevin Kaardal, 2001, Champaign, IL: Human Kinetics.

Offensive—Team

Concept

When passing to a closely guarded teammate, use the bounce pass to pass under the defender's arms.

Skill Analysis

1. Refer to the Common Components of All Passes (see form B.41).
2. Also refer to the Skill Analysis section of the one-handed push pass (form B.42).
3. Aim for the ball to bounce at a point on the floor away from the defender directly beneath his or her denying arm.

Skill Practice

Level A: From 5, 10, and then 15 feet, pass 10 times to a wall target with each hand.

Level B: (1) With a defender, pass to a moving receiver from 10 to 15 feet away, 10 times with each hand. (2) Pass to a defended teammate who is moving to the ball using L-cuts or V-cuts, 10 times with each hand.

Level C: Playing Two-on-Two, pass 20 times to a partner who is practicing L-cuts, V-cuts, steals, and screen-and-rolls.

Skill Mastery

Levels A, B, & C: Perform each task successfully 8 of every 10 trials.

Modified Games

Keep-Away, No-Dribble Basketball, Two-on-Two, and Three-on-Three

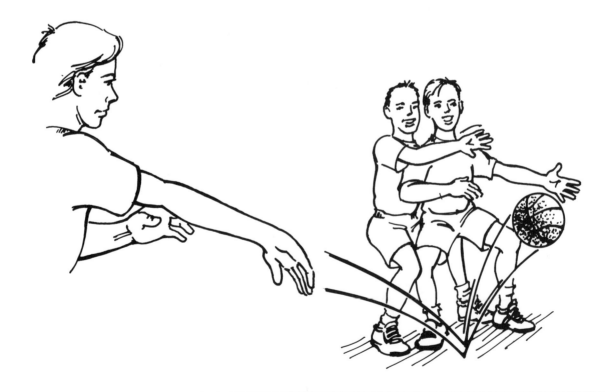

Basketball

From *Learning by Choice in Secondary Physical Education: Creating a Goal-Directed Program* by Kevin Kaardal, 2001, Champaign, IL: Human Kinetics.

Offense—Team

Concept

Create easy scoring opportunities by making a quick transition from defense to offense. When you recover the ball on either rebounds or steals, advance it toward your offensive goal the quickest way possible. If teammates are open ahead of you, this means passing the ball. If no teammates are open ahead of you, dribble quickly toward your goal, watching for teammates who are running to fill open passing lanes.

General Skill Analysis for Fast Breaks

Teams running a fast break generally divide the court into five lanes to spread the defense out, making themselves more difficult to defend. Four principles help teams run successful fast breaks:

1. Move the ball away from the defense quickly, usually by passing to an open player in lanes 1, 2, or 3.
2. Try to outnumber the defense briefly by beating some or all the defensive players up court.
3. Offensive players generally fill lanes 1, 2, and 3 first to make the defense guard a wider area of the court.
4. Players fill lanes 4 and 5, which are called "trail lanes," because the players filling them generally trail behind the initial fast break play.

Note: Three common situations will most often result if an offensive team makes a good transition to offense: the one-on-zero fast break, the two-on-one fast break, and the three-on-two fast break (see forms B.48, a-c).

Skill Mastery

For all fast break types and levels: Score 7 of 10, finishing with successful layups.

From *Learning by Choice in Secondary Physical Education: Creating a Goal-Directed Program* by Kevin Kaardal, 2001, Champaign, IL: Human Kinetics.

Skill Analysis

1. If you, as an offensive player, receive the ball ahead of all the defenders, speed-dribble in a straight line to the basket and finish with a layup.
2. If the defense is close behind you, fake a shot then do a power layup to try to get a more open shot.

Skill Practice

Level A: From at least half-court (10-second line), speed-dribble 10 drives to the basket, finishing in a right- or left-handed layup. Alternate the side of the court and the hand you are dribbling with and perform the corresponding layup. Alternate power layups with running layups.

Level B: Do Level A's practice, but add having a defender chase you. The defensive player starts 15 feet behind you, then passes the ball ahead of you. You catch the ball and drive to the basket. The defensive player tries to stop you from scoring by trying to get into good defensive position ahead of you.

Level C: Do Level B's practice, but have the defensive player start only 10 feet behind you.

From *Learning by Choice in Secondary Physical Education: Creating a Goal-Directed Program* by Kevin Kaardal, 2001, Champaign, IL: Human Kinetics.

Skill Analysis

When the transition into offense results in a two-on-one advantage for the offense, the offensive players should occupy the sideline edges of lanes 4 and 5 as they approach the basket. This creates a minimum of 15 feet between teammates, spreading out the offense, making it harder for the defender to defend both attacking players.

1. Before the players reach the jump circle at the top of the defender's key, the player with the ball should pass the ball to a teammate.

2. The teammate then reads the defensive player's reaction and responds in one of two ways: (a) If the defensive player remains in the middle of the key, the receiver will drive to the basket for a layup or (b) if the defensive player jumps over to guard the receiver, the receiver passes back to the original dribbler in a "give-and-go" play. This player then attacks the basket for a layup before the defender can react and catch up to the ball.

Skill Practice

Level A: Starting at least at half-court, practice 10 two-on-one, give-and-go plays, against a defender who may not use hands to defend.

Level B: Same as Level A, but go against a defender who may play aggressive defense but must react to the first pass by stopping the receiver's drive.

Level C: Starting at least at half-court, practice 10 two-on-one fast breaks, reading and reacting to the defender's reaction to your approach (see Skill Analysis section). Defenders will be working on faking to defend the fast break and will attempt different strategies to disrupt the offensive players.

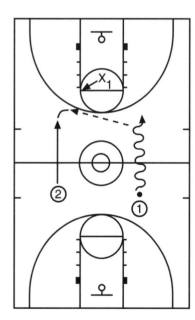
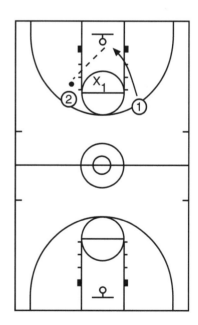

Skill Analysis

When transition results in three offensive players' attacking two defensive players, the offensive players should try to fill lanes 1, 2, and 3. A common play for this situation starts with the ball in the middle of lane 1.

1. The dribbler attacks the defense in lane 1 until defended.
2. If the defense does not stop the drive, the dribbler drives to the basket for a layup. If the defense defends the drive, then the dribbler passes to either player in lanes 2 or 3.
3. Once the ball has gone to the wing, the passer in lane 1 drifts to the corner of the foul line nearest to the receiver to wait for the return pass. Players in lanes 2 and 3 cut toward the basket once they reach the foul line extended.
4. The player on the wing, who now has the ball, reads the defensive reaction to the pass and chooses one of four options.

   a. If the defense does not guard the ball handler, the ball handler drives to the basket for a layup.

   b. If the defense guards the ball handler but does not recover quickly to protect the space under the basket, then the ball handler passes to the opposite wing player (a classmate working on the same skills), cutting to the basket.

   c. If the defense recovers quickly and guards both the ball handler and the area under the basket, the ball handler passes the ball back to the player in lane 1, who is now waiting on the corner of the foul line for an open, 15-foot shot.

   d. If none of these first three options is open, the ball handler dribbles out and starts the offensive play or passes to one of the players running in lanes 4 or 5, who are trailing the play, if one is open for a quick shot or drive.

Skill Practice

Level A: Starting at least at half-court, practice 10 three-on-two situations using the options described in the Skill Analysis section. The two defenders, who are playing at half speed, may not use hands to defend.

Level B: Same as Level A, but go against two defenders who may play "tandem defense" at three-quarter speed (see Level B of the Defending Fast Breaks poster [Form B.62], Two-on-Three [Tandem Defense]).

Level C: Same as Level B, but defenders play at full speed.

From *Learning by Choice in Secondary Physical Education: Creating a Goal-Directed Program* by Kevin Kaardal, 2001, Champaign, IL: Human Kinetics.

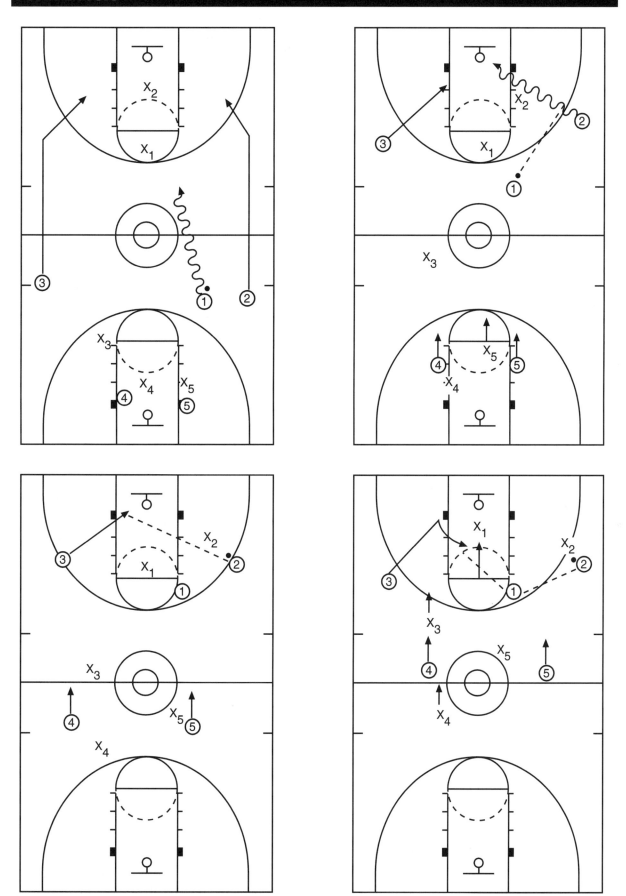

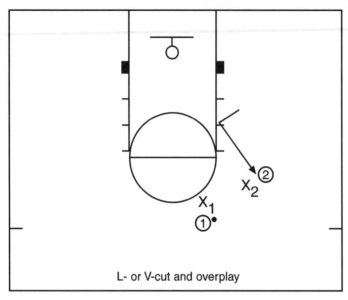

L- or V-cut and overplay

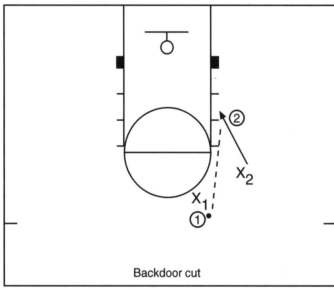

Backdoor cut

Offense—Team

Concept

During play the offensive team tries to isolate two offensive players against two defensive players to run simple plays that may result in open shots. These plays include the backdoor cut, the drive-and-dish, the give-and-go, and the screen-and-roll. The two offensive players will be referred to as Player 1 and Player 2.

Skill Analysis

See diagrams provided for the following:

1. Backdoor cut
2. Drive-and-dish
3. Give-and-go
4. Screen-and-roll

Skill Practice

Level A: In groups of four, practice running each two-on-two play as described in the Skill Analysis sections of the related posters. Alternate playing offense and defense. The defense may not use their hands to defend. Try each play five times per team.

Level B: While playing Two-on-Two, practice running each two-on-two play as described in the Skill Analysis sections of the related posters. Alternate playing offense and defense. The defense should play at full speed. Try each play five times per team.

Level C: While playing Five-on-Five, attempt to isolate two offensive players on a wing and use the two-on-two plays described on the related posters.

Skill Mastery

Levels A, B, & C: Successfully execute each two-on-two play every four of five attempts. You are successful if the play results in an open shot, whether you score or not.

Skill Analysis

Backdoor Cut

1. Player 2 L- or V-cuts to try to get open for a pass in the wing area.
2. Player 2 notices that her or his defender is overplaying the passing lane (guarding Player 2 too closely).
3. Player 1 fakes a pass to Player 2 to get the defender to lean into the passing lane.
4. Immediately after the faked pass, Player 2 cuts hard toward the basket.
5. Player 1 passes the ball to Player 2, who finishes the drive with a layup.

From *Learning by Choice in Secondary Physical Education: Creating a Goal-Directed Program* by Kevin Kaardal, 2001, Champaign, IL: Human Kinetics.

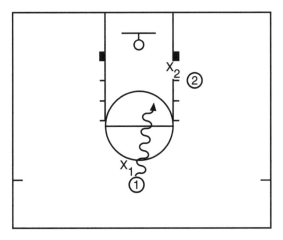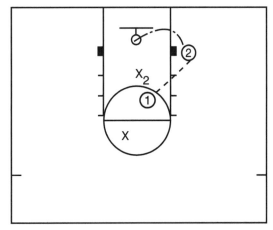

Drive-and-dish

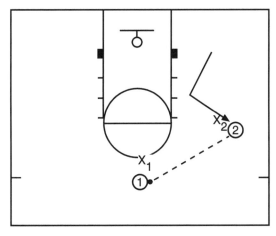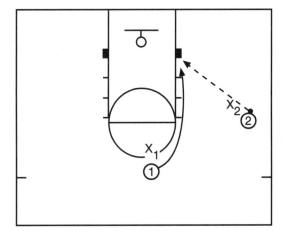

Give-and-go

Skill Analysis

Drive-and-Dish

1. Player 1 drives past the defender toward the basket.
2. Help side defenders leave Player 2 and move to stop Player 1's drive.
3. Player 1 passes to Player 2 who was left open when the help side defender moved to stop the drive.
4. Player 2 shoots the ball. Player 1 blocks out to rebound in case of a missed shot.

Give-and-Go

1. Player 1 passes to an open teammate.
2. After the pass, Player 1 fakes a step or two away from the ball and then uses a change-of-direction step to move in front of the defender toward the ball.
3. Player 1 drives hard to the basket with an arm and target hand extended, expecting a return pass.
4. Player 2 passes the ball back to Player 1.
5. Player 1 shoots the layup. Player 2 drives to the basket to attempt to rebound in case of a missed shot.

From *Learning by Choice in Secondary Physical Education: Creating a Goal-Directed Program* by Kevin Kaardal, 2001, Champaign, IL: Human Kinetics.

Setting the screen

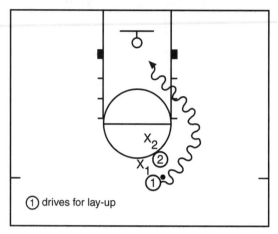

① drives for lay-up

Defense does not react

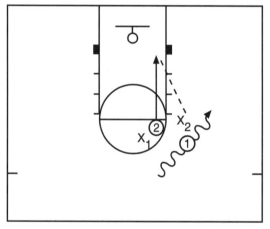

Defense switches

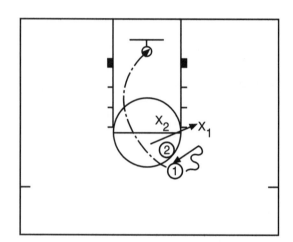

Defense slides through

Skill Analysis

Screen-and-Roll

1. Player 1 has the ball.
2. Player 2 sets a screen for Player 1 by straddling Defender 1's leg in the direction Player 2 wants Player 1 to drive.
3. Player 1 jab-steps in the opposite direction of the screen then drives off Player 2's shoulder toward the basket.
4. Player 1 needs to read the defense's reaction to the screen:
   a. If the defense does not react, Player 1 drives to the basket.
   b. If the defense switches checks, Player 1 dribbles in a diagonal path toward the sideline or baseline to create a passing lane for Player 2. Immediately after Player 1 runs off the screen, Player 2 back-pivots and slides to the basket. This maneuver, known as the "roll," effectively seals Defender 1 behind Player 2, leaving Player 2 open for a return pass from Player 1 and an open shot.
   c. If the defense slides through the screen, Player 1 crossover-dribbles to change direction and creates an open shot by shooting over Player 2, who is still holding the screen.

From *Learning by Choice in Secondary Physical Education: Creating a Goal-Directed Program* by Kevin Kaardal, 2001, Champaign, IL: Human Kinetics.

Offense—Team

Concept

The offensive team tries to create an open shot by bringing offensive players who are positioned on the opposite side of the court from the ball (called the "weak side") to the ball handler's side of the court (the "strong side"). The offense should cut to open spaces on the strong side before the defense can adjust, potentially resulting in open shots. During three-on-three play, offensive teams can use all the skills and plays described in one-on-one play and two-on-two play. Also, the offensive team may use the specific play designed to create an open space for the weak side offensive player: the screen-away.

Skill Analysis

Screen-Away

1. Player 1 has the ball in the wing area.
2. Player 2 sets a screen for Player 3 by straddling Defender 3's leg in the direction Player 2 wants Player 3 to drive.
3. Player 3 jab-steps in the opposite direction of the screen and then cuts off Player 2's shoulder toward the open space created by the screen.
4. Player 2 needs to read the defense's reaction to the screen:
   a. If the defense does not react, Player 3 cuts to the basket.
   b. If the defense switches checks, Player 3 cuts hard toward the ball. Immediately after Player 3 runs off the screen, Player 2 back-pivots and slides to the basket. This roll effectively seals Defender 2 behind Player 2, leaving Player 2 open for a return pass from Player 1 and an open shot. Player 1 may also pass to Player 3.
   c. If the defense slides through the screen, Player 3 uses a change-of-direction step and creates a chance for an open shot by fading to the open spot behind the screen. Player 1 skip-passes the ball to Player 3, who shoots over Player 2's screen.

Skill Practice

Level A: In groups of six, practice running each two-on-two play as described in the Skill Analysis section. Alternate playing offense and defense. The defense may not use their hands to defend. Try each play five times per team.

Level B: While playing Three-on-Three, practice running the screen-away as described in the Skill Analysis section. Alternate playing offense and defense, defense playing at full speed. Try each play five times per team.

Level C: While playing full-sided (five-against-five) games, attempt screen-away plays.

Skill Mastery

Levels A, B, & C: Successfully execute the screen-away play every four of five attempts. You are successful if the play results in an open shot, whether you score or not.

(continued)

From *Learning by Choice in Secondary Physical Education: Creating a Goal-Directed Program* by Kevin Kaardal, 2001, Champaign, IL: Human Kinetics.

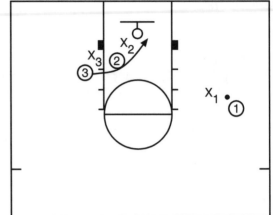

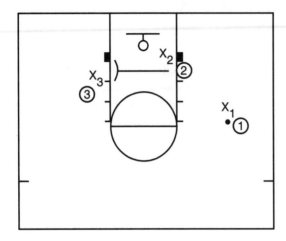

Defense does not react

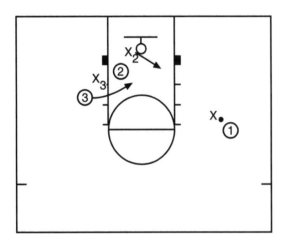

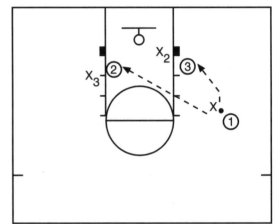

Defense switches

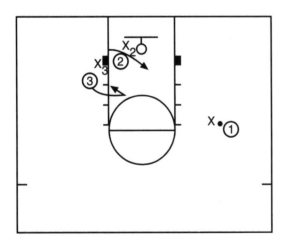

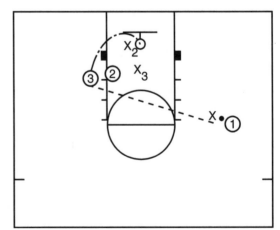

Defense slides through

Offense—Team

Concept

Five-on-five offense uses the same offensive maneuvers that occur in one-on-one, two-on-two, and three-on-three offenses. But the maneuvers described on this poster happen in an organized fashion with five players working together to produce the best opportunity for a teammate to score. Consider the following principles when designing an offense: spacing, timing and triangles, areas of attack, and responsibility (STAR).

Skill Analysis

Refer to the Skill Analysis sections of the five STAR offense diagrams (forms B.51, a-e).

Skill Practice

Level A: Design and practice a STAR-principle offense against player-to-player defense, using a one-two-two formation. Include a screen-away maneuver and a give-and-go maneuver. Draw a diagram of your offense on the court sheets provided. Practice five-on-zero, then after mastering the movement pattern, go against a passive defense, then against an aggressive defense. Teach your offense to a group of your classmates.

Level B: Same as Level A, except the offense must maintain continuity and balance. "Continuity" is when players may change positions through the various maneuvers of the offense, but the positions in the offense are always occupied. It is also when after a set of offensive maneuvers each player finishes in their original starting position. "Balance" is the number of players on each half of the court as divided by an imaginary line down the center of the key. Draw a diagram and practice as in Level A. Teach your offense to a group of your classmates.

Level C: Same as Level A, except research and design offenses against each of the following zone defenses: two-three zone, one-three-one zone, and three-two match-up zone. See the bibliography on page 253 for suggested resources. Draw a diagram and practice as in Level A. Teach your offense to a group of your classmates.

Skill Mastery

Levels A, B, & C: Turn in your diagrams to the teacher. The teacher must believe he or she would be able to help teach your classmates how to perform your offense, using the principles of STAR. The players who were taught your offense must be able to demonstrate it in a five-on-five scrimmage.

From *Learning by Choice in Secondary Physical Education: Creating a Goal-Directed Program* by Kevin Kaardal, 2001, Champaign, IL: Human Kinetics.

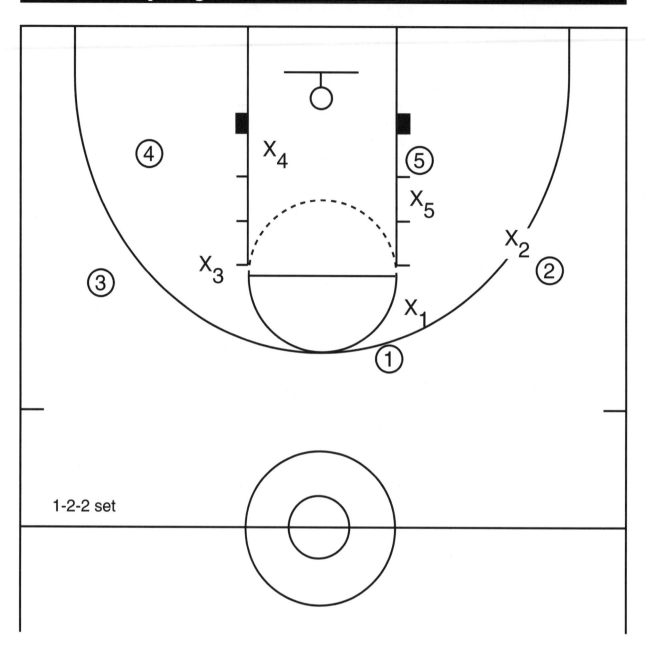

1-2-2 set

Skill Analysis

Consider how your offense may make best use of the court space in the offensive end. Spread out enough to make it difficult for the defense to defend the ball with more than one player at a time. A 12- to 15-foot separation between each offensive player is a good starting point. Consider the court positions each player will take in the offense. The most common formations are one-two-two, one-three-one, or three-two. Against zone defenses, players must space themselves in the "seams" of the zone (the spaces halfway between two defenders in the zone).

From *Learning by Choice in Secondary Physical Education: Creating a Goal-Directed Program* by Kevin Kaardal, 2001, Champaign, IL: Human Kinetics.

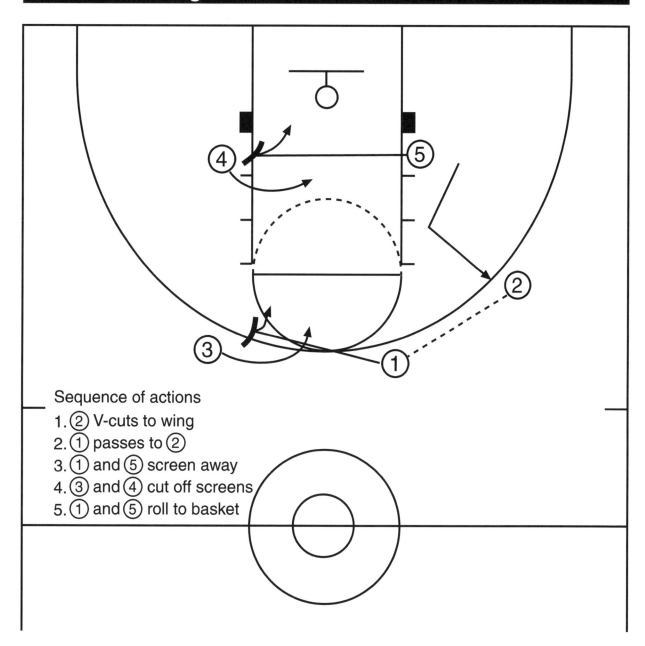

Sequence of actions
1. ② V-cuts to wing
2. ① passes to ②
3. ① and ⑤ screen away
4. ③ and ④ cut off screens
5. ① and ⑤ roll to basket

Skill Analysis

Consider when each offensive maneuver will occur and in what order. For example, picture two players without the ball running a screen, away from the ball-side low post at the same time as the point guard and the wing, running a give-and-go. This will result in two offensive players' occupying and possibly colliding in the same space at the same time. Therefore, it is important to time each maneuver so that you do not interfere with a teammate's moves. In the example, this may involve clearing the ball-side low post before passing in the give-and-go. At the end of the ball cut, the point guard sets the screen-away.

From *Learning by Choice in Secondary Physical Education: Creating a Goal-Directed Program* by Kevin Kaardal, 2001, Champaign, IL: Human Kinetics.

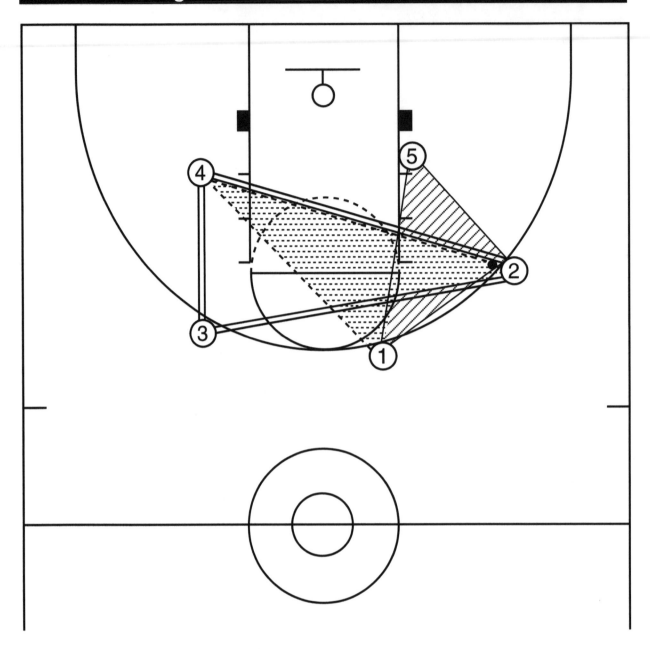

Skill Analysis

Offensive players should try to create deep triangles with each player's body position in relation to the ball. This will make passing easier as the passer will have a greater range of angles to deliver a pass, making it more difficult for the defenders to intercept the ball. Deep triangle formations will spread the defense out, creating space for the offense to maneuver within.

From *Learning by Choice in Secondary Physical Education: Creating a Goal-Directed Program* by Kevin Kaardal, 2001, Champaign, IL: Human Kinetics.

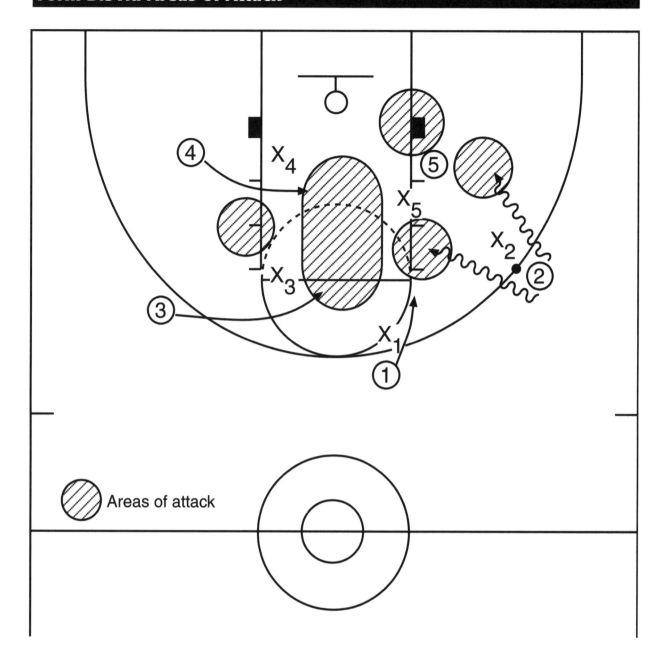

Areas of attack

Skill Analysis

Design the offense to create areas of attack for each maneuver. This is generally done by clearing out weak side defenders or strong side defenders from the area on the court so that one-on-one may occur from that space or an offensive player may cut to that now open space to receive a pass. The offense wants one-on-one situations because there is no help defense to stop the ball handler. Since defense generally reacts to what the offense does, these defenders can be cleared out by positioning offensive players away from the area of attack initially or by using screens and ball cuts (see diagrams).

From *Learning by Choice in Secondary Physical Education: Creating a Goal-Directed Program* by Kevin Kaardal, 2001, Champaign, IL: Human Kinetics.

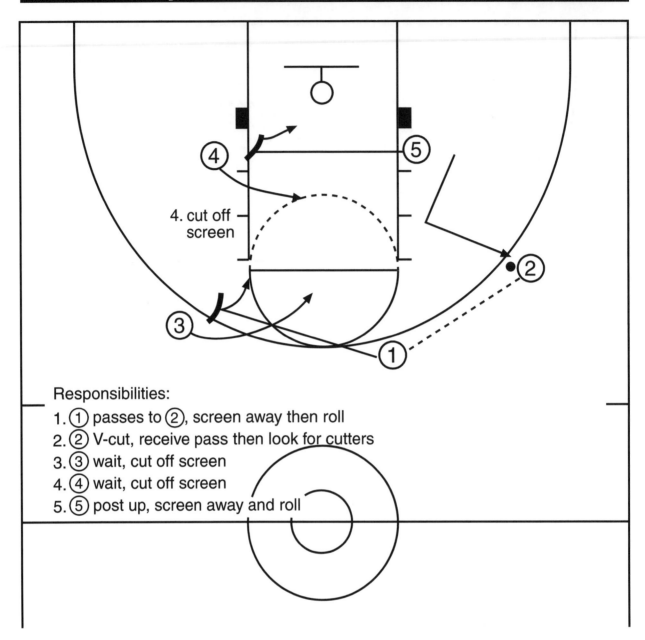

4. cut off screen

Responsibilities:

1. ① passes to ②, screen away then roll
2. ② V-cut, receive pass then look for cutters
3. ③ wait, cut off screen
4. ④ wait, cut off screen
5. ⑤ post up, screen away and roll

Skill Analysis

Each offensive player has to understand the responsibilities he or she has during different phases of the offense—whether setting screens, playing safety (protecting the basket from fast break attacks), or attempting to rebound after a shot attempt. What these responsibilities are depends on the design of the offense and the particular skills of the player. One responsibility you always have, though, is to always be able to see the ball (except when setting a screen away from the ball).

From *Learning by Choice in Secondary Physical Education: Creating a Goal-Directed Program* by Kevin Kaardal, 2001, Champaign, IL: Human Kinetics.

Form B.52 Defensive Stance

Defense—Individual

Concept

As a defender, a slightly exaggerated ready position allows you to move quickly laterally (side to side) and close open spaces.

Skill Analysis

Use the ready position with the following adjustments:

1. Place your feet slightly wider than shoulder-width apart.
2. Hold the arm in line with the ball at ear level to block that passing lane.
3. Hold the arm away from the ball low to prevent crossover dribbling.

Skill Practice

Level A: Practice assuming the defensive stance on command.

Level B: Assume the defensive stance after tossing the ball to a partner.

Level C: During full-sided/five-on-five game situations, assume the defensive stance each time your check (defender) receives the ball.

Skill Mastery

Level A: Demonstrate the defensive stance on command, using correct form.

Level B: Assume the defensive stance correctly 9 of 10 times your partner receives the ball.

Level C: In a three-on-three situation, assume defensive stance 9 of every 10 times your check receives the ball.

From *Learning by Choice in Secondary Physical Education: Creating a Goal-Directed Program* by Kevin Kaardal, 2001, Champaign, IL: Human Kinetics.

Defense—Individual

Concept

Use the defensive shuffle step to direct offensive players away from the basket to the sidelines. Also shuffle-step to direct the ball handler to the help side defense so that the dribbler can be double-teamed.

Skill Analysis

1. In defensive stance, shuffle-step (see form B.19).
2. The defender's (your) head should be in line with the ball. Watch the dribbler's chest.
3. Position your body to angle the dribbler either to the sideline or to the help side (see diagram).

Skill Practice

Level A: Shuffle-step five court lengths in a zigzag pattern.

Level B: Shuffle-step five court lengths in a zigzag pattern while defending a dribbler.

Level C: Shuffle-step to move the dribbler to a help side defender or to the sideline in a game of Two-on-Two, Three-on-Three, or Four-on-Four.

Skill Mastery

Level A: Finish four of five court lengths, staying in defensive stance and keeping your feet from crossing over or touching.

Level B: Finish four of five court lengths, staying between the dribbler and the basket.

Level C: Move the dribbler to a help side defender or to the sideline, 7 of 10 attempts.

From *Learning by Choice in Secondary Physical Education: Creating a Goal-Directed Program* by Kevin Kaardal, 2001, Champaign, IL: Human Kinetics.

Defense—Individual

Concept

If the dribbler runs past you as a defender, back-pivot then sprint to get back between the dribbler and your team's basket to prevent an uncontested layup.

Skill Analysis

1. Drop-step (back-pivot) once the dribbler runs by you.
2. Then turn and chase the dribbler.
3. Run to where the dribbler is going. (Don't follow the dribbler—*anticipate* and run ahead to a spot on the court in the path of the dribbler).
4. Assume defensive stance and begin directing the dribbler's progress away from the basket or to the help side.

Skill Practice

Level A: On a zigzag obstacle course of six or more cones, drop-step and recover the length of the court, recovering to each cone.

Level B: Drop-step and recover in a zigzag pattern for the length of the sideline while defending a dribbler.

Level C: Shuffle-step to move the dribbler to help side or to the sideline in a game of Two-on-Two, Three-on-Three, or Four-on-Four.

Skill Mastery

Level A: Practice the drop step, running at half speed, successfully recovering to a position in front of each cone on four of five attempts.

Level B: Finish four of five lengths, staying between the dribbler and the basket.

Level C: Move the dribbler to the help side or to the sideline, 7 of 10 attempts.

Overhead view of the drop step

Overhead view of the recovery

From *Learning by Choice in Secondary Physical Education: Creating a Goal-Directed Program* by Kevin Kaardal, 2001, Champaign, IL: Human Kinetics.

Defense—Individual

Concept

When a ball handler has picked up the ball and used up his or her dribbles, close the space between you and the ball handler to prevent easy shots or passes.

Skill Analysis

1. Get close, about a half an arm's length away.
2. Follow the ball's movements with both hands, mirroring the actions of the ball handler.
3. Stay low in a defensive stance.

Skill Practice

Level A: Practice mirroring the ball handler's movements five times for 10 seconds each time.

Level B: Play a three-person Keep-Away game, challenging the passer.

Level C: Ball-challenge ball handlers who use up their dribbles during modified game situations.

Skill Mastery

Level A: Keep your hands in front of the ball for the full 10 seconds .

Level B: Deflect 3 of every 10 passes attempted during Keep-Away.

Level C: Change the passer's movement patterns forcing a lob pass or a pass away from the basket. (A lob pass is an overhead pass that takes a flight path that resembles the flight path of a shot.)

From *Learning by Choice in Secondary Physical Education: Creating a Goal-Directed Program* by Kevin Kaardal, 2001, Champaign, IL: Human Kinetics.

Defense—Individual

Concept

You have the right to a body-width space that stretches from where your feet touch the floor straight up to the ceiling. Players causing contact with another player in that player's space are guilty of fouling that player. The defense uses this rule when the defender runs in front of an offensive player's intended path and establishes a legal position by planting both feet on the ground in that path before any contact occurs. This effectively closes that space or lane to the advancing offensive player. Sometimes the offensive player is unable or unwilling to stop and crashes into the defender. This foul is called "charging." If the defender does not prepare and react to the contact properly, injuries could result for both players.

Skill Analysis

1. Get into a defensive stance.
2. Use your hands and arms to help cushion the initial contact with the offensive player by placing them tightly in front of your torso.
3. As the player makes contact with you, sit down quickly, cushioning your fall with your hands, arms, and buttocks.
4. Slide backward when you make contact with the floor.

Skill Practice

Level A: Assume a defensive stance. As a partner pushes you backward, practice sitting down and sliding back quickly, to absorb the force of the push. Do 10 times.

Level B: Same as Level A, but have a partner charge you.

Level C: During small-sided games, try to take the charge of an offensive player if the situation warrants it.

Skill Mastery

Levels A & B: Land safely in control of your body, 8 of 10 trials.

Level C: Legally take the charge, 4 of 5 trials.

Basketball

From *Learning by Choice in Secondary Physical Education: Creating a Goal-Directed Program* by Kevin Kaardal, 2001, Champaign, IL: Human Kinetics.

Defense—Individual

Concept

Rebounding is the way the defense gains possession of the ball after a missed shot, ending the offense's opportunity to score during a given sequence of play. Reduce the number of shot opportunities the offense has by successfully rebounding the first shot taken. Defensive rebounding also begins the transition into offense by starting the fast break with an outlet pass.

Skill Analysis

Blocking Out

1. If the offensive player is outside the key area, watch the player until he or she makes a move toward the missed shot, then step in his or her path to the ball using a front pivot.

2. If the offensive player is inside the key, upon the shooter's release of the ball reverse-pivot into your opponent, putting your body between the ball and the offensive player.

Front pivot blockout

From *Learning by Choice in Secondary Physical Education: Creating a Goal-Directed Program* by Kevin Kaardal, 2001, Champaign, IL: Human Kinetics.

Attack, Land, and Outlet-Pass

1. After blocking out, take off with both feet to attack the ball and catch it at the peak of your jump.
2. Land in the triple threat position, pivot to the outside of the court, and pass to an open teammate.

Reverse pivot blockout

Skill Practice

Level A: (1) Block out a partner 20 times as he or she mimics the shooting action (without a ball). (2) Toss the ball off the wall at a height of 10 feet, take off with both feet to attack the ball aggressively, and catch the ball at the highest point of the jump.

Level B: Block out an active opponent and rebound, 20 times. Practice 10 from outside the key, front-pivoting, and 10 from inside the key, reverse-pivoting.

Level C: Add a defender on the rebounder and intended pass receiver. Make 10 outlet passes to a teammate after successfully rebounding the ball. Low control-dribble to get in an open position to make the pass safely.

Skill Mastery

Level A: (1) Make contact with your opponent, 20 of 20 attempts. Successfully keep the offensive player behind you 16 of 20 attempts. (2) Make 8 of 10 attempts.

Levels B & C: Make 8 of 10 attempts for each type of blocking out.

Modified Games

One-on-One, Two-on-Two, Three-on-Three, Box-Out

From *Learning by Choice in Secondary Physical Education: Creating a Goal-Directed Program* by Kevin Kaardal, 2001, Champaign, IL: Human Kinetics.

Defense—Team

Concept

To stop the offense from moving the ball into high-percentage scoring areas (open spaces close to the basket), the defense must close spaces near offensive players. One skill that helps you do this is the "half-front," or "denial," position, in which defensive players who are one pass away from the ball deny their offensive check's passing lane by positioning their bodies in the half-front defensive stance.

Skill Analysis

1. Assume the defensive stance.
2. Straddle the leg nearest the basket of the potential pass receiver.
3. Place an arm in the passing lane, palm facing the ball and thumb pointing to the floor.
4. Stay between a half and one arm's length away from the pass receiver.
5. Position your head so that you can see both the passer and your check.

Skill Practice

Level A: Assume the half-front position on command, 10 times.

Level B: Play Keep-Away, denying the pass receiver, 20 passes.

Level C: In Three-on-Three, try to deny your offensive check the ball each time he or she becomes a potential pass receiver.

Skill Mastery

Level A: Half-front, demonstrating all Skill Analysis section components 8 of 10 times.

Level B: Deflect four of five passes in Keep-Away.

Level C: Successfully deny three of five pass attempts during the Three-on-Three practice game.

Modified Games

Keep-Away, Two-on-Two, Three-on-Three

From *Learning by Choice in Secondary Physical Education: Creating a Goal-Directed Program* by Kevin Kaardal, 2001, Champaign, IL: Human Kinetics.

Defense—Team

Concept

Defending players full-front to deny a pass into the low post area, a high-percentage scoring area. To full-front, the low post defender will need the help of a teammate in a help side position. Defenders may also full-front when the ball handler has picked up the dribble. The player on the ball closes out and plays aggressive, on-the-ball defense, while all other defensive players full-front their checks to deny passes, forcing a five-second violation.

Skill Analysis

1. Assume the defensive stance.
2. Stand directly between the passer and the potential pass receiver (your check).
3. Position your body so that you can see the ball and still contact your check.
4. Communicate with the help side teammates you are full-fronting so that they are ready to defend the lob pass.
5. Keep your arms up at shoulder height, elbows bent. Move with the pass if attempted.

Skill Practice

Level A: Play Keep-Away, forcing the passer to throw lob passes.

Level B: In a four-person drill (see diagram), position one passer 18 feet from the basket foul line, extended at a 45 degree angle from the basket. Position another pass receiver on the low block, one defender fronting the pass receiver and one help side defender under the basket, with the ball to the low post. Score one point per successful entry pass, two points per basket. For the defense, score one point per successful deflection.

Level C: Full-front the post during full-sided games.

Skill Evaluation

Level A: Force 9 of 10 passes to be lob passes while playing Keep-Away.

Level B: Play five games (of the drill described) up to 10 points. The defense must win at least three of five games.

Level C: Successfully deny four of five passes into the low post.

Modified Games

Keep-Away, Four-on-Four

From *Learning by Choice in Secondary Physical Education: Creating a Goal-Directed Program* by Kevin Kaardal, 2001, Champaign, IL: Human Kinetics.

Defense—Team

Concept

On offense, a screen helps you close the space beside a defender by straddling the defender's leg and standing still. This opens up the space behind the screener for you to use. There are three ways to defend the screen: the switch, the slide-through, and over-the-top. The most effective method is going over the top of the screen.

Skill Analysis

The Switch

1. The defensive player (2), whose check is setting the screen, switches checks, defending the offensive player (A), who is running or dribbling off the screen.
2. The defender (1) who is being screened spins off the screen to establish a position between the screener (B) and the basket.

The Slide-Through

1. The defender (1) being screened slides behind the screen, between the screener (B) and the screener's defender (2) and meets the player cutting off the screen (A) on the other side. This maneuver effectively closes the space opened with the screen.
2. The defender (2) whose check (B) is screening must communicate with the defender (1) who is being screened. The screener's defender (2) makes space by backing off the screen, allowing room for the defender of the cutter (1) to slide through. The screener's defender (2) may also help by pulling the teammate (1) through the screen.

Over-the-Top

1. The defender (2) of the screener communicates to the teammate (1) being screened by shouting, "Screen coming (left or right)."
2. The defender (1) of the cutter jumps closer to the offensive cutter (A) in the communicated direction. Once the screen is set, the defender of the cutter (1) shuffle-steps over the screen and continues to defend the cutter.

Skill Practice for All Screens

Level A: In a two-on-two practice drill at half speed, practice each skill with classmates who are practicing the screen-and-roll. Try each method five times.

Level B: In a three-on-three practice drill, defend screens away from the ball at half speed. Try each method five times.

Level C: In a Three-on-Three or full-sided game, defend screens as they develop. Choose one method until five screens have been set, then switch methods until you have practiced each type.

Skill Mastery

Levels A, B, & C: Defend four of five screens successfully for each method.

Modified Games

Two-on-Two, Three-on-Three, Four-on-Four

From *Learning by Choice in Secondary Physical Education: Creating a Goal-Directed Program* by Kevin Kaardal, 2001, Champaign, IL: Human Kinetics.

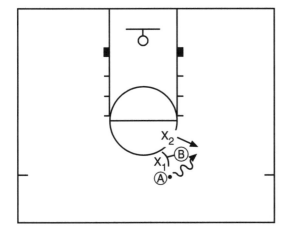 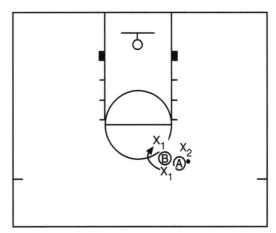

The switch

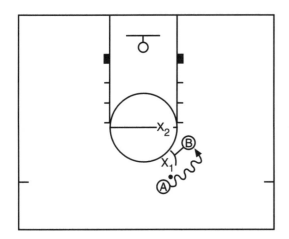 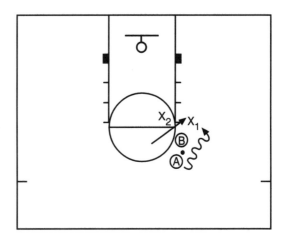

The slide-through

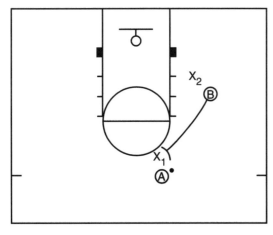 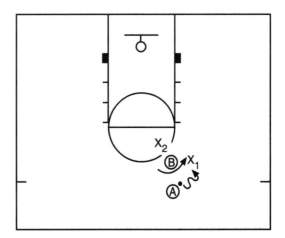

Over-the-top

From *Learning by Choice in Secondary Physical Education: Creating a Goal-Directed Program* by Kevin Kaardal, 2001, Champaign, IL: Human Kinetics.

Defense—Team

Concept

The primary responsibility of the defense is to stop the ball from advancing close to the basket, allowing the offense to shoot short shots or layups. Therefore, every player on defense is responsible for guarding their check and the ball at the same time.

Skill Analysis

In Deny Position

1. As a defender, you should see the ball and your check.
2. Attack the ball handler if she beats her defender on the ball.
3. Stay with the ball handler until she picks up the dribble and her original defender has recovered and is guarding her again.
4. Quickly recover (return) to guard your check.

Away From the Ball

1. Open up your body position to face away from the basket.
2. Point at your check and the ball handler.
3. Assume a position halfway between the ball handler and your check.
4. Attack the ball handler if he beats his defender on the ball.
5. Stay with the ball handler until he begins dribbling and his original defender has recovered and is guarding him.
6. All players may need to switch checks after the help occurs to cover the closest players to the basket in sequence. (After the player nearest the ball carrier switches from the player he was defending to cover the ball handler, his former check will be open to recover or cover all players. So the defending team members may all have to rotate checks in sequence. The nearest player to the open player moves to guard that player, which creates a chain reaction where each player now closest to the next open player moves to check that player until the last player left open is the offensive player farthest from the ball. That player is often picked up by the player who was originally beat or broken down off the dribble, cut, or screen.)

Skill Practice

Level A: Play Two-on-Two, practicing help side defense.

Level B: Play Three-on-Three, practicing help side defense.

Level C: (1) In a four-player shell formation, in which there is no post player and all players defend the perimeter of the key, practice jumping to help position as the ball is passed around the outside of the shell. Offense may not dribble. (2) In the shell, leave your check and jump to help stop the dribbler from penetrating to the basket. After stopping the dribbler, recover to defend your check. Offensive players are limited to three dribbles. (3) Play Four-on-Four, practicing help side defense.

Skill Mastery

Level A: The defender is in help side position four of five opportunities.

Level B: The defender is in help side position four of five opportunities.

Level C: (1) Complete 8 of 10 trials with every player jumping to help side. (2) Complete 8 of 10 trials with every player jumping to help and then recovering to their check or switching to the closest check to the basket. (3) In help side position, react and recover four of five opportunities.

From *Learning by Choice in Secondary Physical Education: Creating a Goal-Directed Program* by Kevin Kaardal, 2001, Champaign, IL: Human Kinetics.

Modified Games

Two-on-Two, Three-on-Three, and Four-on-Four

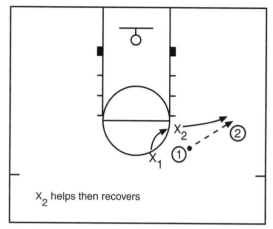

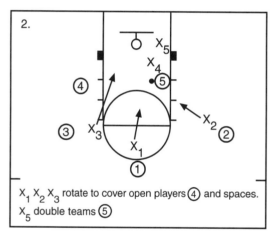

X₂ helps then recovers

In deny position

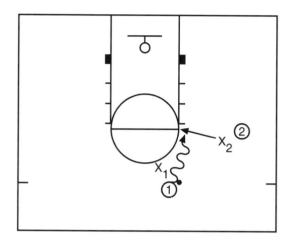

1.

X₄ helps

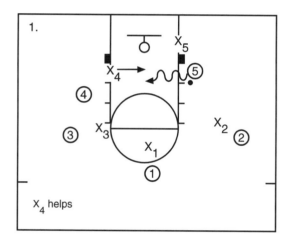

2.

X₁ X₂ X₃ rotate to cover open players ④ and spaces.
X₅ double teams ⑤

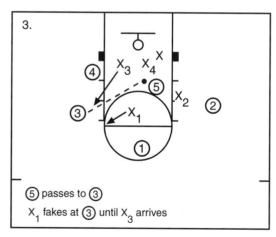

3.

⑤ passes to ③

X₁ fakes at ③ until X₃ arrives

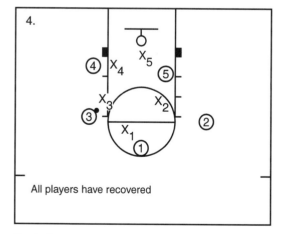

4.

All players have recovered

Away from the ball

Defense—Team

Concept

To create an easy scoring opportunity, the offense tries to advance the ball quickly down court before all defensive players can make the transition from offense to defense. To prevent this, the defense tries to slow the progress of the ball and still protect the basket by defending the ball handler and all players open and ahead of the ball handler. If the offense has already moved the ball even with or past the defenders, the defenders first retreat to the key to prevent an uncontested layup then find the nearest open offensive player to defend. If the offense beats the defense down court and outnumbers them, the defense can adopt movement patterns that give them a better chance of keeping the offense from scoring.

Skill Analysis

1. One-on-Two Defense
2. Two-on-Three, or Tandem, Defense

Skill Practice

One-on-Two Defense

Level A: Practice with players who are working on their two-on-one fast break skills. Practice faking at your opponents to make them pass the ball, then get in front of the path of the receiver; do 10 times.

Level B: Practice aggressive defense against players who are working on two-on-one fast break skills. You must stop the dribbler and then recover quickly to defend the pass receiver; do 10 times.

Level C: Practice aggressive defense against players who are working on two-on-one transition offense skills. Use as many fakes as you can, trying not to commit to guarding anyone until the player begins to drive for the goal; do 10 times.

Two-on-Three Defense (Tandem Defense)

Level A: Practice with players who are working on three-on-two transition offensive skills. At half speed without using your hands to check, practice the rotations as described in the Skill Analysis section; do 10 times.

Level B: Same as for Level A, but at three-quarter speed.

Level C: Same as for Level A, but at full speed.

Skill Mastery

Levels A & B: Recover to a legal defensive position ahead of the offense 7 of 10 times.

Level C: Stop the offense from scoring one of every three attempts.

From *Learning by Choice in Secondary Physical Education: Creating a Goal-Directed Program* by Kevin Kaardal, 2001, Champaign, IL: Human Kinetics.

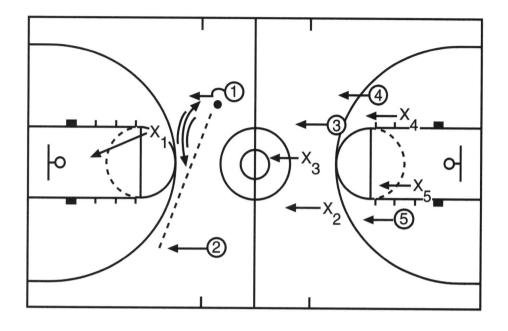

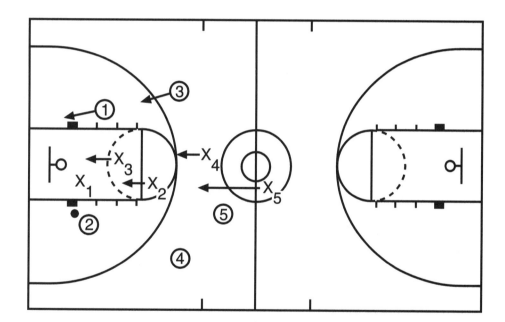

Skill Analysis

One Defender Versus Two Offensive Players

1. Retreat to the center of the key area, looking at both players.
2. Head- and shoulder-fake at the dribbler, trying to get the dribbler to pick up the ball and attempt to pass to the other offensive player.
3. Jump ahead of the dribbler's path as soon as the dribbler starts to cut to the basket to start a layup.
4. Watch what happens then make a decision to act based on what you see.
   a. If the dribbler continues to drive, hold the defensive position and take the charge.
   b. If the dribbler passes the ball to a teammate, try to intercept the ball. If you can't, follow the flight path of the ball, aggressively defending the pass receiver, hoping to prevent an open shot and giving your teammates time to arrive to help defend the basket.

From *Learning by Choice in Secondary Physical Education: Creating a Goal-Directed Program* by Kevin Kaardal, 2001, Champaign, IL: Human Kinetics.

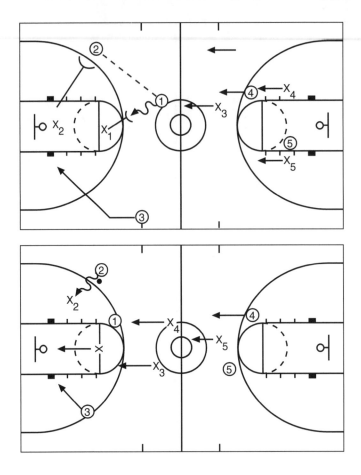

Skill Analysis

Two Defenders Versus Three Offensive Players (Tandem Defense)

1. Retreat to the center of the key, with one player actively waiting for the attacking offense near the top of the key's jump circle (referred to as Defender 1) and the other about halfway up the key (referred to as Defender 2)

2. Defender 1 stops the dribbler from advancing by checking closely.

3. Defender 2 reacts to the dribbler's first pass and closes out on the wing to guard the pass recipient.

4. Defender 1 then leaves the dribbler and retreats to the back of the key just in front of the basket and guards against any attempt to pass the ball across the key to the other wing player who is driving to the basket. This defender must also react to the next pass whether it goes cross-court or back to the original dribbler who is likely waiting at the corner of the foul line.

5. If the wing player who received the first pass passes the ball after receiving it, Defender 1 (who has rotated to the bottom of the key) must go and defend the new pass receiver. As Defender 1 leaves the area just in front of the basket, Defender 2 must run to replace Player 1 in this area and defend against any cross-court passes or drives to the basket until help arrives.

From *Learning by Choice in Secondary Physical Education: Creating a Goal-Directed Program* by Kevin Kaardal, 2001, Champaign, IL: Human Kinetics.

Defense—Team

Concept

Sometimes the defense applies extra pressure to the ball handler by "double-teaming," when two defensive players guard the ball handler at the same time to cause the player to throw a bad pass or lose control of the ball. Double-teaming, or "trapping," is risky. If done poorly, the ball handler will pass to the teammate left open by the defensive player who came to double-team. The offensive player receiving the pass is then undefended and able to take an open shot. If done well, the defense can disrupt the offense's timing, causing a turnover or a hurried, difficult shot.

Skill Analysis

To double-team effectively, the ball handler must be in a position so that all or some of the following conditions are met: facing away from and unable to see the rest of the offensive players; near a sideline or just over the 10-second line; or in an area very close to the basket, preparing to shoot. When two players are double-teaming, the other three defensive players must play help side defense, denying the passing lanes.

1. If the dribbler is facing away from the rest of the offensive team, an effective double-team can occur. The defender guarding a player near the dribbler can sneak up quickly, trapping the dribbler before she can turn back to face the offensive team and see who is open for a pass.

2. If the dribbler is near a sideline or has just come over the 10-second line, the defender coming to set the double-team positions his body to dictate the dribbler's movements back toward the boundary line. This limits the dribbler's options and space to play. Try this only when the first condition of double-teaming is also occurring (step 1 of this description). If not, the offensive player passes to the teammate left open by the defensive player who came to double-team the ball handler.

3. If the ball handler is near the basket and initiates a move toward the basket, then the help side defensive player closest to the attacker should double-team the ball handler. After stopping the drive, the player who double-teams should recover to her check. All other players should rotate to cover the remaining four players as described on form B.61 Help Side and Recovering and form B.64 Five-on-Five Disrupting STAR defense posters.

Skill Practice

Level A: Playing Two-on-Two from at least half-court, practice double-teaming a dribbler and dictating the dribbler to the sidelines. (Position your defensive stance to encourage the dribbler to move in a given direction, hedging your court position in relation to the dribbler so you close a particular path on the floor. If the dribbler continued in that direction he would charge the defender.) Double-team as near the sidelines as possible. The dribbler may not pass the ball until the double-team has occurred. Each team tries 10 times.

Level B: Playing Three-on-Three from at least half-court, practice double-teaming a dribbler and dictating the dribbler to the sidelines. The third player not involved in the pass must try to intercept the pass made by the dribbler. The dribbler may not make a forward pass. Each team tries 10 times.

Level C: Playing a full-sided game, double-team offensive players whenever the correct conditions exist (see Skill Analysis section).

(continued)

From *Learning by Choice in Secondary Physical Education: Creating a Goal-Directed Program* by Kevin Kaardal, 2001, Champaign, IL: Human Kinetics.

Skill Mastery

Levels A, B, & C: Your team is successful if you force a bad pass, cause the offense to commit a violation, or force an offensive player to work hard and make a difficult pass or maneuver to beat the double-team. As a result of the extra work the offensive players made to beat the double-team, the defenders were able to recover and play defense so that no open shot resulted. The team must be successful 8 of 10 attempts.

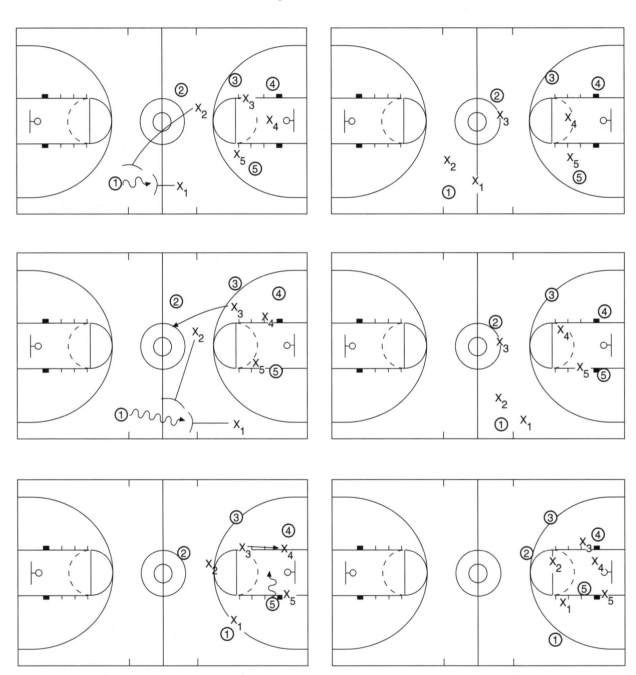

Defense—Team

Concept

Team defense when playing full-sided basketball uses all the concepts introduced in the defensive posters in this program in concert. To stop the offense from executing the maneuvers they want to, the defense may play player-to-player or any number of zone defenses (usually two-three, one-three-one, or three-two match-up zones), or a combination of player-to-player and zone defenses such as the triangle-and-two or box-and-one. Defensive principles can also be broken down into the STAR principles.

Skill Analysis

See diagrams on this poster.

Skill Practice

Level A: Playing Four-on-Four against a stationary (standing-still) offense (then later an offense limited to two dribbles), practice adjusting defensive positions as the ball moves around the offense. The defenders' positions should be as outlined in the Responsibilities section of this poster (form B.64.b).

Level B: Playing a full-sided game against an offense limited to two dribbles (then later against a live offensive unit), practice adjusting defensive positions as the ball moves around the offense. The proper defenders' positions are outlined in the Responsibilities section of this poster (form B.64.b). Alternate practicing half-fronting and full-fronting the post player.

Level C: (1) Research and design one of each of the following zone defenses: two-three zone, one-three-one zone, and three-two match-up zone. Ask the teacher to suggest resources. Draw a diagram of your defense on the court sheets provided. Explain the defense in terms of STAR principles. (2) Practice mastering the movement patterns of the defense, then progress against a stationary offense, then an offense limited to two dribbles, then finally a live offensive unit. Practice adjusting defensive positions as the ball moves around the offense.

Skill Mastery

Level A: Demonstrate proper defense in a four-on-four scrimmage situation.

Level B: Demonstrate proper defense in a full-sided scrimmage situation.

Level C: Turn in your diagrams to the teacher. The teacher should be able to teach your classmates how to perform your defenses, using STAR principles and your research, based on your diagrams. The players taught your defenses must be able to demonstrate them in a full-sided scrimmage.

From *Learning by Choice in Secondary Physical Education: Creating a Goal-Directed Program* by Kevin Kaardal, 2001, Champaign, IL: Human Kinetics.

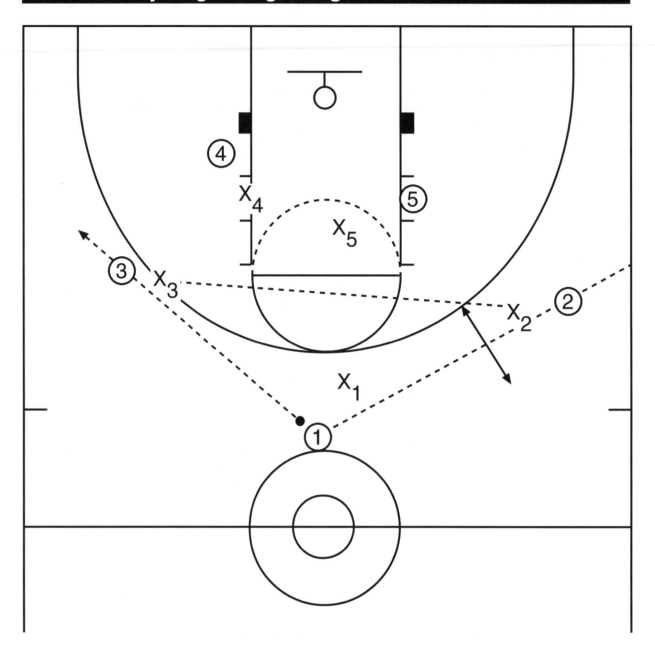

Skill Analysis

The defense's objective is to disrupt the offense's spacing and timing, to flatten the triangles, and take away the areas of attack that the offense attempts to establish. The defense accomplishes this objective by denying passing lanes, beating players making cuts to their intended destination, and playing help side defense.

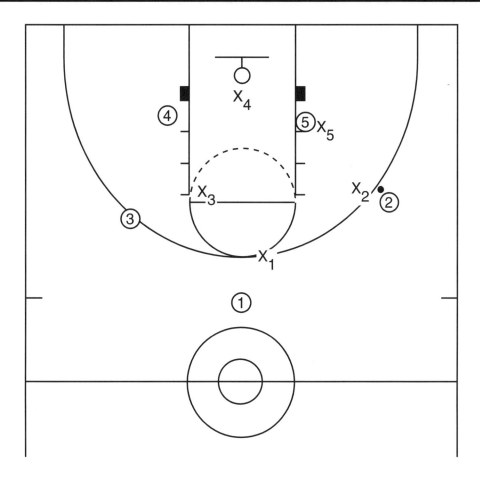

Skill Analysis

To disrupt the offense, defenders must understand their responsibilities in relation to the type of defense they are playing (player-to-player or zone) and the checks' positions on the floor. The responsibilities vary slightly with each type of defense but can be generally summarized as follows:

1. Always see the ball and your check.
2. Respond appropriately to the specific situation:
   a. If your check has the ball, play one-on-one defense, dictating the ball handler to go to the sideline away from the basket.
   b. If your check is one pass away from the ball, play deny defense in the line of the pass toward the ball and be ready to help and recover if the ball handler drives.
   c. If your check is two passes away from the ball, play help side defense toward the ball.
   d. If your check is one pass away from the ball in the post, either half- or full-front this player.

From *Learning by Choice in Secondary Physical Education: Creating a Goal-Directed Program* by Kevin Kaardal, 2001, Champaign, IL: Human Kinetics.

Passing	Improving Accuracy
Inside-of-the-Foot Pass	Diving Header
Instep Pass	
Outside-of-the-Foot Pass	**Shooting**
Raised Pass	Instep and Outside-of-the-Foot Shots
Ball Control	**Game Skills**
Foot	Give-and-Go
Thigh	Takeover
Chest	Overlap
Juggling	
Heading	**Rules**
Controlled Header	
Distance/Clearing Header	**Modified Games**

Note: Instructors can create their own rules poster for the soccer unit. Rules are posted at **www.fifa.com**, the website of Fédération Internationale de Football Association.

Concept

Pass the ball with the inside of your foot when you're looking for a quick, accurate short pass along the ground.

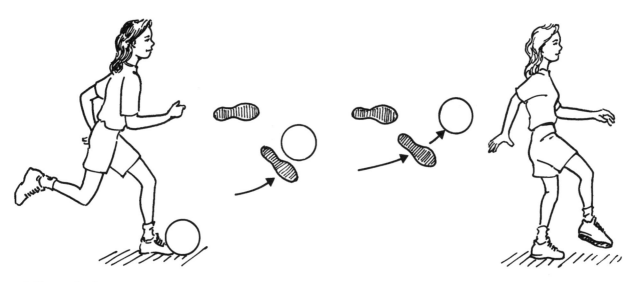

Skill Analysis

1. The approach: The step before the plant is a magic hop. (The magic hop is a transition step where your running momentum is transferred from forward momentum to kicking power by planting the nonkicking foot after an elongated step—the magic hop—to help generate power by allowing for hip rotation.)
2. Plant nonkicking foot directly beside ball.
3. Turn kicking foot 90 degrees so that toes are pointing away from ball.
4. With a short backswing, swing kicking foot crisply through ball, striking the lower middle of ball.
5. Follow through with a step by the nonkicking foot.

Skill Practice

Level A: From 6, 8, and 10 yards away, pass a stationary ball through a set of cones 1 yard apart, 8 of 10 tries.

Level B: Same as Level A, but pass while body and ball are moving (variations: three-touch maximum, two-touch maximum, both feet one-touch total).

Level C: In a game of Three-on-Three, pass the ball to teammates within 1 yard, 10 times in a row.

Skill Mastery

Levels A & B: Each task, 8 of 10 tries successfully.

Level C: Successfully complete 10 passes in a row under pressure.

Modified Games

Keep-Away, Three-on-Three, Four-on-Four. In all games, you score only with an inside pass and must trap with one touch or control the pass by cushioning with two touches, using your feet.

From *Learning by Choice in Secondary Physical Education: Creating a Goal-Directed Program* by Kevin Kaardal, 2001, Champaign, IL: Human Kinetics.

Concept

Use an instep pass when you need more power over a longer distance.

Skill Analysis

1. Approach: Use a magic hop with the last step elongated (stretched out).
2. Place the nonkicking foot next to the ball.
3. Strike the ball lower than the midline of the ball with shoelaces (instep) of kicking foot.
4. Follow through with toes pointed.

Skill Practice

Level A: With a partner 10, 15, 20 yards away, receive a pass, set up the ball while on the move, and pass the moving ball back with the instep, 20 passes each foot.

Level B: Play Keep-Away with three players, passing with each foot. Attempt 10 passes, then change defender.

Level C: Play Three-on-Three, with 10 successful instep passes in a row worth one point.

Skill Mastery

Level A: Complete 16 of 20 passes with each foot.

Level B: Complete 10 passes in a row.

Level C: In a game situation, successfully complete 10 passes in a row with each foot.

Modified Games

Keep-Away, Three-on-Three

From *Learning by Choice in Secondary Physical Education: Creating a Goal-Directed Program* by Kevin Kaardal, 2001, Champaign, IL: Human Kinetics.

Concept

Pass with the outside of your foot when you are trying to deceive the defender or when you want to put an outward spin on the ball.

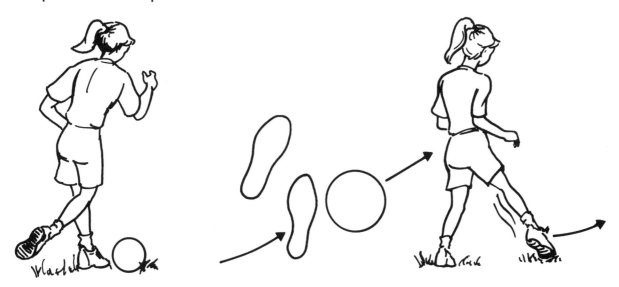

Skill Analysis

1. Approach: Use a magic hop with the last step elongated (stretched out).
2. Place nonkicking foot even with ball.
3. Overrotate kicking foot inward.
4. Strike the ball midway near the side of your little toe.
5. Follow through with your big toe, moving through the plane of the kick.

Skill Practice

Level A: With cones 2 yards apart, pass the ball through the cones with the outside of your foot, from 5, 10, and 15 yards away.

Level B: Play Keep-Away with three players. Five consecutive outside-of-the-foot passes earns one point, but if defender intercepts, change defender. The object is to avoid being in the middle. The game can be modified so everyone plays in the middle; the person with the fewest interceptions over a time limit wins.

Level C: Play Three-on-Three. Five consecutive outside-of-the-foot passes earns one point; five points wins the game.

Skill Mastery

Level A: Successfully complete 8 of 10 tries with each foot.

Levels B & C: Successfully complete five passes in a row.

Modified Games

Keep-Away, Two-on-Two, Three-on-Three

From *Learning by Choice in Secondary Physical Education: Creating a Goal-Directed Program* by Kevin Kaardal, 2001, Champaign, IL: Human Kinetics.

Concept

This long, lofted pass works best when crossing the ball, switching the field sides, or trying to pass over a defender.

Skill Analysis

1. Approach ball with elongated last step (magic hop).
2. Plant nonkicking foot slightly behind ball.
3. Strike ball with your instep below the midline of the ball. As you strike, lean back slightly.
4. Follow through straight forward.

Skill Practice

Level A: Standing 20 yards apart from a partner, see how many times of 10 you can lift the ball and get it to within two steps of your partner. Alternate feet.

Level B: Play Crossbar, passing the ball back and forth.

Level C: Play Any Goal. Playing on teams of three to six, score on any goal, focusing on long passes to switch the momentum of the game and score quick goals.

Skill Mastery

Level A: Successfully complete 8 of 10 passes.

Level B: Score 12 points for mastery.

Level C: Assist on 10 goals; first team to score 15 goals wins game.

Modified Games

Keep-Away, Crossbar, Any Goal, Trick Your Neighbor

From *Learning by Choice in Secondary Physical Education: Creating a Goal-Directed Program* by Kevin Kaardal, 2001, Champaign, IL: Human Kinetics.

Concept

To control the ball and therefore maximize chances to move forward and score, controlling the ball with your thigh and foot is vital.

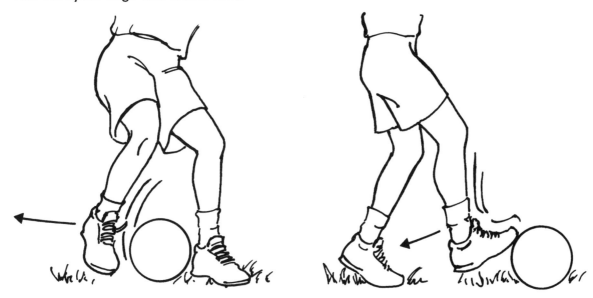

Skill Analysis

Think of your body as a pillow, absorbing the momentum of the ball.

1. Watch the ball onto the inside of your foot.
2. As the ball approaches, allow your foot to retract (pull back) with ball to slow it down and keep it close to your body.
3. Step down, brushing against ball, making it backspin.
4. The ball should end up one step ahead of you.

Skill Practice

Level A: Pass with a partner 10, 15, and 20 yards away, controlling the ball with the inside and outside of the foot, 20 passes each foot. Not moving, then moving across the field facing each other, pass and control the ball.

Level B: Inside a circle of six people, one person controls the ball and one person defends. The people forming the circle start with two balls. The controller must receive the ball from someone forming the circle, then control and pass to a different person. Players play one minute per position, then switch.

Level C: In a Three-on-Three Keep-Away game, control the ball with the inside and outside of the foot. ten controls earn one point. Play to five points. Combine this drill with inside-of-the-foot and outside-of-the-foot passes.

Skill Mastery

Level A: Complete 16 of 20 passes for each foot.

Level B: Control ball for the entire minute without giving it away to the defender.

Level C: Complete 50 controls under pressure, in five sets of 10.

Modified Games

Two-on-Two, Three-on-Three, Keep-Away, Touch Soccer (two- or three-touch limit)

From *Learning by Choice in Secondary Physical Education: Creating a Goal-Directed Program* by Kevin Kaardal, 2001, Champaign, IL: Human Kinetics.

Concept

Using your thigh to control a ball too high to control with your feet keeps the game moving quickly.

Skill Analysis

Think of your body as a pillow, absorbing the momentum of the ball.

1. Face the ball as it approaches you at thigh level. Watch it onto the front of your thigh. Lift leg up so that knee is bent 90 degrees.
2. As the ball hits your thigh, lower your leg to the ground, absorbing the momentum and dropping the ball right at your feet. (Hint: If the ball is bouncing up when you contact it, you are raising your leg too early. Bring your thigh up before the ball hits it.)

Skill Practice

Level A: (1) Have a partner toss a ball to you. Control the ball within one step of yourself, 10 tries each leg. (2) Move across the field with a partner facing you. One of you moves backward and tosses ball to the partner moving forward, who traps ball and passes it back with three touches. Change roles at end of field.

Level B: Inside a circle of 6 to 10 people, one player controls and one defends. The people forming the circle start with two balls. The controller must receive a toss from someone forming the circle, then control and pass it to a different person. Play one minute, then change positions.

Level C: In a Three-on-Three Keep-Away game, control the ball with your thigh whenever possible. Combine these drills with raised passes.

Skill Mastery

Level A: (1) Control 8 of 10 passes, each leg. (2) Control ball entire width of the field.

Level B: Control ball for the entire minute.

Level C: Control under pressure and finish the trap with a productive pass at game speed.

Modified Games

Three-on-Three, Four-on-Four, Touch Soccer (three-touch limit), Relay Races

---

From *Learning by Choice in Secondary Physical Education: Creating a Goal-Directed Program* by Kevin Kaardal, 2001, Champaign, IL: Human Kinetics.

Concept

When the ball is too low to head or too high to trap with your thigh, a chest trap allows you to control the ball and look at the field options at the same time.

Skill Analysis

Think of your body as a pillow, absorbing the momentum of the ball.

1. As the ball is approaching you, lean back slightly, creating a platform with your upper chest.
2. Watch the ball onto that platform.
3. As the ball strikes, bend your knees to absorb the momentum of the ball.
4. The ball should end up at your feet, about one step in front of you.

Skill Practice

Level A: (1) Toss ball so that a partner may chest-trap it, 10 tries. (2) Move across the field with a partner facing you. One of you moves backward and tosses ball to the partner moving forward, who traps the ball and passes it back. Change roles at end of field.

Level B: Inside a circle of 6 to 10 people, one person controls and one defends. The people forming the circle start with two or three balls. The controller must receive a toss from someone who is part of the circle, then control and pass it to a different person. Play one minute, then have the controller and the defender change positions.

Level C: In a Three-on-Three or Four-on-Four Keep-Away game, control the ball with your chest whenever possible (combine with a raised pass when possible).

Skill Mastery

Level A: (1) Control 8 of 10 passes. (2) Control ball entire width of the field.

Level B: Control ball for the entire minute.

Level C: Control under pressure and finish the trap with a productive pass at game speed.

Modified Games

Two-on-Two, Three-on-Three, Four-on-Four, Touch Soccer (two-touch limit)

From *Learning by Choice in Secondary Physical Education: Creating a Goal-Directed Program* by Kevin Kaardal, 2001, Champaign, IL: Human Kinetics.

Concept

If you don't have a passing partner or you want to improve, juggling is the best way to improve your control.

Skill Analysis

Using different parts of your body, keep the ball in the air as long as possible.

Skill Practice

Level A: Juggle the ball, allowing it to bounce once between each strike.

Level B: Juggle the ball without allowing it to bounce between strikes.

Level C: Do milkshakes—up one side of your body and down the other.

Small milkshake: You must strike the ball in this order—foot, knee, head, knee, foot.

Large milkshake: You must strike the ball in this order—foot, knee, shoulder, head, shoulder, knee, foot.

Skill Mastery

Levels A & B: Complete 50 consecutive strikes.

Level C: Complete the sequence of juggles as described in Skill Practice Level C—small milkshake and large milkshake. How many can you do in a row?

From *Learning by Choice in Secondary Physical Education: Creating a Goal-Directed Program* by Kevin Kaardal, 2001, Champaign, IL: Human Kinetics.

Concept

When you have time to create another option, controlled heading allows you to do so.

Skill Analysis

Think of your body as a pillow, absorbing the momentum of the ball.

1. Position your body underneath the ball. Bend knees and keep neck strong.
2. Ball will strike the middle of your forehead at the hairline, which is the hardest part of the skull. Watch the ball onto your forehead. Do not close your eyes—they will close on their own.
3. As the ball strikes your head, bend your knees to absorb the impact.
4. The ball should land at your feet within one step of you.

Skill Practice

Level A: Toss the ball to yourself and practice getting the ball to your feet, 10 tries. Increase toss height as you gain confidence.

Level B: Move across the field with a partner facing you. One of you moves backward and tosses ball to partner moving forward, who heads ball, passing it back with no more than three touches. Change roles at end of field.

Level C: During a Three-on-Three or Four-on-Four Keep-Away game, control the ball with your head whenever possible (combine with a raised pass when possible).

Skill Mastery

Level A: Control 8 of 10 passes.

Level B: Control ball entire width of the field.

Level C: Control under pressure and finish the trap with a productive pass at game speed.

Soccer

From *Learning by Choice in Secondary Physical Education: Creating a Goal-Directed Program* by Kevin Kaardal, 2001, Champaign, IL: Human Kinetics.

Concept

When a ball is too high to trap or there is too much pressure to control it, the best option may be to clear the ball by heading it for distance.

Skill Analysis

1. Make sure your body is underneath the ball. Lean back slightly.
2. Watch the ball onto your forehead. Do not close your eyes. Keep your neck tense.
3. As you contact the ball, tighten your abdominal muscles and push your shoulders forward. You will be meeting the ball; don't wait for it.
4. The force of your movement plus the strong neck should power the ball forward.

Skill Practice

Level A: (1) Have a partner toss ball from 10, 15, and 20 yards. Power through, trying to head it past tosser, 10 tosses at each distance. (2) Move across field, facing partner. The partner moving backward tosses at controller. Controller must head the ball past tosser. Get off the ground. Change roles at end of field.

Level B: Form a group of three: defender, offender, and thrower. Thrower throws ball toward offender. Offender tries to head ball toward a target while defender tries to head ball away; repeat 10 times at each position. Offensive and defensive players are not allowed to contact each other. Contact stops the play, and a new throw is undertaken. Combine with accuracy heading (see form C.12).

Level C: Play a crossing game in 18-yard box with three defenders and four offenders. Wingers from left and right cross ball into box. Defenders try to clear the ball out of box. Offenders try to score 10 times in each position.

Skill Mastery

Levels A, B, & C: Head the ball 8 of 10 times past tosser or defender.

Concept

Accurately heading the ball works as a pass or shot, strengthening your game.

Skill Analysis

1. Position your body under the approaching ball.
2. Note where you are in relation to your target.
3. As you contact ball with your forehead, turn your shoulders toward target. This should direct ball to target. (Hints: Watch ball onto your forehead all the time. Your eyes will close automatically. Use your arms for balance and protection.)

Skill Practice

Level A: Set up three targets (hoops or small goals) to aim for. Have a partner toss ball to you. Name in advance which target you are aiming for. Switch roles after 20 tries.

Level B: Form groups of three: defender, offender, thrower. Practice accuracy heading over defender. Thrower throws ball toward offender. Offender tries to hit one of three targets while defender tries to clear ball, 10 times each position. Combine with distance heading.

Level C: Heading Soccer: Play a Four-on-Four soccer game to five points in which the only way you can move the ball is by throwing, heading, and catching the ball (with your hands) with teammates.

Skill Mastery

Level A: Make 16 of 20 successful hits on target.

Level B: Make 8 of 10 successful hits on target.

Level C: Make 8 of 10 heads under game speed pressure to teammates.

Modified Games

Three-on-Three, juggling circles (form C.9)

From *Learning by Choice in Secondary Physical Education: Creating a Goal-Directed Program* by Kevin Kaardal, 2001, Champaign, IL: Human Kinetics.

Concept

When the ball is not low enough to the ground to trap or high enough to control, a diving header allows for accuracy and power . . . most often on goal! Exciting!

Skill Analysis

1. When ball is moving across your body at about hip level, dive forward so that your forehead (at the hairline) will strike ball. Do not look away from ball or close eyes.

2. After hitting ball, land on palms and push body forward to absorb impact.

3. Watch the ball score!

Skill Practice

Level A: For safety considerations, Level A players do not need to master this skill.

Level B: Perform crosses from outside the 18-yard box, finishing with diving headers on net, 10 times (combine with raised passes).

Level C: Play Four-on-Four or Five-on-Five. A goal by a diving header is worth three points, and a regular goal is worth one. The losing team adds one player from the winning team. If the winning team (now with just four players) wins again, they send another player to the losing team. If, however, the losing team wins, they send a player back.

Skill Mastery

Levels B & C: Accurately judge when to attempt a diving header into the net, 8 of 10 times.

From *Learning by Choice in Secondary Physical Education: Creating a Goal-Directed Program* by Kevin Kaardal, 2001, Champaign, IL: Human Kinetics.

Concept

Accuracy in shooting is far more important than speed or power. So practice shooting with both the instep and outside of the foot with each foot.

Skill Analysis

Note: The basic skills of shooting are the same as passing with the instep and passing with the outside of the foot.

1. When you shoot, do not look anywhere but at the ball. The net will never move.
2. To keep ball low as you strike it, make sure nonkicking foot is beside ball and head and shoulders are over ball.
3. To raise ball, plant nonkicking foot slightly behind ball and raise head slightly as you strike ball.
4. When striking ball with the outside of your foot, the shot should curve outward.

Skill Practice

Level A: (1) Create a goal with two pylons any size you and a partner agree on. Stand 10 yards back, one person on each side of the net. How many times can you score out of 10? (2) Challenges: Move farther back from goal or make goal smaller.

Level B: In a group of up to five, have one player with his or her back to the goal, acting as passer. All other players (shooters) face the goal, 10 to 20 yards back from passer. A shooter passes ball to passer, who flicks/passes the ball to the left or right side. The shooter runs to the *moving* ball and shoots best of 10 shots.

Level C: Shooting Game. This is a small-sided game (two to six players a side) with players shooting at net every chance they get. There is one ball on the field, and other balls waiting to be put into play behind each goal. When a player shoots and misses, play continues by the goalie taking one of the balls in waiting and kicking a quick goal kick. This occurs while the shooter retrieves the missed shot and places the ball behind the net. For the brief period while the shooter is retrieving the missed shot, his or her team plays short-sided.

Skill Mastery

Levels A & B: Score 8 of 10 attempts.

Level C: Choose a good shot, 8 of 10 times, and score under pressure, 6 of 10 shots.

Modified Games

Trick Your Neighbor, World Cup Shoot-Out, scrimmaging

From *Learning by Choice in Secondary Physical Education: Creating a Goal-Directed Program* by Kevin Kaardal, 2001, Champaign, IL: Human Kinetics.

Concept

A quick give-and-go gives the offense a chance to exploit the defense with a quick change of pace, change of direction, and pass.

Skill Analysis

1. Offense 1 dribbles ball while Defense 1 marks him.

2. Offense 2 gives Offense 1 a passing angle of 45 degrees.

3. Offense 1 passes to Offense 2, sprints past Defense 1, and receives the one-touch return pass from Offense 2.

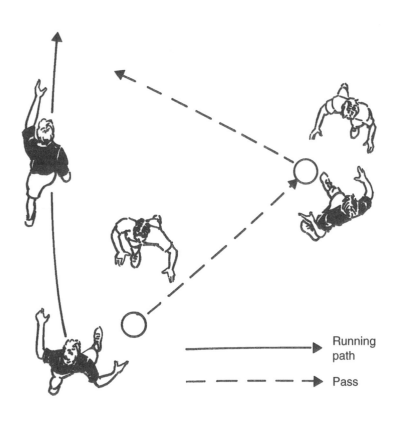

Running path

Pass

Skill Practice

Level A: Form groups of three and set up a triangle of pylons, 10 yards apart from each other. Offense 1 dribbles ball toward pylon 1. Offense 2 approaches pylon 2. Defense 1 plays simple, noncontact defense. Offense 1 passes to Offense 2, changes pace and direction drastically, and receives ball at pylon 3. Make 10 attempts at each position.

Level B: Grid work, two-on-one: Playing in a 10-yard square, focus only on give-and-goes. Make 10 in a row without losing control, then switch from offense to defense.

Level C: Play a small-sided game, using the give-and-go to exploit the defense once before you can score. First team to score five points wins.

Skill Mastery

Level A: Control 8 of 10 give-and-goes with one-touch passing.

Level B: Make 9 of 10 in a row without losing control.

Level C: Use successfully in game, making 8 of 10.

Modified Games

Trick Your Neighbor, Three-on-Three

From *Learning by Choice in Secondary Physical Education: Creating a Goal-Directed Program* by Kevin Kaardal, 2001, Champaign, IL: Human Kinetics.

Concept

While moving across the field, taking the ball from a teammate combined with a quick change of pace creates a chance to exploit the defense.

→ Running path
∿→ Dribble path

Skill Analysis

This is not a pass: It is a takeover.

1. Offense 1 carries the ball across the field while Defense 1 marks him.
2. Offense 2 moves across the field toward Offense 1.
3. When they meet, Offense 2 takes the ball and quickly moves away while Offense 1 sprints in the opposite direction.

Skill Practice

Level A: Divide into two groups: dribblers and takeover players. The first dribbler moves the ball toward the first takeover player, who moves toward the dribbler. When they reach each other, the takeover player takes the ball and sprints away, while the first dribbler sprints in the opposite direction.

Level B: Form groups of three. Moving in a half field, pass the ball in a combination including short passes, long passes, and takeovers. Keep the same combination in the same order. After 10 passes, change the order so that you get a chance at each pass or add one other play (e.g., give-and-go).

Level C: Play Three-on-Three up to Five-on-Five, except require one takeover before a goal can be scored. First team to five points wins, then create new teams. Play full scrimmage when ready.

Skill Mastery

Level A: Complete 8 of 10 takeovers at game speed under control.

Level B: Complete 8 of 10 successful combinations, each pass.

Level C: Make good choices for when to use a takeover, 8 of 10 times.

Modified Games

World Cup Tag, Trick Your Neighbor

From *Learning by Choice in Secondary Physical Education: Creating a Goal-Directed Program* by Kevin Kaardal, 2001, Champaign, IL: Human Kinetics.

Concept

A way to include a defender in an offensive strike down the side.

_____▶ Running path

– – – – – – –▶ Pass

Skill Analysis

This is a skill usually performed along the sideline.

1. Offense 1 receives the ball from anyone on the field. She turns to face Defense 1.
2. Offense 2 runs past Offense 1 into the corner space.
3. As Offense 2 begins her run past Offense 1, Offense 1 passes the ball on the ground to the space for Offense 2 to run into.

Skill Practice

Level A: Offense 1 has the ball in the center of the field. Offense 1 passes to Offense 2, who turns to face the goal. Offense 3 overlap-runs and calls for the ball. Offense 2 makes a strong pass on the ground with the correct pace to have the ball arrive just ahead of the receiving player. Offense 3 runs onto the ball, dribbles it to the end line, and tries to cross it to Offense 1, who is running for the goal; 10 attempts.

Level B: Form groups of three on a half field. Create a pattern of passes and plays to follow, including an overlap run (other suggestions: short pass, long pass, give-and-go, takeover). Practice the play as many times as you can for five minutes, then switch roles.

Level C: Play Three-on-Three to Six-on-Six, but you must overlap-run once before scoring. First team to five points wins.

Skill Mastery

Level A: Complete 8 of 10 successful passes with good pace.

Level B: Complete 25 to 30 passes in five minutes.

Level C: Make 8 of 10 good decisions for when to overlap-run.

Modified Games

World Cup Tag or Kings (or Queens) of the Pitch, Trick Your Neighbor, scrimmaging

From *Learning by Choice in Secondary Physical Education: Creating a Goal-Directed Program* by Kevin Kaardal, 2001, Champaign, IL: Human Kinetics.

Tag-Type Games: One person is "It" and runs after other players, trying to tag them by touching with a hand. The person tagged then becomes "It," and the game continues. You may also have (1) the "It" people join hands as they are tagged and chase after other players in a chain, splitting the chain after it grows to eight people (Amoeba Tag); (2) the tagged person freeze until a free player ducks under the tagged person's arms (Frozen Tag); or (3) the players try to run from one safe zone at one end of the gym to another safe zone at the other end. After the "It," people call "British Bull Dog" (the name of this game).

Control Tag: One person is "It." All students control their own soccer balls. If you are tagged you become "It." You may move only if you are in control of the ball. You may be tagged "It" while you are stopped.

World Cup Tag: Every person is "It" and must control a ball within the same confined space, e.g., a 10-yard-square area. Work to force an opponent's ball outside the confined space or cause them to lose control of their ball. Then they are eliminated from the game and must practice juggling drills. The last player left wins. For more of a challenge, try reducing the space size as the number of players is reduced until the final two players are left.

World Cup Shoot-Out: Form groups of five, each with one goalie. The object of the game is to score a goal from a penalty shot. If you miss, you are out and must do juggling drills. Players keep shooting until one player per group is left. Then the goalie who had the least goals scored on him or her plays goalie for the final shoot-out in which all winners continue the game until only one player is left.

Two-on-Two: Play two against two, practicing skills as indicated on the posters. Players call their own violations.

Three-on-Three: Play three against three, practicing skills as indicated on the posters. Players call their own violations. Modify the rules to give you more trials of the skill you are practicing.

Four-on-Four to Six-on-Six: Focus on the skill you are practicing. Players call their own violations. Modify the rules to give you more trials of the skill you are practicing (e.g., limiting the number of touches will force players to pass).

Keep-Away: Practice creating space for passing, using pivots, target hands, and seals in 10-yard-square. Two offensive players face each other, 5 to 7 yards apart. In the three-player game, one defender tries to deflect the pass between the offensive players. If the pass is deflected out of the playing area or the offense loses control, the passer becomes the defender. Stay on offense as much as possible. Every turn as defender earns a point. Set a time limit; the player with the fewest points wins. Add another defender for a four-player game. Keep-Away can also be played with evenly balanced teams that attempt to keep the ball from the other team and score points by how many passes they can successfully make before the ball is intercepted.

Any Goal: Play Six-on-Six, using a half field with a two-yard goal (with no goalie), on each side (for four total). Pass to open players near one of the goals. Control each pass and shoot to score. First team with 15 points wins.

Crossbar: Face a partner with a crossbar between you. Chip pass or shoot at the crossbar from about 10 yards. First player to hit the crossbar 10 times wins.

(continued)

From *Learning by Choice in Secondary Physical Education: Creating a Goal-Directed Program* by Kevin Kaardal, 2001, Champaign, IL: Human Kinetics.

Relay Races: In teams, dribble through a course of cones, one or two players at a time. Each player has a ball. The players can go one after another or at the same time, so they must not only navigate the cones but avoid each other as well. Each dribbler passes off to the next player or group of players in the line. First team done wins.

Kings (or Queens) of the Pitch: Divide one or more soccer pitches into several grids. In its simplest form, six people play Two-on-Two, with two players rotating in. The offensive players become the "kings (or queens) of the pitch" when they score, and the one scored upon leaves to be replaced by another. If a defender gets the ball, the offense and defense switch. Players leave the grid only if scored upon. The game goes up to as many goals as the players decide (one to three is usual). See who can stay kings or queens of the pitch as much as possible.

Touch Soccer: During scrimmage play, limit the number of touches a player can use before passing the ball. The fewer touches, the more difficult the game.

Fool Your Neighbor: This is a dribbling or passing game similar to Any Goal. On a small-sided pitch, you have up to two balls. The object of the game is to trap the ball on one of the endlines or sidelines. This game can be played individually or in teams of two or three. There are three to four teams to a pitch. It is every team for themselves on offense, but on defense, teams cooperate to stop the offensive team. Transitions from defense to offense become very important and happen very quickly once the ball has been stolen by one of the defending teams from the team that was in possession of the ball. You are instantly on offense when your team possesses the ball. Teams try to fool the defending teams about which sideline they are trying to score on as all sidelines are in play at all times and offensive teams can change their objectives quickly and fool the defenders.

From *Learning by Choice in Secondary Physical Education: Creating a Goal-Directed Program* by Kevin Kaardal, 2001, Champaign, IL: Human Kinetics.

Form D.1 Fitness Assessment Record Sheet

Name: _____ Class: _____ Initial level: A B C D

Tasks	Baseline	Goals	Term 1 Level___	Term 2 Level___	Final Test Level___

Muscular endurance
  Push-ups:
 	
  Crunches:
	#___/
	___%
		#___/
		___%
			#___/
			___%
				#___/
				___%
					#___/
					___%

Rating for muscular endurance and strength tests (form D.3):	#___/ ___% 1. 2. 3. 4. 5.	#___/ ___% 1. 2. 3. 4. 5.	#___/ ___% 1. 2. 3. 4. 5.	#___/ ___% 1. 2. 3. 4. 5.	#___/ ___% 1. 2. 3. 4. 5.
Flexibility Hamstrings (toe touches):	_____	_____	_____	_____	_____
Aerobic fitness 12-min. run laps:	#___/ ___%	#___/ ___%	#___/ ___%	#___/ ___%	#___/ ___%
Things I can and want to change about my fitness: List specific fitness goals (e.g., lose 5 kg [11 lb], improve 12-min. run score by 4 laps):	Term 1: Term 2: Term 3: Term 4:				

From *Learning by Choice in Secondary Physical Education: Creating a Goal-Directed Program* by Kevin Kaardal, 2001, Champaign, IL: Human Kinetics.

Form D.2 Leveled Fitness Evaluation Grid

Grade	Level A			Level B			Level C			Level D		
	CR	PU	Run	CR	PU	Run	CR	PU	Run	CR	PU	Run
10%	2	10	5									
20%	4	13	7									
30%	6	15	10									
40%	8	17	12									
50%	10	10	15	20	15	20	30	25	25	50	35	35
60%	15	13	20	25	20	25	40	30	30	60	40	40
70%	20	17	25	33	25	30	50	35	35	70	45	45
80%	26	20	30	40	30	35	60	40	40	80	50	50
90%	33	25	35	50	35	40	70	45	45	90	55	55
100%										100	60	60

Key:

CR = crunches done continuously in one minute

PU = Push-ups done continuously in one minute

Run = 12-min. run in number of laps

Do abdominal curl-ups.

Do regular push-ups, arms flexing to about 90°.

Run around the main volleyball court.

How to Find Your Percent Average for These Three Fitness Tests

1. Record only your best scores from the term.
2. Choose a level at which your highest possible score will fall between 80 and 90%, improving your "attitude" mark from challenging yourself—improving your overall unit mark. If you get 100% for skill, your attitude mark will suffer from not challenging yourself to improve.
3. Circle the three numbers that correspond with your performance on each test at the level you have chosen. Match these numbers with the corresponding percent grade. Add the percent grades and divide by three to get your average.

From *Learning by Choice in Secondary Physical Education: Creating a Goal-Directed Program* by Kevin Kaardal, 2001, Champaign, IL: Human Kinetics.

Form D.3 Muscular Endurance and Strength Test

1. Familiarize yourself with the five lifts used for this test: bench press, arm curl, lateral pull-down, leg extension (quad lift), and leg curl.
2. Find your body weight in pounds.
3. Find the amount of resistance to use by multiplying your weight by the number given for each lift:

Lift	Percent of Body Weight	
	Men	Women
Lateral (lat.) pull-down	.70	.45
Leg extension	.65	.50
Bench press	.75	.45
Leg curl	.32	.25
Arm curl	.35	.18

4. Perform the maximum continuous number of repetitions possible.
5. Based on the number of repetitions performed, look up the percentile rank for each lift in the column of the Muscular Endurance and Strength Scoring Table.
6. Find your overall strength fitness category by averaging your percent scores for all five lifts.

Determine your overall muscular endurance fitness rating according to the following:

Average Repetition Score	Endurance Classification
81+	Excellent
61–80	Good
41–60	Average
21–40	Fair
Less than 20	Poor

(continued)

From *Learning by Choice in Secondary Physical Education: Creating a Goal-Directed Program* by Kevin Kaardal, 2001, Champaign, IL: Human Kinetics.

Muscular Endurance and Strength Scoring Table

Women

Percentile Rank	Lat. Pull-Down	Leg Extension	Bench Press	Leg Curl	Arm Curl
99	30	25	27	20	25
95	25	20	21	17	21
90	21	18	20	12	20
80	16	13	16	10	19
70	13	11	13	9	14
High Physical Fitness Standard					
60	11	10	11	7	12
50	10	9	10	6	10
Health Fitness Standard					
40	9	8	7	5	8
30	7	7	3	4	7
20	6	5	1	3	6
10	3	3	0	1	3
5	2	1	0	0	2

Men

Percentile Rank	Lat. Pull-Down	Leg Extension	Bench Press	Leg Curl	Arm Curl
99	30	25	26	24	25
95	25	20	21	20	21
90	19	19	19	19	19
80	16	15	16	15	15
70	13	14	13	13	12
High Physical Fitness Standard					
60	11	13	11	11	10
50	10	12	10	10	9
Health Fitness Standard					
40	9	10	7	8	8
30	7	9	5	6	7
20	6	7	3	4	5
10	4	5	1	3	3
5	3	3	0	1	2

From *Learning by Choice in Secondary Physical Education: Creating a Goal-Directed Program* by Kevin Kaardal, 2001, Champaign, IL: Human Kinetics.

Dates I Will Work Toward My Goals	Goals I Will Be Working Toward	What I Will Have Accomplished

From *Learning by Choice in Secondary Physical Education: Creating a Goal-Directed Program* by Kevin Kaardal, 2001, Champaign, IL: Human Kinetics.

Use this calendar to plan and record your fitness workouts for a month. Fill in the days of the week on which you work out.

Month: _____

From *Learning by Choice in Secondary Physical Education: Creating a Goal-Directed Program* by Kevin Kaardal, 2001, Champaign, IL: Human Kinetics.

HR = Heart rate taken during a 10-sec. count.

Activity	Resting HR	HR at Finish	HR After 3 Min.
1.			
2.			
3.			
4.			
5.			
6.			
7.			
8.			
9.			
10.			
11.			
12.			
13.			
14.			

From *Learning by Choice in Secondary Physical Education: Creating a Goal-Directed Program* by Kevin Kaardal, 2001, Champaign, IL: Human Kinetics.

Psychomotor Goals

A: Uses an active-living and a total wellness fitness program. Demonstrates assimilation into everyday life.

B: Performs three single-session personal fitness workouts: aerobics, circuit training, and supercircuit/muscular endurance.

C: Safely and effectively performs nonstop 15 push-ups, 26 crunches, and 12 min. of continuous jogging, completing 28 laps.

Exemplars

A: Completes the Canadian Active Living Challenge (CALC) with more than 210 points within 8 weeks.

B: Maintains heart rate (HR) within the active-living (target) zone (TZ), 20 consecutive min. during workouts.

C: Runs at an even pace while able to talk and reach TZ. Achieves 80% performance mark for exercises as outlined for level one.

Cognitive Goals

A: Demonstrates knowledge of safe and effective exercising practices.

B: Designs the workouts described under Psychomotor Goals "B."

C: Understands how to find HR, health benefits of active living, cost to society of sedentary lifestyles, types of activity contributing to healthy life, and required activity level to achieve health and training benefits.

Exemplars

A: Teachers and expert students, as well as expert examples on videotape and diagrams on posters, demonstrate models.

B: Workouts include three phases: warm-up with safe stretching, 30-min. workout, and cool-down with large-muscle activities.

C: Same as "A" and completes an active-living diary as outlined and modeled. Student-made handouts and posters present information highlighting the benefits of living actively. Personal records in motor skill performance, demonstrations of leadership and knowledge, and student fitness packets also serve as positive models.

Affective Goals

A: Demonstrates appreciation and enjoyment of physical activity by participating in health-related physical activities outside of class.

B: Same as "A" but also sets and works toward personal fitness goals over the school year.

C: Same as "B" but also displays the positive behavior traits listed in the Mastery section of the Affective Evaluation chart, form A.4.

Exemplars

A: Completes the CALC activity log book including entries about physical activities engaged in outside the formal classroom setting.

B: Achieves all personal fitness goals and sets some personal records.

C: Achieves the behavioral criterion listed under the 80% or higher category outlined in the table.

From *Learning by Choice in Secondary Physical Education: Creating a Goal-Directed Program* by Kevin Kaardal, 2001, Champaign, IL: Human Kinetics.

Instructional Strategies

Initial Instruction—Overview of process, materials, and marking criteria through information packets, problem solving, lectures, guided practice, questioning, and student or teacher demonstrations and videotape or poster presentations. ("Guided practice" is teacher-directed practice and support, such as reciprocal peer teaching, guided discovery, independent or group task card work, modified games and drills.)

Independent Activity—Individualized student research, reading, and/or practice time, enabling achievement of unit goals (e.g., independent work on personal fitness goals, fitness task and self-evaluation sheets, personal fitness contracts, and CALC log book).

Expanded Opportunities

Speak to alternative learning styles and add meaning to learning through individualized study, tutorials, computer-assisted instruction, flextime, and review and testing. Students may, for example, use the fitness center when it is supervised outside of class time or improve fitness by participating in intramural activities or on school teams or clubs. Students set personal goals and choose the performance test that suits their unique abilities. (See also chapters 1 to 6 of this book.) Expect students to demonstrate work toward goals, subject integration, and social value, through knowledge and participation in school, extracurricular, and cooperative community service and participation opportunities. Give class credit base on student documentation in log book and contract work. (See also Reassessment under Assessment Instruments.)

Assessment Instruments

Be sure to reflect a collection of data, measuring indicators of progress toward unit goals:

Diagnostic—Informal assessment of the student's level of understanding, attitudes, and what the student would like to find out before the beginning of the unit (e.g., interest inventories, pretests, observations, brainstorming, informal questioning, class webs).

Formative—Ongoing assessment as the student progresses through unit toward personal goals (e.g., checklists, assignments, quizzes, observations of work in progress, journal writing, fitness assessment demonstrations, conferences, peer evaluation, self-evaluation).

Reassessment—After initial assessment and further learning opportunities, retest students.

Summative—Pictures achievement at end of unit (e.g., self-evaluation; teacher's formal report; completion of CALC; attainment of personal goals, personal bests, and leveled fitness assessment standards; completion of fitness activity and test packages for level one [may be compared to performance norms and graded]).

From *Learning by Choice in Secondary Physical Education: Creating a Goal-Directed Program* by Kevin Kaardal, 2001, Champaign, IL: Human Kinetics.

Form D.8 Levels of Performance Rubric

This rubric is for Level A. Instructors should develop similar rubrics for Levels B, C, and D.

Rubric
Levels of Performance
(Use for planning unit goals.)

	Minimal Reassessment required	Acceptable Reassessment recommended	Mastery Reassessment not required	Going Beyond Reassessment not required
Goal 1	A: Doesn't earn 210 points in Canadian Active Living Challenge (CALC) in 10 wks; meets less than 70% of goals. B: Workouts maintain HRs in target zone (TZ) under 12 min. C: Meets less than 65% of level A requirements.*	A: Completes CALC with 210 in 10 wks; meets 70–80% of goals. B: Workouts maintain HRs in TZ for 15–20 min. C: Meets 65–79% of level A performance requirements.*	A: Completes CALC with 210 in 8 wks; meets all goals. B: Workouts maintain HRs in TZ for 20 min. or more. C: Meets 80–89% of level A requirements.*	A: Completes CALC with 210 or more points in 6 wks or less. Students meet all of their personal goals. B: Workouts maintain HRs in TZ for 30 min. or more. C: Meets 90% or more of level A requirements.*
Goal 2	A: Doesn't show safe and effective exercise practices. B: Doesn't complete 3 single-session workout sheets. C: Doesn't correctly and neatly complete assignments in unit packs; manual HR counts don't match those on HR monitor.	A: Usually shows safe and effective exercise practices. B: Correctly and neatly completes 3 single-session workout sheets, but doesn't describe all exercises in detail. C: Correctly and neatly completes 80-89% of assignments in unit pack. 1-min. manual HR counts reflect count on HR monitor within 5 beats.	A: Shows safe and effective exercise practices. B: Correctly and neatly completes 3 single-session workout sheets, in detail. Workouts include warm-ups with safe stretching techniques, a 30-min. workout phase, and cool-down phase with large muscle (e.g., walking and safe stretching). C: Correctly and neatly completes all assignments included in unit pack. Manual HR counts match those of HR monitor within 15-sec. count.	A: Models safe and effective exercise practices. B: Correctly and neatly completes 3 single-session work-out sheets, in detail. Workouts include warm-ups with safe stretching, 30-min. workouts, and large muscle cool-downs. C: Models correct and neat completion of all assignments in unit pack. Manual HR counts match those of HR monitor within 15-sec. count.

From *Learning by Choice in Secondary Physical Education: Creating a Goal-Directed Program* by Kevin Kaardal, 2001, Champaign, IL: Human Kinetics.

	Minimal Reassessment required	**Acceptable** Reassessment recommended	**Mastery** Reassessment not required	**Going Beyond** Reassessment not required
Goal 3	A: Journal records no physical activity outside PE. B: Doesn't improve fitness level. C: Displays behaviors in 64% or less range (see Form A.4 Affective Evaluation Chart).	A: Journal records 1–2 vigorous physical activities outside PE per wk. B: Meets 65–79% of goals. C: Displays behaviors in 65–79% range (see form A.4).	A: Journal records 3–5 vigorous physical activities outside PE per wk. B: Meets 80–100% of goals. C: Displays behaviors in 80%$^+$ range (see form A.4).	A: Journal records 3–5 vigorous physical activities outside PE per week. B: Meets 80–100% of goals. C: Displays behaviors in 80%$^+$ range (see form A.4).
Descriptive scale:	1	2 3.25	4	5

Descriptive scale: Minimal (1) to mastery (5). See detailed description of indicators in each box.

Indicators: Answers questions (e.g., "How do you know?" and "What do you see?" in ongoing monitoring and evaluating of each unit goal).

*As outlined in the appropriate fitness test package.

From *Learning by Choice in Secondary Physical Education: Creating a Goal-Directed Program* by Kevin Kaardal, 2001, Champaign, IL: Human Kinetics.

Form E.1 Badminton Skill Practice and Tournament Record Sheet

Name: _____ **Class:** _____ **Teacher:** _____

Instructions: In the skill practice part of the lesson, choose task learning experiences or do drills, using the related task card posters. Then write the number of the task in the small box provided.

Task Learning Experience and Drill Practice Record

Stretch, grip, ready position															
Serve (high)															
Serve (underhand)															
Backhand, short serve															
Return of serve															
Basic stroke															
Overhand clear															
Underhand net shots															
Drop shot															
Drive															
Smash															
Modified games															

Instructions: After playing a game, record a "W" for a win or an "L" for a loss in the win/loss box and the score in score box. Have your opponent sign in the box provided.

Games and Tournament Personal Record

Win/Loss	Score	Opponent's Signature	Win/Loss	Score	Opponent's Signature	Win/Loss	Score	Opponent's Signature
	/			/			/	
	/			/			/	
	/			/			/	
	/			/			/	
	/			/			/	
	/			/			/	
	/			/			/	
	/			/			/	
	/			/			/	
	/			/			/	
	/			/			/	
	/			/			/	

From *Learning by Choice in Secondary Physical Education: Creating a Goal-Directed Program* by Kevin Kaardal, 2001, Champaign, IL: Human Kinetics.

Name: _____   **Class:** _____

Teacher: _____   **Partner:** _____

Grip and ready position: Have your partner demonstrate the grip and ready position and check off whether he or she demonstrates the following performance points. The skill posters have diagrams of the skills. Score one point for each key point present.

Key Performance Points	Present	Not Present
Feet are shoulder-width apart.		
Weight is on balls of feet.		
Back is straight and head is up.		
Racket points at opponent.		
"V" is to the opposite shoulder grip.		

Score of 5 = _____

Forehand overhead clear: Have your partner feed you 10 high serves. Using the forehand clear, return the serve deep to the back of the court. Let the clear drop to the court. Score one point for each bird that lands toward the side boundaries within three feet (one meter) of the back boundary line and travels above the partner's head. Also score one point for each of the following performance points present.

Score of 10 = _____

Key Performance Points	Present	Not Present
"V" is to the opposite shoulder grip.		
Racket starts behind head.		
Arm fully extends on contact.		
Wrist snaps down and turns away.		
Shuttle flight is high and deep.		

Score of 5 = _____

Backhand clear: Have your partner feed you 10 high serves. Using the backhand clear, return the serve deep to the back of the court. Let the clear drop to the court. Score one point for each bird that lands toward the side boundaries within three feet (one meter) of the back boundary line and travels above your partner's head. Also score one point for each of the following performance points present.

Score of 10 = _____

(continued)

From *Learning by Choice in Secondary Physical Education: Creating a Goal-Directed Program* by Kevin Kaardal, 2001, Champaign, IL: Human Kinetics.

Form E.2 *(continued)*

Key Performance Points	Present	Not Present
"V" is to the opposite shoulder grip.		
Racket starts over opposite shoulder.		
Arm fully extends on contact.		
Wrist snaps down and turns away.		
Shuttle flight is high and deep.		

Score of 5 = _____

High serve: Serve to your partner 10 times. Aim the serve deep to the back of the court. Let the serve drop to the court. Score one point for each bird that lands within three feet (one meter) of the corners of the back boundary lines and travels above your partner's head. Also score one point for each of the following performance points present.

Score of 10 = _____

Key Performance Points	Present	Not Present
Server creates alley for racket.		
Racket head is below waist and wrist.		
Wrist snaps up and turns toward body.		
Follow-through travels toward opposite shoulder.		
Shuttle flight is high and deep.		

Score of 5 = _____

Form E.3 Badminton Skills Test Level B

Name: _____ **Class:** _____
Teacher: _____ **Partner:** _____

Short serve: Serve to your partner 10 times. Aim the serve short and to the front side corners of the service court. Let the serve drop to the court. Score one point for each bird that lands within two feet (62 centimeters) of the side corners and travels no higher than a racket length above net. Also score one point for each of the following performance points present.

Score of 10 = _____

From *Learning by Choice in Secondary Physical Education: Creating a Goal-Directed Program* by Kevin Kaardal, 2001, Champaign, IL: Human Kinetics.

Key Performance Points	Present	Not Present
Server creates an alley for racket.		
Racket head is below waist and wrist.		
Racket head slices bird.		
Follow-through is short; follows shuttle's flight path.		
Shuttle flight is low and short.		

Score of 5 = _____

Underhand clear: Have your partner feed you 10 low, short serves. Using the underhand clear, return the serve deep to the back of the court. Let the clear drop to the court. Score one point for each bird that lands toward the side boundaries within three feet of the back boundary line and travels above the partner's head. Also score one point for each of the following performance points present.

Score of 10 = _____

Key Performance Points	Present	Not Present
Receiver starts in ready position.		
Receiver creates an alley for racket.		
Wrist snaps up and turns toward body.		
Follow-through travels toward opposite shoulder.		
Shuttle flight is high and deep.		

Score of 5 = _____

Drop shot: Have your partner feed you 10 high serves. Using the drop shot, return the serve short to in front of the side corners of the service court. The closer to net, the better. Let the shot drop to the court. Score one point for each bird that lands in front of the service court's corners and drops no higher than a racket length above net. Also score one point for each of the following performance points present.

Key Performance Points	Present	Not Present
"V" is to opposite shoulder grip and racket starts over opposite shoulder.		
Arm fully extends on contact.		
Racket head slices bird.		
Follow-through is short; follows shuttle's flight path.		
Shuttle flight is low and short.		

Score of 5 = _____

Net shots, forehand and backhand: Stand at net across from a partner and attempt to keep a continuous rally of nets going. Keep the bird no higher than half a racket length above net. Alternate between the forehand and backhand net shots.

Scoring: 10 points for a rally of 20 net shots in a row; 9 points for a rally of 18 net shots in a row; and so on down to 5 points for a rally of 10 net shots in a row, and 0 points for less than 10 shots.

From *Learning by Choice in Secondary Physical Education: Creating a Goal-Directed Program* by Kevin Kaardal, 2001, Champaign, IL: Human Kinetics.

Name: _____ **Class:** _____

Teacher: _____ **Partner:** _____

Backhand doubles service: Serve the shuttle backhanded five times to the front corners of the service court and five times to the back corners of the doubles service court. Also score one point for each of the following performance points present.

Key Performance Points	Present	Not Present
Stands with racket in front of body, pointing down.		
Racket head is below waist and wrist.		
Snaps wrist on high serves; lightly flicks wrist on short serves.		
Follow-through is short; follows shuttle's flight path for short serve; is long and finishes above head for deep serve.		
Disguises type of serve until shuttle is struck.		

Score of 5 = _____

The smash: Begin a rally with your partner. When appropriate, try to smash the bird at two cones placed on yard up from the doubles services lines and one foot inside the singles court sideline boundaries. Repeat five times, scoring one point for every bird that lands within a racket length of the cones. Also score one point for each of the following performance points present.

Score of 5 = _____

Key Performance Points	Present	Not Present
"V" is to opposite shoulder grip.		
Racket starts behind head.		
Body position is behind bird.		
Arm fully extends on contact.		
Wrist snaps down and turns away.		
Shuttle flight is quick and moves sharply downward.		

Score of 6 = _____

Shot control test: With a partner, stand at net and try to keep a continuous rally of clears, smashes, and net shots going in a set pattern of clear, smash, and net shots.

Scoring: Shots in a row: _____ = _____ points. 10 points for a rally of 20 net shots in a row; 9 points for a rally of 18 net shots in a row; and so on down to 5 points for a rally of 10 net shots in a row, and 0 points for less than 10 shots.

From *Learning by Choice in Secondary Physical Education: Creating a Goal-Directed Program* by Kevin Kaardal, 2001, Champaign, IL: Human Kinetics.

Form E.5 Level A Tennis Skills Evaluation

Level A Skills

Skill: Ready Position	Present	Needs Improvement/ Evaluator's Suggestions
Weight on balls of feet.		
Knees relaxed.		
Feet slightly apart.		
Right hand relaxed on grip.		
Left hand on racket throat.		
Elbows slightly bent.		
Racket in front of body.		
Racket head higher than grip.		

Rubric

1 2 3 3.5 Acceptable	4 Mastery	5 Going Beyond
Performed in drill on command.	Performed in half-court singles on return of serve.	Performed in rally, returning to ready position after each stroke.

Level A Skills

Skill: Eastern Grip	Present	Needs Improvement/ Evaluator's Suggestions
Shakes hands with racket.		
"V" between forefinger and thumb.		
"V" over back edge of racket.		
Thumb around handle.		
Hand relaxed.		
Fingers spread slightly.		

(No rubric: For this skill, subtract one point from five for each performance point that is not present.)

Level A Skills

Skill: The Forehand	Present	Needs Improvement/ Evaluator's Suggestions
Right foot moves first.		
Left moves ahead of right foot.		
Transfers weight to left foot.		
Racket perpendicular to ball.		

(continued)

From *Learning by Choice in Secondary Physical Education: Creating a Goal-Directed Program* by Kevin Kaardal, 2001, Champaign, IL: Human Kinetics.

Level A Skills

Skill: The Forehand *(cont.)*	Present	Needs Improvement/ Evaluator's Suggestions
Racket at waist height.		
Racket directly behind ball.		
Hits ball at a point opposite to front (left) foot.		
Wrist firm.		
Number of balls returned from toss into service court:		/10
Maximum number of balls rallied between partners:		

Rubric

1 2 3 3.5 Acceptable	4 Mastery	5 Going Beyond
Number of balls returned from toss into service court. Score out of 10 and multiply by 0.4.	Performed in half-court singles on return of serve. Controls ball; creates rally, directing ball to opponent.	Hits solid ground strokes: winners or opponent misses hit. Forehand ground strokes make opponent move around court.

Level A Skills

Skill: The Backhand	Present	Needs Improvement/ Evaluator's Suggestions
Rotates racket 1/4 turn to right.		
Right shoulder is toward net.		
Right foot points to sideline.		
Draws back racket at waist level.		
Hits ball 1 ft. (31 centimeters) in front of right foot.		
Racket is perpendicular to ball.		
Wrist firm.		
Number of balls returned from toss into service court:		/10
Maximum number of balls rallied between partners:		

Rubric

1 2 3 3.5 Acceptable	4 Mastery	5 Going Beyond
Number of balls returned from toss into service court. Score out of 10 and multiply by 0.4.	Performed in half-court singles on return of serve. Controls ball; creates rally, directing ball to opponent.	Hits solid ground strokes: winners or opponent misses hit. Backhand ground strokes make opponent move around court.

From *Learning by Choice in Secondary Physical Education: Creating a Goal-Directed Program* by Kevin Kaardal, 2001, Champaign, IL: Human Kinetics.

Form E.6 Level B Tennis Skills Evaluation

Level B Skills

Skill: The Volley	Present	Needs Improvement/ Evaluator's Suggestions	
Eastern grip.			
Nonplaying hand holds racket at throat.			
Uses ready position.			
Crossover-steps with foot opposite to direction of volley.			
Wrist firm.			
Racket stops on contact.			
Racket and arm make short punching action.			
Number of balls volleyed from toss into service court:		Forehand /5	Backhand /5
Maximum number of balls rallied between partners:			

Rubric

1 2 3 3.5 Acceptable	4 Mastery	5 Going Beyond
Number of balls volleyed from toss into service court. Score out of 10 and multiply by 0.4.	Performed in half-court singles on return of serve. Controls ball; returns strokes at net with forehand/backhand volleys, directing ball to opponent.	Hits good volleys: winners or opponent misses hit. Controls ball; returns strokes at net with forehand/backhand volleys, making opponent move around court.

Level B Skills

Skill: The Volley	Present	Needs Improvement/ Evaluator's Suggestions	
Eastern grip.			
Nonplaying hand holds racket at throat.			
Uses ready position.			
Crossover-steps with foot opposite to direction of volley.			
Firm wrist.			
Racket stops on contact.			
Racket and arm make short punching action.			
Number of balls volleyed from toss into service court:		Forehand /5	Backhand /5
Maximum number of balls rallied between partners:			

(continued)

Racket Sports

227

From *Learning by Choice in Secondary Physical Education: Creating a Goal-Directed Program* by Kevin Kaardal, 2001, Champaign, IL: Human Kinetics.

Rubric

1 2 3 3.5 Acceptable	4 Mastery	5 Going Beyond
Number of balls volleyed from toss into service court. Score out of 10 and multiply by 0.4.	Performed in half-court singles on return of serve. Controls ball; returns strokes at net with fore-hand or backhand volleys, directing ball to opponent.	Hits good volleys: winners or opponent misses hit. Controls ball; returns strokes at net with forehand/backhand volleys, making opponent move around the court.

Level B Skills: The Serve

Skill: The Serve	Present	Needs Improvement/ Evaluator's Suggestions	
Eastern grip.			
Left foot on diagonal, pointed to service court from behind baseline. Nonplaying hand holds ball at racket throat.			
Racket points at service court; back diagonal to service court.			
Shifts weight from back to front foot as racket drops down past the knees at take away.			
Racket arcs up and behind head. Racket head scratches back. Elbow is high.			
Tosses ball about 4 inches above the total height of the upwardly extended arm, and racket extends in front.			
Hits ball at hightest point, and body is fully ex-tended on contact.			
Follows through by swinging racket across body. Finishes in ready position, facing service court.			
Number of balls served into service court:		Left court /5	Right court /5
Maximum number of balls rallied between partners after serve:			

Rubric

1 2 3 3.5 Acceptable	4 Mastery	5 Going Beyond
Number of balls served into service court. Score out of 10 and multiply by 0.4.	Performed in half-court singles on return of serve. Controls ball; serves to opponent.	Hits hard serves: winners or opponent misses hit. Controls ball; serves make opponent move around court.

From *Learning by Choice in Secondary Physical Education: Creating a Goal-Directed Program* by Kevin Kaardal, 2001, Champaign, IL: Human Kinetics.

Level C Skills: The Slice Serve

Skill: The Slice Serve	Present	Needs Improvement/ Evaluator's Suggestions	
Continental grip.			
Left foot on diagonal, pointed to service court from behind baseline. Nonplaying hand holds ball at racket throat.			
Racket pointed at service court. Back diagonal to service court.			
Shifts weight from front to back foot as racket drops down past knees on take away.			
Racket arcs up and behind head. Racket head scratches back. Elbow is high.			
Tosses ball about 4 inches above the total height of the upwardly extended arm, and racket extends in front.			
Racket slices across ball. Hits ball at hightest point, and body is fully extended on contact.			
Follows through by swinging racket across body. Finishes in ready position, facing service court.			
Number of balls served into service court:		Left court /5	Right court /5
Maximum number of balls rallied between partners after serve:			

Rubric

1 2 3 3.5 Acceptable	4 Mastery	5 Going Beyond
Number of balls served into service court. Score out of 10 and multiply by 0.4.	Performed in half-court singles on return of serve. Controls ball; serves to opponent.	Hits hard serves: winners or opponent misses hit. Controls ball; serves make opponent move around court.

Level C Skills: The Drop Shot

Skill: The Volley	Present	Needs Improvement/ Evaluator's Suggestions
Eastern grip.		
Nonplaying hand holds racket at throat.		
Uses ready position.		
Crossover-steps with foot opposite to direction of volley.		

(continued)

From *Learning by Choice in Secondary Physical Education: Creating a Goal-Directed Program* by Kevin Kaardal, 2001, Champaign, IL: Human Kinetics.

Level C Skills: The Drop Shot *(cont.)*

Skill: The Volley *(cont.)*	Present	Needs Improvement/ Evaluator's Suggestions	
Firm wrist.			
Racket cushions ball on contact or slices ball with underspin.			
Ball travels just over net and bounces twice quickly.			
Number of nonreturnable drop shots volleyed from toss into service court by a player running in from baseline:		Forehand /5	Backhand /5

Rubric

1 2 3 3.5 Acceptable	4 Mastery	5 Going Beyond
Number of nonreturnable drop shots volleyed from toss into service court by a player running in from the baseline. Score out of 10 and multiply by 0.4.	Performed in half-court singles on return of serve. Controls ball; returns strokes at net with forehand/ backhand drop shots. Opponent returns only 2 of 5 drop shots.	Hits good drop shots: winners or opponent misses hit. Controls ball; returns strokes at net with forehand/backhand drop shots, making opponent move around court.

Level C Skills: The Lob Shot

Skill: The Volley	Present	Needs Improvement/ Evaluator's Suggestions	
Continental grip.			
Nonplaying hand holds racket at throat.			
Uses ready position.			
Crossover-steps with foot opposite to direction of volley.			
Swing angles racket face up. For topspin lob, hit over top of ball on looping upswing.			
Racket puts topspin on ball.			
Ball travels deep and high to corners.			
Number of lob shots volleyed from toss into service court that land within one foot (31 centimeters) of baseline and near corners of court.		Forehand /5	Backhand /5

(continued)

From *Learning by Choice in Secondary Physical Education: Creating a Goal-Directed Program* by Kevin Kaardal, 2001, Champaign, IL: Human Kinetics.

Rubric

1 2 3 3.5 Acceptable	4 Mastery	5 Going Beyond
Number of lob shots volleyed from toss into service court that land within a foot (31 centimeters) of baseline and near corners of court. Score out of 10 and multiply by 0.4.	Performed in half-court singles on return of serve. Controls ball; returns strokes with forehand or backhand lob shots. Opponent smashes only 1 of 5 lob shots.	Hits good lob shots: winners or opponent misses hit. Controls ball; returns strokes with forehand or backhand lob shots, making opponent move around court.

Level C Skills: The Topspin Winner

Skill: The Volley	Present	Needs Improvement/ Evaluator's Suggestions	
Eastern grip.			
Nonplaying hand holds racket at throat.			
Uses ready position.			
Crossover-steps with foot opposite to direction of volley, creating swing alley.			
Swing angles racket face at about 45° on contact with ball.			
Racket puts topspin on ball.			
Ball travels deep and fast to corners of court away from opponent and is not returnable.			
Number of topspin winners volleyed from toss into service court that land within one foot (31 centimeters) of baseline and near corners of court.		Forehand /5	Backhand /5

Rubric

1 2 3 3.5 Acceptable	4 Mastery	5 Going Beyond
Number of topspin winners volleyed from toss into service court that land within one foot (31 centimeters) of baseline and near corners of court. Score out of 10 and multiply by 0.4.	Performed in half-court singles on return of serve. Controls ball; returns strokes with forehand or backhand topspin shots. Opponent returns only 2 of 5 drop shots.	Hits good hard topspin: winners or opponent misses hit. Controls ball; returns strokes with forehand or backhand topspin shots, making opponent move around court.

(continued)

From *Learning by Choice in Secondary Physical Education: Creating a Goal-Directed Program* by Kevin Kaardal, 2001, Champaign, IL: Human Kinetics.

Level C Skills: The Smash

Skill: The Slice Serve	Present	Needs Improvement/ Evaluator's Suggestions	
Continental grip.			
Uses ready position. Nonplaying hand holds ball at racket throat.			
Moves to lob shot.			
Shifts weight from back to front foot, pointing at ball with nonplaying hand as setup is begun.			
Racket arcs up and behind head. Racket head scratches back. Elbow is high.			
Racket slices across the ball. Hits ball at highest point, and body is fully extended on contact, aiming to open court.			
Follows through with racket swing across body. Finishes in ready position, facing direction of smash.			
Number of balls smashed into the open service court from a toss:		Forehand /5	Backhand /5

Rubric

1 2 3 3.5 Acceptable	4 Mastery	5 Going Beyond
Number of balls smashed into the open service court from a toss. Score out of 10 and multiply by 0.4.	Performed in half-court singles on return of serve. Controls ball; smashes ball over net. Directional control is random.	Hits hard smashes to open court: winners or opponent misses hit. Controls ball; smashes in game situation. As result, opponent stops using lob shot.

From *Learning by Choice in Secondary Physical Education: Creating a Goal-Directed Program* by Kevin Kaardal, 2001, Champaign, IL: Human Kinetics.

Skills

Demonstrates the abilities to do the following:

1. Throw the ball to a partner 65 feet away (the distance between the bases) so the partner can receive the throw without having to take more than one step in any direction
2. Catch a ball thrown by a partner from 65 feet away. Remembers to cushion the ball while catching it
3. Hit a ball with a bat, using a self-toss
4. Field a ground ball hit within 10 feet of player's defensive position, using the blocking method (as demonstrated in class). Must hit the ball from 50 feet or more, using a self-toss.

Exemplars: Teacher and expert student demonstrations.

Knowledge

Demonstrates the abilities to do the following:

5. Understand and play the modified games, Move-Ups or 500-Up. Move-Ups is played with three hitters and six to nine fielders, each playing a position on the field. When a hitter is put out, the fielders move up a postion starting at right field, continuing to center, left field, third base, short stop, second base, first base, pitcher, catcher, after which you're up as a batter. An exchange of positions with the batter occurs instantly if the batter is caught out by someone catching a fly ball or line drive. 500-Up is played with one batter self-tossing and hitting to two or more fielders. A ground ball is worth 50 points, a one bouncer 100, line drive 200, and a fly ball 300 points. You gain points with a successful catch and you subtract points with a missed catch. The first person to 500 points becomes the batter and the game then starts again.
6. Understand the basic rules of slow-pitch, including those regarding the number of outs per team per inning, the four basic situations resulting in a player's being called out, and how strikes are determined in slow-pitch
7. Demonstrate or diagram the basic defensive lineup against a right-handed hitter

Exemplars: Teacher and expert student demonstrations.

Attitudes

8. Demonstrates the "Superior" characteristics listed on form A.4, Affective Evaluation Chart.

Exemplars: "Superior" behaviors listed on form A.4, Affective Evaluation Chart.

From *Learning by Choice in Secondary Physical Education: Creating a Goal-Directed Program* by Kevin Kaardal, 2001, Champaign, IL: Human Kinetics.

To be used in planning unit goals.

	Minimal Reassessment required	**Acceptable** Reassessment recommended	**Mastery** Reassessment not required	**Going Beyond** Reassessment not required
Skill	1. Completes less than 3 of 5 throws. 2. Catches ball thrown by partner from 65 feet away less than 3 of 5 tries. 3. Hits ball, using self-toss less than 3 of 5 tries. 4. Fields ball less than 3 of 5 tries.	1. Completes 3 of 5 throws. 2. Catches ball thrown by partner from 65 feet away 3 of 5 tries. 3. Hits ball, using self-toss 3 of 5 tries. 4. Fields ball 3 of 5 tries.	1. Completes 4 of 5 throws. 2. Catches ball thrown by partner from 65 feet away 4 of 5 tries. 3. Hits ball, using self-toss 4 of 5 tries. 4. Fields ball 4 of 5 tries.	1. Completes 5 of 5 throws. 2. Catches ball thrown by partner from 90 feet away 5 of 5 tries. 3. Hits ball, using pitched toss 4 of 5 tries. 4. Fields ball 5 of 5 tries.
Knowledge	5. Doesn't demonstrate understanding of Move-Ups or 500-Up and can't play without a lot of direction from teacher. 6. Scores less than 65% on written assignment. 7. Scores less than 65% on diagram.	5. Demonstrates understanding of and plays Move-Ups or 500-Up with minimal direction from teacher. 6. Scores 65–79% on written assignment. 7. Scores 65–79% on diagram.	5. Demonstrates understanding of and plays Move-Ups or 500-Up without direction from teacher. 6. Scores 80–89% on written assignment. 7. Scores 80–89% on diagram.	5. Creates new modified games. 6. Scores 90–100% on written assignment. 7. Scores 90–100% on diagram.
Attitude	8. Scores 6.4 or less as listed in form A.4 (Affective Evaluation Chart).	8. Demonstrates the "Acceptable" characteristics listed in form A.4.	8. Demonstrates the "Mastery" characteristics listed in form A.4.	8. Demonstrates "Superior" characteristics listed in form A.4 at highest level.

Descriptive scale: Minimal (1) to going beyond (4). See detailed description of indicators in each box.

Indicators: Answers the questions "How do you know?" and "What do you see?" in ongoing monitoring and evaluating of each unit goal.

From *Learning by Choice in Secondary Physical Education: Creating a Goal-Directed Program* by Kevin Kaardal, 2001, Champaign, IL: Human Kinetics.

Skills

Demonstrates the abilities to do the following:

1. Throw the ball to the first-base player from shortstop after fielding a ground ball hit within 20 feet of your defensive position
2. Catch a ball thrown by a partner to first base from shortstop
3. Hit a ball pitched into the strike zone
4. Field a ground ball, line drive, or fly ball hit within 20 feet of his or her defensive position

Exemplars: Teacher and expert student demonstrations.

Knowledge

Demonstrates the abilities to do the following:

5. Understand the specific rules of slow-pitch, including rules regarding infield fly balls, the strike zone, foul balls on a third strike, the number of players on the field, and leading off
6. Play and self-umpire a game of slow-pitch with classmates
7. Demonstrate or diagram the basic defensive lineup against a right-handed hitter, a left-handed power hitter, and a ground-ball hitter

Exemplars: Teacher and expert student demonstrations.

Attitudes

8. Demonstrates the "Superior" characteristics listed in form A.4, Affective Evaluation Chart.

Exemplars: "Superior" behaviors listed in form A.4, Affective Evaluation Chart.

From *Learning by Choice in Secondary Physical Education: Creating a Goal-Directed Program* by Kevin Kaardal, 2001, Champaign, IL: Human Kinetics.

To be used in planning unit goals.

	Minimal Reassessment required	**Acceptable** Reassessment recommended	**Mastery** Reassessment not required	**Going Beyond** Reassessment not required
Skill	1. Throws ball to first-base player less than 3 of 5 tries. 2. Catches a ball thrown by partner to first base from shortstop less than 3 of 5 tries. 3. Hits ball pitched into strike zone 0 or 1 of 5 tries. 4. Fields ball less than 3 of 5 tries, in each drill.	1. Throws ball to first-base player 3 of 5 tries. 2. Catches ball thrown by partner to first base from shortstop 3 of 5 tries. 3. Hits ball pitched into strike zone 2 of 5 tries. 4. Fields ball 3 of 5 tries, in each drill.	1. Throws ball to first-base player 4 of 5 tries. 2. Catches ball thrown by partner to first base from shortstop 4 of 5 tries. 3. Hits ball pitched into strike zone 3 of 5 tries. 4. Fields ball 4 of 5 tries, in each drill.	1. Throws ball to first-base player 5 of 5 tries even if fielding ball off hit makes thrower have to regain balance before throwing. 2. Catches ball thrown by partner to first base from shortstop position 5 of 5 tries even if throw is not accurate (within 3 feet). 3. Hits ball pitched into strike zone 4 of 5 tries. 4. Fields ball 5 of 5 tries in each drill.
Knowledge	5. Scores less than 65% on written assignment. 6. Plays and self-umpires game of slow-pitch with classmates but needs many interventions by and directions from teacher. 7. Scores less than 6.5 of 10 on all diagrams.	5. Scores 65–79% on written assignment. 6. Plays and self-umpires game of slow-pitch with classmates with few interventions required by teacher. 7. Scores 6.5 to 7.9 of 10 on all diagrams.	5. Scores 80–89% on written assignment. 6. Plays and self-umpires game of slow-pitch with classmates with no interventions required by teacher. 7. Scores 8 to 8.9 of 10 on all diagrams.	5. Scores 90% on written assignment. 6. Umpires game of slow-pitch with classmates with no interventions required by teacher. 7. Scores 9 of 10 or better on all diagrams.
Attitudes	8. Scores 6.4 or less as listed in form A.4 (Affective Evaluation Chart).	8. Demonstrates the "Acceptable" characteristics listed in form A.4.	8. Demonstrates the "Mastery" characteristics listed in form A.4.	8. Demonstrates the "Superior" characteristics listed in form A.4.

Descriptive scale: Minimal (1) to going beyond (4). See detailed description of indicators in each box.

Indicators: Answers the questions "How do you know?" and "What do you see?" in ongoing monitoring and evaluating of each unit goal.

From *Learning by Choice in Secondary Physical Education: Creating a Goal-Directed Program* by Kevin Kaardal, 2001, Champaign, IL: Human Kinetics.

Skills

Demonstrates the abilities to do the following:

1. Throw the ball to the home-plate player from deep center field after fielding a ball hit within 40 feet of his or her defensive position
2. Pitch a ball into the strike zone
3. Hit a pitched ball to each field on command
4. Field a ground ball, line drive, or fly ball hit within 40 feet of his or her defensive position

Exemplars: Teacher and expert student demonstrations.

Knowledge

5. Demonstrates an understanding of the defensive strategies and offensive strategies of slow-pitch. Writes out case studies that explain five specific defensive strategies and five offensive strategies.

Exemplars: Teacher and expert student demonstrations.

Attitudes

6. Demonstrates the "Superior" characteristics listed in form A.4, Affective Evaluation Chart.

Exemplars: "Superior" behaviors listed in form A.4, Affective Evaluation Chart.

From *Learning by Choice in Secondary Physical Education: Creating a Goal-Directed Program* by Kevin Kaardal, 2001, Champaign, IL: Human Kinetics.

To be used in planning unit goals.

	Minimal Reassessment required	**Acceptable** Reassessment recommended	**Mastery** Reassessment not required	**Going Beyond** Reassessment not required
Skill	1. Throws ball to relay from deep center field less than 3 of 5 tries in time for relay to make play on bases. 2. Pitches ball into strike zone less than 3 of 10 tries. 3. Hits pitched ball to each field on command less than 3 of 5 hits. 4. Fields ground balls, line drives, or fly balls hit within 40 feet of defensive position less than 3 of 5 tries.	1. Throws ball to relay from deep center field 3 of 5 tries in time for relay to make play on bases. 2. Pitches ball into strike zone 3 of 10 tries. 3. Hits pitched ball to each field on command 3 of 5 hits. 4. Fields ground balls, line drives, or fly balls hit within 40 feet of defensive position 3 of 5 tries.	1. Throws ball to home plate from deep center field 3 of 5 tries with one bounce and no relay. 2. Pitches ball into strike zone 5 of 10 tries. 3. Hits pitched ball to each field on command 4 of 5 hits. 4. Fields ground balls, line drives, or fly balls hit within 40 feet of defensive position 4 of 5 tries.	1. Throws ball to home plate from deep center field 5 of 5 tries with one bounce and no relay. 2. Pitches ball into strike zone 7 of 10 tries. Consistently causes batters to strike out or hit pop flies. 3. Hits pitched ball to each field on command 5 of 5 hits. Reads defensive alignment and hits to holes in defensive set. 4. Fields ground balls, line drives, or fly balls hit within 40 feet of defensive position 5 of 5 tries. Makes diving catches.
Knowledge	5. Scores less than 65% on 10 case studies.	5. Scores 65–79% on 10 case studies.	5. Scores 80–89% on 10 case studies.	5. Scores 90–100% on 10 case studies.
Attitudes	6. Scores 6.4 or less as listed in form A.4 (Affective Evaluation Chart).	6. Demonstrates the "Acceptable" characteristics listed in form A.4.	6. Demonstrates the "Mastery" characteristics listed in form A.4.	6. Demonstrates "Superior" characteristics listed in form A.4.

Descriptive scale: Minimal (1) to going beyond (4). See detailed description of indicators in each box.

Indicators: Answers the questions "How do you know?" and "What do you see?" in ongoing monitoring and evaluating of each unit goal.

From *Learning by Choice in Secondary Physical Education: Creating a Goal-Directed Program* by Kevin Kaardal, 2001, Champaign, IL: Human Kinetics.

Form F.7 Student Softball Skills Test

Name: _____ Class: _____ Teacher: _____

Skills—Level A

Demonstrates the abilities to do the following:

1. Throw the ball to a partner 65 feet away (the distance between the bases) so the partner can receive the throw without having to take more than one step in any direction   1. /5

2. Catch a ball thrown by a partner from 65 feet away. Remembers to cushion the ball as he or she catches it   2. /5

3. Hit a ball with a bat, using a self-toss   3. /5

4. Field a ground ball hit within 10 feet of his or her defensive position, using the blocking method (demonstrated in class). The ball must be hit from 50 feet or more, using a self-toss.   4. /5

Skills—Level B

Demonstrates the abilities to do the following:

1. Throw the ball to the first-base player from shortstop after fielding a ground ball hit within 20 feet of his or her defensive position   1. /5

2. Catch a ball thrown by a partner to first base from shortstop   2. /5

3. Hit a ball pitched into the strike zone   3. /5

4. Field a ground ball, line drive, or fly ball hit within 20 feet of his or her defensive position   4. /5

Skills—Level C

Demonstrates the abilities to do the following:

1. Throw the ball to the home plate player from deep center field after fielding a ball hit within 40 feet of his or her defensive position   1. /5

2. Pitch a ball into the strike zone   2. /5

3. Hit a pitched ball to each field on command   3. /5

4. Field a ground ball, line drive, or fly ball hit within 40 feet of his or her defensive position   4. /5

From *Learning by Choice in Secondary Physical Education: Creating a Goal-Directed Program* by Kevin Kaardal, 2001, Champaign, IL: Human Kinetics.

Form F.8 Slow-Pitch Softball Written Assignment

Knowledge—Level A

1. Describe the basic rules of slow-pitch. Include the four most common ways players are called out, how teams score runs, when players are allowed to run in slow-pitch, how much arc must be on a pitch, what a strike is, when players "walk," and when runners must tag up before running.

2. Draw a diagram showing where your team's players should line up in the field to defend against a left-handed power hitter.

3. Draw a diagram showing where your team's players should line up in the field to defend against a right-handed hitter who hits a high percentage of ground balls.

Knowledge—Level B

1. The count is one away. There are runners on first and third. The ball is hit and fielded by the shortstop. What is the correct play for the shortstop to make?

2. The count is two away. There are runners on first and third. The ball is hit deep into left center field and fielded by the center fielder. What is the correct play for the center fielder to make?

3. Describe the seven reasons a player will be called out by a slow-pitch umpire.

4. There are two outs and nobody on base. The fourth hitter in the batting order, a right-handed batter, is up to bat. Draw a diagram showing where your team's players should line up in the field to defend against this hitter.

5. Draw a diagram showing where your players should line up in the field to defend against the first hitter of the inning who happens to be left-handed.

6. Define the following terms in your own words:

   Full count—

   Fielder's choice—

   Error—

   RBI—

Knowledge—Level C

1. Select an all-star team of any 10 classmates. Draw a lineup of where you would position your classmates for both hitting and fielding. Explain your decisions.

2. Design three softball practices you might typically use with a competitive team: one for a preseason practice, one for a midseason practice, and one for the night before a play-off game.

From *Learning by Choice in Secondary Physical Education: Creating a Goal-Directed Program* by Kevin Kaardal, 2001, Champaign, IL: Human Kinetics.

Form G.1 Student Contract for Volleyball

I, _____ of _____ agree to work toward mastering the
(Student name)   (Class)
following skills in volleyball.

I will have a peer evaluate me during skill practices, and I will demonstrate these skills in a game or modified game situation for the teacher to assess me.

Skill	Peer-Evaluated Skill Mark	Teacher-Applied Skill Mark	Average of Both Marks
Serving			
Passing			
Attacking			
Blocking			

For my written assignment I will complete the following (circle one):
1. Question sheet on the history, rules, and strategies of volleyball
2. A test on history, rules, and strategies of volleyball
3. An essay on the history of volleyball
4. An athlete or a team profile paper analyzing the player's or team's strengths and weaknesses

I understand my affective (attitude and effort) mark will be based on observable behaviors outlined on the Affective Evaluation Chart (form A.4) and these marks will be recorded on my teacher's class grid sheet.

I wish to select the optional fitness training component and complete the volleyball fitness test outside of class as a part of my mark (circle one): Yes No

I wish the weighting of my assessment to be as follows (choose a percentage for each category within the range allowed; total of all categories when added must equal 100):

Category and Minimums and Maximums	Weighting Selections
Skill performance (10–40%)	
Skill improvement (10–40%)	
Knowledge (20–40%)	
Attitude and effort (10–40%)	
Fitness through volleyball training (10–40%)	
Total (must be 100)	

I agree to complete this contract by _____.
(date)

Student's signature: _____ Teacher's signature: _____

From *Learning by Choice in Secondary Physical Education: Creating a Goal-Directed Program* by Kevin Kaardal, 2001, Champaign, IL: Human Kinetics.

Form G.2 Volleyball Skills Test

Underhand Serve	Not Present	Present
Foot on opposite side to serving hand is forward.		
Arm is straight on swing.		
Contacts ball under ball.		
Steps through on contact and follows through to target.		

Accuracy test: Serve 10 times to a partner so he or she may contact, catch, or pass your serve after moving two steps or fewer: _____/10.

Sidearm Serve	Not Present	Present
Foot on opposite side to serving hand is forward.		
Arm swings on a plane almost level with shoulder.		
Arm is straight on swing.		
Contacts just under midline of ball.		
Steps through on contact and follows through to target.		

Accuracy test: Serve 10 times to a partner so he or she may contact, catch, or pass your serve after moving two steps or fewer: _____/10.

Overhand Serve	Not Present	Present
Foot on opposite side to serving hand is forward.		
Tossing arm is exactly even with shoulder holding ball.		
Hitting arm is up, thumb down, and elbow high.		
Tosses directly in front of the serving shoulder.		
Contacts just under midline of ball.		
Shows the rhythm: "step, toss, and contact."		

Accuracy test: Serve 10 times to a partner so he or she may contact, catch, or pass your serve after moving two steps or fewer: _____/10.

From *Learning by Choice in Secondary Physical Education: Creating a Goal-Directed Program* by Kevin Kaardal, 2001, Champaign, IL: Human Kinetics.

Forearm Pass	Not Present	Present
Thumb pads are together.		
Wrists are hyperextended.		
Elbows are locked.		
Contacts ball on forearms.		
Forearms and thighs are parallel on contact.		
Tranfers weight through ball toward target.		

Accuracy test: Have a partner toss the ball to you 10 times. Pass back to your partner so he or she may contact, catch, or overhead-pass your forearm pass after moving two steps or fewer: _____/10

Overhead Pass	Not Present	Present
Points thumbs at nose; spreads fingers comfortably.		
Arms are parallel to floor.		
Contacts ball near forehead height.		
Extends elbow fully toward target after contact.		
Palms face partner on follow-through.		
Transfers weight through ball toward target.		

Accuracy test: Have a partner toss the ball to you 10 times. Pass back to your partner so he or she may contact, catch, or hit your overhead pass after only moving three steps or fewer in a simulated attack: _____/10.

Overhead "Back Set" Pass	Not Present	Present
Points thumbs at nose; spreads fingers comfortably.		
Arms are parallel to floor.		
Contacts ball slightly above forehead height.		
Extends elbow fully toward target after contact.		
Thumbs point to roof on follow-through.		
Head stays stationary (still) throughout pass.		

Accuracy test: Have a partner toss the ball to you 10 times. Pass back to your partner so he or she may contact, catch, or hit your overhead pass after moving three steps or fewer in a simulated attack: _____/10.

(continued)

From *Learning by Choice in Secondary Physical Education: Creating a Goal-Directed Program* by Kevin Kaardal, 2001, Champaign, IL: Human Kinetics.

Down Ball	Not Present	Present
Nonhitting hand is high, pointing at airborne ball.		
Thumb of hitting arm is down, and elbow is high.		
Hitting arm contacts ball high and fully extended.		
Elbow is straight on contact.		
Wrist is firm, and full hand contacts.		
Transfers weight through ball toward target.		
Ball travels in a flat trajectory or downward after going over net due to topspin.		

Accuracy test: Have a partner toss the ball to you 10 times. Hit ball over net to a target 10 times. Target hits: _____/10.

The Attack: "Spike"	Not Present	Present
Uses proper footwork (left, right, left).		
Feet are at a 45-degree angle to the net.		
Nonhitting hand is high, pointing at airborne ball.		
Thumb of hitting arm is down, and elbow is high.		
Hitting arm swings fully, quickly, and powerfully.		
Elbow is straight on contact.		
Hitting arm contacts ball high and fully extended.		
Wrist is firm, and full hand contacts ball.		
Ball travels downward.		

Accuracy test: Have a partner toss the ball to you 10 times. Hit ball over net to a target 10 times. Target hits: _____/10.

The Attack: "Tip"	Not Present	Present
Uses proper footwork (left, right, left).		
Feet are at a 45-degree angle to each other.		
Nonhitting hand is high, pointing at airborne ball.		
Thumb of hitting arm is down, and elbow is high.		

From *Learning by Choice in Secondary Physical Education: Creating a Goal-Directed Program* by Kevin Kaardal, 2001, Champaign, IL: Human Kinetics.

The Attack: "Tip" *(cont.)*	Not Present	Present
Stops swing of hitting arm short of full contact, punching or tipping ball to an open space over or past blockers.		
Hitting arm contacts ball high and fully extended.		
Wrist is firm, and player contacts with fingertips.		
Ball travels downward.		

Accuracy test: Have a partner toss the ball to you 10 times. Hit ball over a blocker and net to a target 10 times. Target hits: _____/10.

The Block: Single-Person	Not Present	Present
Uses ready position.		
Sees the backs of own hands.		
Spreads fingers.		
Bends knees.		
Times jump to meet ball above net.		
Fully extends arms.		
Hands are together, and forearms are touching partner.		
Presses over net. (Rotates shoulders up and forward to press the ball back at the opposing team.)		

Accuracy test: Have a partner toss the ball to you 10 times. Block ball back over net 10 times: _____/10

The Block: Two-Person	Not Present	Present
Uses ready position.		
Sees the backs of own hands.		
Spreads fingers.		
Bends knees.		
Times jump with partner to meet ball above net.		
Fully extends arms.		
Hands are together, and forearms are touching partner.		
Presses over net. (Rotates shoulders up and forward to press the ball back at the opposing team.)		

Accuracy test: Have a partner toss the ball to you 10 times. Block ball back over net 10 times: _____/10

Instructions: For each category, mark the group out of 10, based on the descriptors and questions in the rubric.

Number of evaluating group: _____ **Dance style:** _____

	Number of Group Being Evaluated								
Skill Criterion	**1**	**2**	**3**	**4**	**5**	**6**	**7**	**8**	**9**
Time (2.5–4 min.)									
Form (Do you see tight lines, good posture?)									
Dance steps or moves									
(Are 7 different steps or moves present?)									
Harmony (Did costumes and dance theme fit the music?)									
Flow (Did routine seem to fit together smoothly? Were steps and moves repeated to connect each phase of routine?)									
Creativity (Was routine entertaining and original?)									
Aesthetics (Was routine pleasing to watch?)									
Rhythm (Did dancers keep time to the music?)									
Difficulty (More than 6 difficult steps is a 10.)									
Total average									

Form H.2 Dance Group Production Peer Evaluation for Attitude and Effort

Using form A.4, Affective Evaluation Chart, assess how well and hard your peers worked to put this presentation together, scoring out of 10.

Your name: _____ **Group number:** _____

Write each group member's first and last names and record your assessment of each member's effort.

:___/10	:___/10	:___/10
:___/10	:___/10	:___/10
:___/10	:___/10	:___/10
:___/10	:___/10	:___/10

I believe I deserve the following mark out of 10: _____

Please write a short paragraph explaining why you believe you have earned this mark for your effort:

_____

_____

_____

_____

_____

_____

_____

_____

_____

_____

_____

_____

_____

_____

_____

_____

Dance and Stuntnastics

From *Learning by Choice in Secondary Physical Education: Creating a Goal-Directed Program* by Kevin Kaardal, 2001, Champaign, IL: Human Kinetics.

Form H.3 Fox-Trot or Waltz Peer Evaluation

Name:_____ Class: _____

Peer evaluator: _____

Level	Skill	Number of Times Step or Move Was Used	Form: /5 (Do you see good form—tight lines, good posture?)	Rhythm: /5 (Did dancers keep time to the music?)	Peer Mark (Combine Form and Rhythm.)	Teacher/Peer Combined Mark
A	Basic box					
	Forward travel					
B	Backward travel					
	Quarter turn					
	Lady's turn					
	Star turn					
	Man's backward turn					
C	Crossover					
	Weave					

General evaluation of entire dance performance, out of 10

Flow

(Did routine seem to fit together smoothly? Were steps and moves repeated to connect each phase of routine?)

Circle one: 1   2   3   4   5   6   7   8   9   10

Aesthetics

(Was the routine pleasing to watch?)

Circle one: 1   2   3   4   5   6   7   8   9   10

Creativity

(Was routine entertaining and original?)

Circle one: 1   2   3   4   5   6   7   8   9   10

Total: Calculate the average skill mark and the average performance marks. Add together and divide by 2 to get a final mark for skill performance.	Average of Skill Mark	Average of Performance Mark	Final Mark

Dance and Stuntnastics

From *Learning by Choice in Secondary Physical Education: Creating a Goal-Directed Program* by Kevin Kaardal, 2001, Champaign, IL: Human Kinetics.

To be used in planning unit outcomes.

	Minimal Reassessment required	**Acceptable** Reassessment recommended	**Mastery** Reassessment not required	**Going Beyond** Reassessment not required
Pyramids	Pyramids not stable, not held for 3 sec., and not selected from group's chosen evaluation level.	Pyramids a little shaky but held for 3 sec. and selected from group's chosen evaluation level.	Pyramids stable, held for 3 sec., and selected from group's chosen evaluation level.	Pyramids stable, with sharp and aesthetically exceptional lines, held for 3 sec., and selected from group's chosen evaluation level.
Individual	Individual balances don't have straight lines and are not held for 3 sec.	Individual balances have almost straight lines (but bent limbs, toes not pointed) and are held with some instability for 3 sec.	Individual balances have straight lines and are held cleanly for 3 sec.	Individual balances have straight lines, with excellent form, demonstrating strength and superb balance, and are held cleanly for 3 sec.
Movement flow	Dance steps, stunts, and gymnastics moves not performed well. Landings missed, and gymnastic moves or stunts not completed successfully. Doesn't flow smoothly, and some confusion as to what the performers are to do next exists.	Dance steps, stunts, and gymnastics moves performed with slightly open tucks and good form (moderate height, toes not pointed, and one- or two-step landings). Flows smoothly and routine is aesthetically pleasing.	Dance steps, stunts, and gymnastics moves performed with tight tucks or excellent form (good height, clean lines, pointed toes, and clean landings). Flows smoothly and routine is aesthetically pleasing.	Dance steps, stunts, and gymnastics moves performed with tight tucks and excellent form (good height, clean lines, pointed toes, and clean landings). Moves flow smoothly and routine is aesthetically pleasing. Appeared exceptional beyond expectations.
Choreography	Final routine not creative: Combinations of dance steps, pyramids, balances, and gymnastics didn't flow together or fit the music; audience wasn't impressed.	Final routine fairly creative: Had some unique and surprising combinations of dance steps, pyramids, balances, and gymnastics, flowing together and fitting the music; audience appreciated routine.	Final routine creative: Had more unique and surprising combinations of dance steps, pyramids, balances, and gymnastics, flowing together and fitting the music; audience appreciated routine.	Final routine creative and surprising: Had unique and surprising combinations of dance steps, pyramids, balances, and gymnastics, flowing together and fitting the music; audience appreciated strongly.

Descriptive scale: Minimal (1) to going beyond (5). See detailed description of indicators in each box.

Indicators: Answers the questions "How do you know?" and "What do you see?" in ongoing monitoring and evaluating of each unit goal.

From *Learning by Choice in Secondary Physical Education: Creating a Goal-Directed Program* by Kevin Kaardal, 2001, Champaign, IL: Human Kinetics.

Teacher: _____ **Class:** _____

Music: _____ **Level:** _____

Be sure to include at least one move of each of the following: strength, balance, rotation, locomotion, asymmetrical pyramid, symmetrical pyramid, and partner balance. Your routine must last at least two minutes, have a definite beginning and end, include music, and demonstrate a high quality of skill performance and smooth flow. The level of your routine is determined by the level of the majority of your group's stunts and skills (e.g., a group that chooses mostly Level C stunts is a Level C group).

List group member names (first and last) below:

_____

_____

_____

Draw diagrams of the stunts, transitions, and/or formations you will be using to perform your routine in sequence:

1. Level __	8. Level __	15. Level __
2. Level __	9. Level __	16. Level __
3. Level __	10. Level __	17. Level __
4. Level __	11. Level __	18. Level __
5. Level __	12. Level __	19. Level __
6. Level __	13. Level __	20. Level __
7. Level __	14. Level __	21. Level __

From *Learning by Choice in Secondary Physical Education: Creating a Goal-Directed Program* by Kevin Kaardal, 2001, Champaign, IL: Human Kinetics.

Instructions

1. Fill in your group number but not your name.
2. For each category, check a performance rating from 1–10, based on the rubric descriptors.
3. Give one bonus point to the difficulty category if a group incorporates a stunt or pyramid from a skill level higher than their own. Level C groups automatically get the bonus in every category in which they attempt only Level C skills.

Number of evaluating group: _____

Skill Criterion	Number of Group Being Evaluated								
	1	**2**	**3**	**4**	**5**	**6**	**7**	**8**	**9**
Asymmetrical pyramid (1 minimum)									
Symmetrical pyramid (1 minimum)									
Balances (held for 3 or more seconds)									
Stunts (Do you see good form—tight lines, tight tucks?)									
Dance steps (3 styles minimum)									
Flow (Did routine seem to fit together smoothly?)									
Creativity (Was routine entertaining and original?)									
Aesthetics (Was routine pleasing to watch?)									
Difficulty: Level A—Start at 6. Level B—Start at 7. Level C—Start at 8.									
Total average									

From *Learning by Choice in Secondary Physical Education: Creating a Goal-Directed Program* by Kevin Kaardal, 2001, Champaign, IL: Human Kinetics.

Using form A.4, Affective Evaluation Chart, assess how well and hard your peers worked to put this presentation together, scoring out of 10.

Your name: _____ **Group number:** _____

Write each group member's first and last names and record your assessment of each member's effort.

:___/10	:___/10	:___/10
:___/10	:___/10	:___/10
:___/10	:___/10	:___/10
:___/10	:___/10	:___/10

I believe I deserve the following mark out of 10: _____

Please write a short paragraph explaining why you believe you have earned this mark for your effort:

_____

_____

_____

_____

_____

_____

_____

_____

_____

_____

_____

_____

_____

_____

_____

_____

_____

From *Learning by Choice in Secondary Physical Education: Creating a Goal-Directed Program* by Kevin Kaardal, 2001, Champaign, IL: Human Kinetics.

Bibliography

Active Living Alliance for Canadians With Disabilities. 1993. *Moving to Inclusion.* Ottawa, Ontario: Fitness Canada.

Adolphe, R., and W. Kozak. 1998. Student self-evaluation in physical education. *Runner Magazine—The Journal of the Health and Physical Education Council of the ATA,* vol. 34, no. 1.

Alberta Education Department. 1988. *The Secondary Physical Education Curriculum Guide, Grades 7 to 12.* Alberta, Canada: Alberta Education Department.

Boschee, F., and M.A. Baron. 1993. *Outcome-Based Education: Developing Programs Through Strategic Planning.* Lancaster, PA: Technomic Publishers.

Burton, A.W., and D.E. Miller. 1998. *Movement Skill Assessment.* Champaign, IL: Human Kinetics.

CAHPERD (**www.cahperd.ca**).

CAHPERD. 1994. *The Canadian Active Living Challenge Resource Book and Tool Kit.* Ottawa, Ontario: CAHPERD.

CAHPERD. 1992. *Gender Equity Through Physical Education.* Ottawa, Ontario: CAHPERD.

CIRA (**www.intramurals.ca**).

The Canadian Association for Health, Physical Education and Recreation. 1990. *The Quality Daily Physical Education Leaders Annual Report.* Ontario, Canada: CAHPERD.

The Canadian Association for Health, Physical Education and Recreation. 1993. *The Quality Daily Physical Education Leaders Kit.* Ontario, Canada: CAHPERD.

The Canadian Association for Health, Physical Education and Recreation. 1993. *The Quality Daily Physical Education Leaders Annual Report.* Ontario, Canada: CAHPERD.

The Canadian Association for Health, Physical Education and Recreation. 1994. *The Quality Daily Physical Education Leaders Annual Report.* Ontario, Canada: CAHPERD.

The Canadian Association for Health, Physical Education, Recreation and Dance. 1996. *The Quality Daily Physical Education Leaders Annual Report.* Ontario, Canada: CAHPERD.

Recreation Association. 1994. *The Canadian Active Living Challenge Leader's Kit.* Ontario, Canada: CAHPERD and CIRA.

Colorosso, B. 1989. *Winning at Parenting . . . Without Beating Your Kids.* A Pannonia International Film Creative Technology Design.

Crespo, C.J. 1999. Exercise and the prevention of chronic disabling illness. In *Exercise in Rehabilitation Medicine.* Champaign, IL: Human Kinetics.

Dupree, M. 1989. *Leadership Is an Art.* New York: Del Trade Publishers.

Dupree, M. 1993. *Leadership Jazz.* New York: Del Trade Publishers.

Durante, F. 1997. Let your students choose! The PCAB method. *Runner Journal,* vol. 35, no. 3.

Eichstaedt, C.B., and B.W. Lavay. 1992. *Physical Activity for Individuals With Mental Retardation.* Champaign, IL: Human Kinetics.

Evans, K.M., and J.A. King. 1994. Research on OBE: What we know and what we don't know. *Educational Leadership,* vol. 51, no. 6.

Griffin, L.L., S.A. Mitchell, and J.L. Oslin. 1997. *Teaching Sport Concepts and Skills: A Tactical Games Approach.* Champaign, IL: Human Kinetics.

Lieberman, L.J., and J.F. Cowart. 1996. *Games for People With Sensory Impairments.* Champaign, IL: Human Kinetics.

McCarthy, J. 1995. *Handouts from EDPA 621.* Calgary: University of Calgary.

Morris, D., and J. Stiehl. 1999. How to change any game. In *Changing Kids' Games,* 2nd ed. Champaign, IL: Human Kinetics.

Morris, D., and J. Stiehl. 1999. Helping others change games. In *Changing Kids' Games,* 2nd ed. Champaign, IL: Human Kinetics.

Mosston, M. 1981. *Teaching Physical Education.* Columbus, OH: Charles E. Merrill Publishing.

National Consortium for Physical Education and Recreation for Individuals With Disabilities. 1995. *Adapted Physical Education National Standards.* Champaign, IL: Human Kinetics.

Safrit, M. 1995. *Complete Guide to Youth Fitness Testing.* Champaign, IL: Human Kientics.

Sizer, T. 1992. *Horace's School—Redesigning the American High School.* Boston, MA: Houghton Mifflin Company.

Spady, W.G. 1994. Choosing outcomes significance. *Educational Leadership,* vol. 51, no. 6.

U.S. Department of Health and Human Services. 1996. Physical activity and health: A report of the Surgeon General. Atlanta, Georgia: U.S. Department of Health and Human Services, Public Health Service, CDC, National Center for Chronic Disease Prevention and Health Promotion.

Wiggins, G., and McTighe, J. 1998. *Understanding by Design.* Alexandria, VA: Association for Supervision and Curriculum Development.

Winnick, J.P. 2000. *Adapted Physical Education and Sport,* 3rd ed. Champaign, IL: Human Kinetics.

Worthen, B., and J. Sanders. 1987. *Educational Evaluation—Alternative Approaches and Practical Guidelines.* New York: Longman Publishing.

Index

Note: Tables are indicated by an italicized *t* following the page number; figures by an italicized *f*. Page numbers of forms are italic.

About the Author

Kevin Kaardal is vice principal at Reynolds Secondary School in British Columbia, Canada. He drew upon his 11 years of teaching physical education in grades 3 to 12 to develop and perfect the approach presented in this book. He was vice principal at Bishop Grandin High School; coordinating teacher of physical education at Bishop McNally High School; and a physical education contact teacher at Bishop Kidd Junior High School and Hugh Sutherland School, where he created programs that earned six Quality Daily Physical Education awards from 1988 to 1996. Recognized by his colleagues, he won a Young Professional's award from CAPHERD, a HPEC Commendation, and a Teacher Plus award. He also has been recognized by students and parents, winning two Excellence in Teaching awards. Kaardal earned a master's degree in curriculum and instruction in kinesiology from the University of Calgary, Alberta, Canada.